Textile Design Theory in the Making

Textile Design Theory in the Making

Elaine Igoe

with contributions by Daniela Calabi, Elena Caratti,
Marianne Fairbanks, Tom Fisher, Marion Lean,
Mark Roxburgh and Rose Sinclair

BLOOMSBURY VISUAL ARTS
LONDON • NEW YORK • OXFORD • NEW DELHI • SYDNEY

BLOOMSBURY VISUAL ARTS
Bloomsbury Publishing Plc
50 Bedford Square, London, WC1B 3DP, UK
1385 Broadway, New York, NY 10018, USA
29 Earlsfort Terrace, Dublin 2, Ireland

BLOOMSBURY, BLOOMSBURY VISUAL ARTS and the Diana logo are trademarks
of Bloomsbury Publishing Plc

First published in Great Britain 2021
Paperback edition first published 2023

Copyright © Elaine Igoe, 2021

Chapter 6 © Elena Caratti and Daniela Calabi, 2021
Chapter 9 © Marion Lean, 2021
Chapter 10 © Rose Sinclair, 2021
Chapter 12 © Tom Fisher, 2021
Chapter 14 © Mark Roxburgh, 2021
Epilogue © Marianne Fairbanks, 2021

Elaine Igoe has asserted her right under the Copyright, Designs and Patents Act,
1988, to be identified as Author of this work.

For legal purposes the Acknowledgements on p. xi constitute an extension
of this copyright page.

All rights reserved. No part of this publication may be reproduced or transmitted in
any form or by any means, electronic or mechanical, including photocopying, recording,
or any information storage or retrieval system, without prior permission in writing
from the publishers.

Bloomsbury Publishing Plc does not have any control over, or responsibility for, any
third-party websites referred to or in this book. All internet addresses given in this
book were correct at the time of going to press. The author and publisher regret any
inconvenience caused if addresses have changed or sites have ceased to exist, but
can accept no responsibility for any such changes.

A catalogue record for this book is available from the British Library.

Library of Congress Cataloging-in-Publication Data

Names: Igoe, Elaine, editor.
Title: Textile design theory in the making / edited by Elaine Igoe.
Description: London ; New York : Bloomsbury Visual Arts, 2021. | Includescontributions
by Elena Caratti, Daniela Calabi, Marion Lean, RoseSinclair, Tom Fisher, Mark Roxburgh,
and Marianne Fairbanks. | Includesbibliographical references and index.
Identifiers: LCCN 2021001766 (print) | LCCN 2021001767 (ebook) |
ISBN9781350061569 (HB) | ISBN 9781350254107 (PB) | ISBN 9781350061576 (ePDF)|
ISBN 9781350061583 (eBook)
Subjects: LCSH: Textile design.
Classification: LCC NK8805 .T49 2021 (print) | LCC NK8805 (ebook) | DDC677/.022–dc23
LC record available at https://lccn.loc.gov/2021001766
LC ebook record available at https://lccn.loc.gov/2021001767

ISBN: HB: 978-1-3500-6156-9
PB: 978-1-3502-5410-7
ePDF: 978-1-3500-6157-6
eBook: 978-1-3500-6158-3

Typeset by Deanta Global Publishing Services, Chennai, India

To find out more about our authors and books visit www.bloomsbury.com and
sign up for our newsletters.

Contents

List of figures	vii
List of contributors	viii
Acknowledgements	xi
Introduction	1
1 Too much to tell	9
2 Matrixial meaning	20
3 Talking textiles: A story	26
4 Design, thinking and textile thinking	31

Mesh one

5 Translating and transforming	47
6 The translation paradigm for design culture *Elena Caratti and Daniela Calabi*	57

Mesh two

7 A story of hard and soft: Modernism and textiles as design	73
8 The gendered textile design discipline	86
9 Taking on textile thinking *Marion Lean*	99
10 Tracing back to trace forwards: What does it mean/take to be a Black textile designer *Rose Sinclair*	111

Mesh three

11 Paraphernalia and playing for design	127
12 Patterns of objects *Tom Fisher*	140

Mesh four

13 Making, problems and pleasures	157
14 Design does/does not solve problems *Mark Roxburgh*	173

15 Elevated surfaces 187

Epilogue: Toing and froing: On creating an oscillation-based
    practice   *Marianne Fairbanks* 202

Glossary of terms 215
References 218
Contributors' references 229
Index 237

Figures

1	Table of textile design activity (2020)	34
2	Press image from Première Vision trade fair, February 2019. Textile designers (standing) showing and selling their designs to buyers (seated)	92
3	Expanded textile thinking entities	105
4	Expanded textile thinking characteristics, attributes and icons used in an interactive exhibit at the Royal College of Art (Lean 2018)	106
5	Textile thinking interactive exhibit at the Royal College of Art, London, UK (2018)	107
6	Portrait of textile designer Althea McNish	119
7	Althea McNish in her design studio for Bachelor Girls Room: Ideal Home Exhibition, London, UK, 1966	120
8	House of Cards (Igoe 2008). Exhibited at the Royal College of Art Work in Progress show, January 2008	131
9	Image of melon-skin object	142
10–11	Images of half-column front and back	143
12	Ten challenges for design education	194
13	*Gradient Slippage* by Marianne Fairbanks (2018) 35.5 × 26 inches. Cotton, Tencel and polyester thread handwoven on TC-2 Loom (framed)	205
14	Detail of *Gradient Slippage* by Marianne Fairbanks (2018). Cotton, Tencel and polyester thread handwoven on TC-2 Loom (framed)	207
15	Fuller Sampler by Marianne Fairbanks (2018). Size variable. Metal blinds, paint, waxed Kevlar. Installed at Living Room, Chicago, IL, United States	208

Contributors

Daniela Calabi is an architect, researcher and Associate Professor at the Department of Design at the Politecnico di Milano. Her research is focused on perception design and visual cultures, in particular, applied to the communication of landscapes and historical and contemporary identities. She also works on design education and basic design, addressing the theme of the translation of signs in texture design and types of texts. From 2005, Daniela Calabi has published numerous articles concerning research on texture design, in particular focusing on the concept of multimedia translation of formats and haptic and visual contents. In 2004 Calabi wrote the first edition of the book *Texture Design. Un percorso Basic*, with the introduction of Professor Attilio Marcolli and Professor Giovanni Baule. She has participated in international conferences promoting research concerning communication design applied to the identity of places through local texture design and craftwork, with experts in environmental design.

Elena Caratti, Architect, MA in e-design and PhD in design, is currently Associate Professor at the Design Department of Politecnico di Milano. Her research interests cover visual cultures and editorial design. She teaches visual cultures at the Design School of Politecnico di Milano and BA and MA courses in communication design. She also teaches research design critique at the PhD School in Design of Politecnico di Milano. In 2017 Caratti was co-editor with Giovanni Baule of the book *Design Is Translation. The Translation Paradigm for Design Culture* (the first edition of the book was published in Italian with Franco Angeli in 2016). It resonates with her contributory chapter reinforcing the concept for the reader and leading them to make comparisons with other fields of design (in this case communication design) while introducing new perspectives. Dr Elena Caratti is also an associate editor of *Studies in Material Thinking*, a peer-reviewed international online journal.

Marianne Fairbanks is an assistant professor in the Design Studies department at the University of Wisconsin–Madison, United States. She received her MFA from the School of the Art Institute of Chicago and her BFA from the University of Michigan. Her work has been shown nationally and internationally in venues including the Museum of Art and Design, New York; the Smart Museum of Art, Chicago; and Copenhagen Contemporary, Denmark. Her work spans the fields of art, design and social practice, seeking to chart new material and conceptual territories, to innovate solution-based design and to foster fresh modes of cultural production.

Tom Fisher has been Professor in the School of Art and Design at Nottingham Trent University, UK, since 2007. He has led research funded by the AHRC and Defra, participating in work funded by WRAP. He is a member of the AHRC Peer Review College and reviews research bids for AHRC, ESRC and EPSRC. He is a member of the Design Research Society Council and lead the Special Interest Group OPEN (Objects, Practices, Experiences, Networks). He has led funded research on sustainable clothing (Defra) and industrial heritage (AHRC).

His background in craft practice (1985–94) has fed his work focused on embodied knowledge, the ethics of design and technologies, design, culture and innovation. He has led research on the textile heritage of Nottingham, particularly, as this relates to future innovation in an international context and has been the basis of his involvement in networks of researchers concerned with innovation. His recent work has included an AHRC-funded network that has focused on innovation in electronic textiles, and he is currently drawing on his work as a maker to develop work in the industrial heritage field on skill acquisition and transmission.

Elaine Igoe is Senior Lecturer in Textiles and Fashion at the University of Portsmouth, UK, and currently Visiting Tutor (Research) in the Department of Textiles at the Royal College of Art, London. Her research is concerned with theories of design as they relate to the creation of textiles, materials and surfaces. Igoe's doctoral study, written autoethnographically, was significant in developing new understandings of textiles within design research. She is a Review Board member for the Journal of Textile Design Research and Practice and for conferences internationally. Her recent articles and chapters focus on textiles in the post-digital era and the ethics of textile production methods.

Marion Lean's doctoral design research at the Royal College of Art, UK, explores methodology for implementing practical material engagement in experiential research encounters including workshops, public exhibition and ethnographic study. The findings suggest new spaces for inquiry and new references for design research which employs material approaches and methods including prototyping and object creation, physical, sensory experience and relationship building. Outcomes are working methods which contribute to the positioning of textile thinking as a means of knowledge production in design research. Previously, Marion worked in design, public engagement and communications roles in London having completed her masters in critical design from Goldsmiths in 2012 and textile design from Dundee in 2011.

Mark Roxburgh is Associate Professor of Design at the University of Newcastle, Australia. Mark's research interests cover design research, visual communication theory and practice, photographic theory and practice and user experience design. His PhD explored the central role that visual images and visual perception play in design, with a specific emphasis on how photographic images condition us to perceive, experience and transform the world in a self-replicating manner. His ongoing research pursuits have been developing a phenomenological theory of photography to counter the dominance of critical theory and semiotic deconstruction and developing a theory of design as a form of embodied perceptual synthesis to counter the dominance of the design problem-solving metaphor.

Rose Sinclair is a Design Lecturer (textiles) in the Design department at Goldsmiths, University of London, UK, where she teaches textiles- and design-related practice at postgraduate level. Her doctoral research focusses on Black British women and their crafting practices, and textiles, through the lens of textiles networks such as Dorcas Clubs and Dorcas Societies, through which she discusses migration, identity and settlement. Rose is also interested in the use of textiles networks as a form of participatory craft practice and public engagement in crafts. Rose continues to explore her textiles practice through participatory immersive workshops in localized pop-up shops, installations and presentations in museums and diverse spaces such as the V&A Museum London, the Bruce Castle Museum and House for An Art Lover. Rose has authored several textile books, her most recent being *Textiles and Fashion, Materials, Design and Technology* (2015). She is a member of the advisory board for Textile: Journal of Cloth and Culture and a member of the AHRC Stitching Together Research Network.

Acknowledgements

The supervisory support and guidance I received during my doctoral studies at the Royal College of Art in the Department of Textiles were the foundation for the ideas developed in this book. I am so grateful to have had the opportunity to have been supervised by Dr Claire Pajaczkowska and Dr Prue Bramwell-Davies – both role models for me in my teaching and research. Likewise my fellow alumna, who remain friends and colleagues. I appreciate the encouragement to go on to publish my research as a book from Professor Jessica Hemmings and Victoria Mitchell back in 2013. More recently, conversations with colleagues and research students in the Department of Textiles at the Royal College of Art have also been key exploring the topics this book covers.

Notably, support and sabbatical funding from the Faculty of Creative and Cultural Industries at the University of Portsmouth has been vital in the development of this manuscript. I thank the fashion and textiles team in particular; helpful dialogue and practical support were given without question and were deeply valued. Thank you Susan Noble, Rachel Homewood, Christine Field and Lara Torres for friendship and unconditional collegiate support.

I acknowledge the contributions of the other authors of this book – not only for their work but also for their advice and patience. I reached out to these individuals to suggest a slightly different approach to academic bookmaking and I am glad to say that I found the right people. I recognize that they too have their own supporting structures to thank. In respect to this I specifically thank Anthony Burton on behalf of Marianne Fairbanks. New academic allegiances have been formed, and existing ones strengthened in the production of this book. In the course of making this book, other individuals have given of their time and energies and although the constraints of professional life meant the involvement had to end, your participation is appreciated. Thank you to the reviewers who give their time to undertake such activities of academic citizenship. I am grateful for the good guidance and support of Frances Arnold and her assistants at Bloomsbury Academic. Many thanks to the committee of the Pasold Trust for supporting this publication with funding for image permissions.

My entire family has offered all types of support as I navigate what it is to be a first-generation academic and author. To my parents, my sisters and my brother, I feel your pride in me. Simon, Nara and Esmé, thank you for giving me joy and balance.

Elaine Igoe, January 2021

Introduction

This book is a conversation about textile design and what it means to approach design from textility.

'Textility' is derived from a common etymological root of the Latin *texere*, meaning 'to weave', and the ancient Greek *techne*, meaning 'to make', and as such offers a model of making that is concerned with the 'slicing and binding of fibrous material' (Mitchell 1997: 7; Ingold 2010: 92). Mitchell goes on to highlight the further connection with 'text', offering textility as inference to a very particular way of making, speaking and writing, but also states: 'It is clear that textiles are not words and the differences between them benefit the conceptual apparatus of thought at the expense of its sensory equivalent' (Mitchell 1997: 8). Webster (1996: 99) explains theories of textuality and writerly texts via Roland Barthes's 'S/Z', in which he frequently uses textile and network metaphors to discuss the structure of texts and describes them as 'a surface over which the reader can range in any number of ways that the text permits'. The tension between the textuality of this publication and its relation to the concept of textility is consistent and apparent throughout this text. Negotiating the tension of this relationship, this *textasis* (see Chapter 15) has become my text-ile practice. I discovered this term 'textasis' in a 2009 essay from Maria Damon. She recounts her residency in Riga in 2008 for the E-text and Textiles Project. Damon's practice combined active poetics with textile practice and she produced small cross-stitched textile works that she sent to friends and colleagues, requesting their interaction and response on the pieces' textuality. One piece, 'B: Tiny Arkhive', was sent to Jewish-Canadian poet Adeena Karasick. BET or b is the second letter of the Hebrew alphabet and in this position is considered as female. Its numeric value is 2, which Karasick sees as signifying a doubling or a multiplicity. It represents a house, an archive – closed on three sides and open on one.

> 'You are an "Open House", which is at once in place, while deprived of any one place. In its place and in place of; re-placed in hyperspatial interplays, you, my tiny archive, displaced en plaisir.' 'Little archive cross-stitched and emanating,

I read you as an embroidered network of socio-linguistic and hermeneutic relations.' (Damon 2009)

Karasick described the piece as 'an inscription of textasis'. This simple term is derived from the ancient Greek *tasis*, meaning stretching, tension or intensity. The example of this collaborative textile work connects ideas of gendering, the matrixial and relational, textuality and textility, representation, symbolism and the quantum, key concepts at various points in this book (Damon 2011).

Mitchell and Ingold's explication of the word 'textilic' should be held as one of the touchstones of this publication. I pick up from Ingold's 2010 paper *The Textility of Making* which outlines the marginalization of textilic approaches to design and making against the primacy of the architectonic model during the Enlightenment. To be textilic is to be textile like – a network, expansive, applicable. It sits between the architectonic and the hylomorphic as paradigms for thinking and making. I expand the notion of a textilic concept of knowledge-making into the matrixial (Ettinger 2005) which allows a feminist expansion of models of design and affords a connection between the exegesis of the design cognition and the designer (maker). The concept of the matrixial denotes trans-subjectivity in regard to the context, the designer(s), the process and the designed outcome.

I suggest that a matrixial approach sets up the connection between the designer and the outcomes and consequences their design spawn. The rhizomatic nature of the matrixial sets up the basis of an unending situation, only broken by external forces acting upon the scenario (see Chapter 13, *Making, Problems and Pleasures*).

Notions of textilic design and matrixial critiques and approaches to design here have been developed from an exploration into what textile design is at a fundamental level. However, my intention is to echo Anni Albers provocation at the start of her book *On Weaving* (1965: IX). *Textile Design Theory in the Making* is not only for those who identify with the disciplinary field of textile design but all those who find it difficult to associate with oversimplified, transactional or convergent models of design. Johan Redström's book *Making Design Theory* (2017) was one of the first to challenge these tenets and suggest that the development of design theory must recognize fluidity, complexity and indeed practice. On a less significant aspect, Redström (2017: 143) points to the lack of imagery in his book and this book too is sparsely illustrated. This may seem unusual, particularly for a book concerned with textile design. It is again an intentional move and an enactment and recognition of relational textile practice. The publication of this book is long preceded by Beverly Gordon's richly illustrated and veritable tome *Textiles: The Whole Story* (Gordon 2013). The image research to be found in Gordon's publication is extraordinary and, to date, unmatched. In many ways, this book cannot be read or fully understood without referring to it; certainly, it provides the best global and historical visualization of notions of how textility exists in the world.

In her preface, Gordon explains her discovery of the story of the Veil of *Maya* within Hindu philosophy (2013: 15). She points out that everything we think we know of our individualistic world is *Maya*. There exists a shimmering veil of Maya which has a purpose of shielding us from the essential wholeness of being but yet is there to remind us of the illusion of our incarnate existence, we are 'caught by its materiality'. Gordon presents her book as a textile installation which mimics the action of the veil of Maya.

I too got caught up in philosophical stories of mesh-like structures when conceptualizing my approach to bookmaking on textiles and the Buddhist philosophy of Indra's net struck me as significant.

> Far away in the heavenly abode of the great god Indra, there is a wonderful net which has been hung by some cunning artificer in such a manner that it stretches out infinitely in all directions. In accordance with the extravagant tastes of deities, the artificer has hung a single glittering jewel in each 'eye' of the net, and since the net itself is infinite in dimension, the jewels are infinite in number. There hang the jewels, glittering 'like' stars in the first magnitude, a wonderful sight to behold. If we now arbitrarily select one of these jewels for inspection and look closely at it, we will discover that in its polished surface there are reflected all the other jewels in the net, infinite in number. Not only that, but each of the jewels reflected in this one jewel is also reflecting all the other jewels, so that there is an infinite reflecting process occurring. (Cook 1973: 2)

Indra's net is an infinite mesh, matrix, grid, lattice, cat's cradle, weave, knit, cloth, fabric: but not only that, it is decorated and decorative, ornamental, glittery, bejewelled, draped so as to please the Gods. But the clever maker of this dazzling matrix remains unnamed. I have responded to the metaphor of Indra's net in both forming and representing the epistemology and methodology that evolved in the structure of this study. But rather than conceal the identity of the maker, through methods of autoethnography, the significance of my identity is not only allowed to surface but is also embodied by the infinite mesh I am adding to. In terms of structure this book is non-linear, borrowing and referencing the notion of an expanding matrix, studded with texts that I hope capture the reflexivity of the research process as they project and reflect onto and into one another in a recursive way. Each chapter is interstitial.

Chapter 1 *Too much to tell* outlines the feminist research approach that has shaped this book. The autoethnographic, narrative style used throughout is explained and the source of the guiding research questions is described. Adams and Holman Jones (2008: 379) outlining the dominant critique of autoethnographic research.

> . . . too much personal mess, too much theoretical jargon, too elitist, too sentimental, too removed, too difficult, too easy, too White, too Western, too colonialist, too indigenous. Too little artistry, too little theorizing, too little connection of the personal and political, too impractical, too little fieldwork, too few real-world applications.

This book's approach may be too much or too little for you. There may simply be too much or too little of its unapologetic narrative style. I intentionally use direct quotes heavily across the text, often suspended between paragraphs as an invitation for personal thought and interpretation before I offer my own. I aim to represent a multitude of voices rather than simply my own singular narration or interpretation. You will have already noted the purposeful use of personal pronouns. It is a monograph in many ways, but one in which I have invited discursive participation from scholars inside and outside of textiles. Their responses are included here alongside mine and collaboratively evidence 'the making' referred to in the title of this book.

Ramia Mazé talks of 'bookmaking as a feminist practice' (Mazé 2018). She describes her experience of being an author, editor and reviewer of several publications and says that

> my work reported here can be understood as a kind of 'practice-led' research, in which my reflections and conceptualizations have accumulated gradually on the basis of multiple experiences of bookmaking.

Mazé refers to and applies Jane Rendell's five modes of critical practice to her feminist bookmaking practice/practise (Rendell 2011 in Mazé 2018), namely collectivity, interiority, alterity, materiality and performativity. In *Textile Design Theory in the Making*, *collectivity* is manifested in the presentation of the book as a report on a methodology that is an actively and collectively developing one. *Interiority* supports philosophical approaches that explore connectedness and interdependency and here is developed through Ettinger's concept of the matrixial in Chapter 2: *Matrixial meaning*. *Alterity* is explored in the discussion of gendering in design history and the development of its theories in Chapter 7: *A story of hard and soft*. This book is *performative* in its autoethnographic approach

(Chapter 1) as well as the breadth of genres and ideologies it espouses and is played out in its structure, its *materiality*.

Chapter 3: *Talking textiles* is a short reflective text that encapsulates my research methods and tells a story – a truth about how interactions with the subject of my study – textile designers – played out and my agency within it as the researcher.

Chapter 4: *Design, thinking and textiles thinking* outlines research into the industrial structure of textile designing as well as pedagogic research in the field. This is contrasted with the development of design research and subsequently design thinking. Textile thinking as a concept is traced through the literature and 'textilic design' proposed as a development of such. After which begins a series of chapters whose content is extrapolated directly from conversations with textile designers and makers. Anonymous excerpts from these conversations are blended into polyphonic, non-linear texts called 'meshes' that intersperse the chapters.

Chapter 5: *Translating and transforming* investigates the role of the textile designer and textile as translator and semantic object, looking at design as an action of response, pledging back and gift- giving. It is paired with a chapter from Elena Caratti and Daniela Calabi on design as translation which is explored through notions of texture design.

Jessica Hemmings (2010) advocates the scholarly application of fiction, narrative and populist writings to develop an academic canon for textiles. Chapter 7: *A story of hard and soft: Modernism and textiles as design* takes a work of fiction by Paul Scheerbart entitled *The Gray Cloth* as a metaphor for the marginalization of textiles within modernist ideology and the subsequent impact on conceptions of textiles as design. The metaphoric comfortable emerald room (Scheerbart 2001) was for too long a space where textile designers quietened their expertise and subscribed to ideologies of craft and applied art.

This is further expanded in Chapter 8: *The gendered textile design discipline* which also draws on aspects of Chapter 5 to define how the discipline of textile design became gendered. In this chapter I expose a number of gendered metaphors for the entity of textiles, encompassing designers, designed outcomes, process and contexts. This is balanced by work from both Marion Lean and Rose Sinclair. In Chapter 9, Lean extends these ideas in the context of contemporary textile design practice and recent applications of textile thinking. Sinclair's contribution in Chapter 10 exposes the specific challenges for women of colour within the field and the invisibility of both race and craft skills in our understanding of textile design.

In Chapter 11: *Paraphernalia and playing for design* I take on notions of playing in the process of designing, particularly with reference to playing cognitively as well as with materials at hand. The role of objects – stuff – for textile designers is the starting point for this chapter which picks back up notions of translation and taciturnity discussed earlier in the book. In Chapter 12, Tom Fisher provides us with a text in which he turns his attention to some objects he has made or found and their function in his career in 'making' with wood and in furniture design and design academia.

In Chapter 13: *Making, problems and pleasure* I return to earlier questions explored regarding design as problem-solving. I apply this to the field of textile design; mainstream textiles as well as innovation-led textile research. What 'problems' does textile design address itself to? Following this Mark Roxburgh develops an argument against the problematization of design. Through the work of Merleau-Ponty and Flusser and his own field of practice as an image-maker, Roxburgh critiques the prescriptive foundations of design theory and posits the perceptual basis of design as an alternative model for our understanding.

The concluding chapter, Chapter 15: *Elevated surfaces*, returns to relational conceptions of design and picks up the topics of the preceding chapters as it proposes definitions for what textile design is and how textilic design could be expanded. I have deliberately avoided approaches to concluding this book neatly; it is after all *in the making*. Instead the last pages provide an interruption of play, a breakage of the rhizome (Deleuze and Guattari 1980: 10), a point of inflection in the Deleuzian fold or a jewel in the (Indra's) net of textilic practice. In fact, this book closes not with my own words but an offshoot into the work of others – an epilogic account from Marianne Fairbanks, a textile practitioner across art, design and innovation. It is her work in fact that wraps this book, so, fittingly, she provides a co-emergent insight into how the thoughts drawn together in this chapter influence her textilic practice.

Writing this book has been an activity of looping, mending and reweaving. Repair as reparation to older ideas that myself and others have built upon. I naturally weave in work from others that has been created in the meantime or that now seems to have a place. My previous work has been cited by others and their work naturally critiques, builds, extends and applies those ideas. I wish to present this truthfully, allowing the layers or time and thinking to be apparent. My aim for my writing practice is that it similarly unfolds using feminist practices through narrative inquiry methods – representing multiple voices and truths through story, metaphor and critique.

This emerges from observations made through the contextualization of the textile design discipline within modernism, reappropriation and re-signification of textile metaphors, conversation, storytelling and restorying as analysis, often subsequently blended and meshed. You will notice that each of these research methods involves a dynamic: something is in something, something is in relation to something else, something combines with something else; notions of relationality, in inevitable partnership with tension, permeate the epistemology of this book at every level. This is attended to in the contextual discussion of design in regard to metamodernism in the concluding chapter, Chapter 15: *Elevated surfaces*.

My research methodology is a montage of qualitative methods, using autoethnography, storytelling and conversation to support textile designers in describing their own process and thinking. My aim is to situate these different stories in relation to the established context of design research. This volume aims to find a location between the types of fictional, poetic, social, cultural, political, historical writing found in textile culture publications and the current and broadest discourse of design theory. Daniela Rosner's book *Critical Fabulations: Reworking the Methods and Margins of Design* (2018) provides a significant influence on this publication. Rosner's work similarly uses narrative, first-person, feminist approaches to expose and 'rework' the margins of design. Key to her study is her exploration of textile structure and computation. Indeed a 'critical fabulation', as defined by Saidiya Hartman and later Rosner, is what I propose. This book aims to sit alongside *Critical Fabulations* in developing a body of alternative writings on what designing is.

I have invited contributions from authors whose research practice varies across forms of art, design and craft and who can offer additional viewpoints on the propositions of the key chapters. At the outset the editing relationship was set up as a dialogue. Their contributions are responses to my draft chapters and subsequently my final texts have been influenced by theirs. Their chapters have been minimally edited to retain style and voice and to respect authorship, avoiding any perceived hierarchy. The contributors include early to mid-career academics and distinguished professors. Three of the contributors I have never met but I sought out to find individuals who would be able to extend and probe my ideas in an interesting way. One is a long-standing and respected associate and another is one of my completed doctoral students. Our grouping of authors does not yet go far enough in terms of diverse representation or in decolonizing academia. Initial proposals for this book included further contributions that could address these long-standing issues. The inevitable permutations of personal lives and global pandemics alongside the structural machinations of academic bookmaking prevented the realization of this initial proposal. Where this project has fallen short, I have engaged in citation politics (Mott and Cockayne 2017) referencing a majority of woman scholars. As mentioned earlier, Mazé and her collaborators' approach was not without obstacles set in place by the conventions of academia and publishing. This is my attempt to develop an additional example of how bookmaking can be a form of feminist design practice.

As you read, you will note marked differences in the style of writing and research approach throughout. This is intentional and communicates a very real shift that I experienced from an objective research style to one where my subjectivity became vital to the research. This shift occurred in response to several contingent factors in both the personal and academic realms of my lived experience.

> The individual is both site and subject of these discursive struggles for identity and for remaking memory. Because individuals are subject to multiple and competing discourses in many realms, their subjectivity is shifting and contradictory, not stable, fixed, rigid. (Richardson 2000: 929)

I wanted to make my own discursive struggle evident across these pages, to use mine and others' writing, as Richardson suggests, as a method (and as such, record) of qualitative inquiry.

When I learnt printed textile design, ensuring that you trim your sample so that it appears as if it is cut from a roll of fabric with no borders was one of the first presentation conventions we encountered. In terminology borrowed from graphic design or photography this would be called a 'full-bleed' method of presentation. My textile practice bleeds into and reflects onto the written and visual work of others, some of which have been directly referenced and some not; some give their names and contributions here, others not. All are respectfully acknowledged as essential to this polyphony.

> There is no longer a tripartite division between a field of reality (the world) and a field of representation (the book) and a field of subjectivity (the author). Rather, an assemblage establishes connections between certain multiplicities drawn from each of these orders, so that a book has no sequel nor the world as its object nor one or several authors as its subject. (Deleuze and Guattari 1980/2008: 25)

1

Too much to tell

Autoethnography

Developed over the past fifty years as a response to colonialism and issues of representation, autoethnography is used as a critical approach to knowledge-making across a range of fields. Carolyn Ellis, a leading autoethnographer, tells how she came to develop her autoethnography as a poststructuralist, postmodern, feminist researcher contesting issues of authority, representation, voice and method (Adams, Holman Jones and Ellis 2015: 3). She describes how, as an approach to her field of ethnography, it united her 'sociological eye with a communicative heart'. Autoethnography was a way to overcome the crisis of representation, to avoid generalizing and homogenous positivism and to recognize the subjectivity of the situated researcher.

> Autoethnography is a qualitative method – it offers nuanced, complex, and specific knowledge about particular lives, experiences, and relationships rather than general information about large groups of people. (Adams, Holman Jones and Ellis 2015: 21)

The research presented in this book began as personal questions, doubts and stories I told myself, about myself and my situation. I came to a point in my career in design academia where these feelings and thoughts surfaced in direct confrontation to what I was rationally, objectively researching. It got to a point where I was forced to deal with them. Autoethnography permitted me to take the route that allowed for complexity and subjectivity, recognizing this juncture as a 'personal-cultural entanglement' (Adams, Holman Jones and Ellis 2015: 22). I aim to achieve the four principles for evaluating autoethnography as set out by Adams, Holman Jones and Ellis (2015: 102–4).

1. Make contributions to knowledge
2. Value the personal and experiential

3. Demonstrate the power, craft and responsibilities of stories and storytelling
4. Take a relationally responsible approach to research practice and representation

This book seeks to contribute to design research and develop design theory. It does this through valuing collective subjective experience in the field of textile design, expressed through narrative methods, both directly told and restoried or fabulated. It is structured through and upon a framework of critical relationality – informing both its premise and its delivery.

Ellis and Bochner's paper *Autoethnography, Personal Narrative, Reflexivity: Researcher as Subject* (2000) tells us a story about what it is to be an autoethnographer, what it is to learn about autoethnography and how the approach developed within the broader field of narrative enquiry. Its storied style makes it easy to read and accessible, even though its content is complex. Reading Ellis and Bochner's work inspired me to write large the changes that have happened throughout my research journey, accepting that edges of my various bits of writing are ragged and frayed, not smooth and sharp. They overlay, enmesh and entangle; they don't tessellate. And I won't try to make them, either.

> [T]he researcher's personal experience becomes important primarily in how it illuminates the culture under study. Reflexive ethnographies range along a continuum from starting research from one's own experience to ethnographies where the researcher's experience is actually studied alongside with other participants, to confessional tales where the researcher's experience of doing the study becomes the focus of investigation. (Ellis and Bochner 2000)

Through reflective writing, through co-creating stories with other textile designers, through the structuring and presentation of this book, I am expressing an autoethnography. I am expressing my life, my character, my constraints, my relationships and my position on textile design in the world. In this book can be seen the evidence of the story of its development. In some ways I wish I could be braver, dating each piece of writing, placing it firmly at the point at which it was thought, written and rewritten, resisting polishing and tessellation. I do consider this text as my creative research practice. My textile design aesthetic is experimental, conceptual, revolving around processes, drawn to texture and nature. My research approach is drawn to equivalent qualities within research methods and methodological design.

Conversation

The key tool I have used to retrieve the fragments of experience is the recorded conversation. The key thoughts presented in this book were based on a series of fifteen recorded conversations which took place between February 2009 and March 2011 and developed through countless informal conversations, emails and further academic work in the years since. These recorded conversations were initially set up as unstructured/semi-structured interviews, but most played out as conversations. At the time, I berated myself as researcher for jumping in and talking, but it was too difficult not to. I was talking to textile designers. I am a textile designer. I teach textile designers. Most of the so-called 'interviews' had been arranged through mutual contacts, or we were fellow alumni. I was inextricably connected to the people I was talking with. I felt at ease and let myself seep into the talking. The individuals I spoke to were students of textile design, world-famous textile designers, textile studio owners, designer makers, textile innovators, commercial textile designers, textile design lecturers, embroidery designers, print designers and weave designers. Some I was in awe to be speaking to, others were literally old friends. They took place in my research space, in cafes, in their studios; I spoke to friends over the phone while they were at work and strangers invited me into their kitchens to talk over homemade soup. Each scenario was interpersonal: trans-subjective encounters, to use Ettinger's terminology.

For the first set of conversations in 2009, I arrived with a list of specific questions that I hoped to pop when the moment should arise. They covered these main areas: working and thinking methods for textile design, communicating design ideas and outcomes for textiles, self-awareness and identification with the concept of textile design. This list of questions often stifled the conversation as it began to emerge. The talk would then begin to loosen and I would steer it ridiculously back to my questions, the dialogue jumping about wildly.

One particular question proved problematic: why do we design textiles? The designers found this question difficult, both to understand and to answer. This question later morphed into me asking about the 'role of textile design'. I wanted to know how the textile designers see the significance of their work.

For the ensuing conversations from 2010 and 2011, I allowed a more natural flow of conversation. At this stage I was more comfortable with open-endedness and had set down some of the specificities I was targeting in the initial conversations.

My personality, my relationships, my research expertise (or lack of it) and my textile knowledge were all brought to bear on each conversation. This is evident as the textile designers talked to me about tutors we had had in common, shortened names for our alma mater and initialisms for certain trade events. In *Living Narrative*, Elinor Ochs and Lisa Capps champion the conversation, specifically personal narratives and everyday storytelling, as a means of exploring narrative for three key reasons. It affords an inherent open-endedness, is a medium for airing unresolved events and it elicits familiarity (2001: 6). They describe how conversational narratives reveal the vernacular and a way of ordering, explaining and establishing a position on experience (2001: 57).

Some of the mutual connections we held were unknown at the outset, only coming to light precisely through conversation, in turn simultaneously building and altering the nuance of the talk. The familiarity that was often established at times turned the direction of the conversation back to myself, the textile designers asking me about my design work and research. Other times, I do this for myself, offering up thoughts and comments for debate that are unique to that specific conversation. This dialogue meant that although I was always the initiator of the talk, I did not hold all the control over it. It became a conversation rather than interview because of its dialogical content. The active participation from both parties changed and altered the direction and content of the talk (Ochs and Capps 2001: 55).

Informal conversations and encounters have naturally influenced my approach to bookmaking. It so often goes without saying but it shouldn't. Conference presentations and invitations to speak at events that seemed to me at first to be a tangent opened up new areas and connections – new words too. Academics finding my (old) work for the first time allowed me to see its currency as well as its flaws. Students using, testing and challenging my work to make their own new work is so directly encouraging and invigorating. Being part of that process as a PhD supervisor is a privilege as well as a prompt as a researcher.

Stories and fabulations

The outcomes of these conversations can be read as narratives, or 'everyday stories', as Ochs and Capps put it, about the lives of these textile designers. These stories include elements of delight, regret, humour, anger, nostalgia, mundanity and reflection. Some aspects have been well rehearsed in prior conversations;

others show new ideas and perspectives surfacing within that moment. The notion of extracting rational 'truth' from these stories is nonsensical. Each textile designer has told me a story about their experience of being a textile designer. Walter Benjamin parallels everyday storytelling with the physicality and materiality of making.

> [A story] does not aim to convey the pure essence of the thing, like information or a report. It sinks the thing into the life of the storyteller, in order to bring it out of him again. Thus, traces of the storyteller cling to the story the way the handprints of the potter cling to the clay vessel. (Benjamin 1936: 91)

And the structure and content of the stories told to me at that time were affected by me: my own story and my own questions.

> For it is granted to him to reach back to a whole lifetime (a life, incidentally, that comprises not only his own experience but no little of the experience of others; what the storyteller knows from hearsay is added to his own.) His gift is the ability to relate his life; his distinction, to be able to tell his entire life. (Benjamin 1936: 108)

These stories do not hold truths but commonalities of experience that might develop new knowledge and understanding, 'openly or covertly, something useful'(1936: 86):

In fact, one can go on and ask oneself whether the relationship of the storyteller to his material, human life, is not in itself a craftsman's relationship, whether it is not his very task to fashion the raw material of experience, his own and that of others, in a solid, useful and unique way. (Benjamin 1936: 107)

The *Talking Textiles* chapter offers a piece of creative writing for which I used a process recommended by Ellis and Bochner (2000: 752). They suggest using a process of emotional recall where the writer revisits a scene emotionally and physically. In this piece, I blended two conversation scenarios together to help indicate the trans-subjective encounter that took place, focusing on motifs of interconnectedness and reflexivity. Ellis and Bochner highlight the advantage of recalling these emotions as close to the experience as possible; however, for me, it was what I experienced in the years between that allowed me to reflect and connect the two scenarios, offering a perspective on my research methodology and methods.

The writing methods myself and the contributing authors employ are a combination of conventional academic writing interspersed with examples of creative non-fiction (Tedlock 2011: 336). Tedlock characterizes creative non-fiction as factually accurate, polyphonic and scenical, and centrally positions the researcher/author as character. The various pieces of creative non-fiction that punctuate this book were written at different times: they are independent but are connected through my experience as textile designer and researcher.

Ronald Pelias (2011: 660) describes how writing might function as a both a realization and record. He cites M. L. Rosenthal's quote from 1987 suggesting that writing is 'the unfolding of a realization, the satisfying of a need to bring to the surface the inner realities of the psyche', and remarks on the difference of 'writing up' and 'writing into'. I use words to help me discover what I want to say. Pelias goes on to explain how realizations recorded and brought about through writing can be felt with confidence or some level of doubt, but that these realizations importantly 'unfold on a continuum from the personal to the public', supporting feminist ideology; he then quickly cautions on separating the personal and the public/political. The writing that makes up this book moves between and conjoins both objective and subjective writing styles as required, recognizing that both have their place and that all writing is a record. Older pieces of work have been cut and spliced with very recent writing and reconfigured. Personal narratives sit alongside conventional styles; mythologies and literature are incorporated into analytical texts; the sections do not flow directly into one another but largely rely on the heuristics of the reader to establish the connections.

In *Critical Fabulations* (2018) Daniela Rosner uses 'fabulation' to displace established understandings of design. To fabulate is to talk or narrate in fables – to invent, concoct and fabricate. Rosner takes this concept from writer Saidiya Hartman who developed critical fabulation in her own work as an approach to re-storying. Rosner describes how in her fabulated account of a project which combined quilting and electrical engineering in a design context, she hopes to expand the opportunities for the groups and spaces in which design takes place and in doing so 'reorient what lies ahead' (Rosner 2018: 1). Rosner clearly sets out her feminist technoscience research approach and based on this challenges established design theory. She designates these as four dimensions:

- Individualism – design as an aggregation of individuals.
- Objectivism – design as science paradigm promotes rationality and objectivity.
- Universalism – designers 'imagine' things about their target 'users'.
- Solutionism – to identify opportunities, designers often direct towards predefined solutions.

Avoiding setting up a binary position, Rosner describes the tactics (Rosner 2018: 15) with which she challenges these dimensions:

- Alliances – demands that design recognizes that it operates in concert with and not on behalf of the groups for whom it works.
- Recuperations – 'the possibility of design to ignite recuperations enlivening neglected histories of encounter' (Rosner 2018: 14).
- Interferences – propose alternative frames of analysis to expand and change existing regimes.
- Extensions – design is remade over time, across contexts and in circulations of practice.

There are two stories or fabulations I wish to tell about this research journey. Both are true.

The first might be considered a tragedy (Booker 2004). The protagonist (myself) embarks on a quest, only to find that the quest takes her into unpredictable territories, ones she is unfamiliar with and unprepared for. She finds that the decisions she makes are naïve and ungrounded and she realizes that she cannot go back. Only the guidance of her elders can lead her back to safety.

The second, a tale of rebirth (Booker 2004). Our main character is captivated by a dream of a new reality and works doggedly to achieve the status she so desires. The voices and actions of others reinforce her fascination. Only those who know her best realize that she is looking in the wrong places to fulfil her dreams. The story builds to a crescendo that results in a moment of clarity for the protagonist, who comes to recognize that she already possesses the knowledge and material required to manifest a new reality of greater worth and meaning than she could have ever dreamt of.

The ontological paradigm or 'world view' of this study can be considered to oscillate between the constructivist and participatory/postmodern, as outlined by Lincoln, Lynham and Guba (2011: 102), and its connected epistemology is well illustrated by Ettinger's matrixial, intersubjective encounter. Holding this 'world view' means that for me, of the two tales, I must select the second as my plot. It's a story that emphasizes the socially constructed nature of knowledge, and also that:

> Realities are taken to exist in the form of multiple mental constructions that are socially and experientially based, local and specific, and dependent on their form and content on the persons who hold them. (Guba 1990 in Lincoln, Lynham and Guba 2011: 107)

The 'multiple mental constructions' that I show here are stories of what it is to design textiles: my own story and those of others. The aim of gathering and thinking around these stories is to prompt a deeper understanding and articulation of the knowledge and thinking crucial to textile design in others and myself.

I intend that the stories, gathered in different ways and at different times over fifteen years and hermeneutically told through my own research practice, should create a layered polyphony, not one singular, uniform voice.

Enmeshing

As an analysis method I have elected to 're-story' the stories (Craig and Huber 2007) I have co-created. Using transcripts from recorded conversations and notes and memories from other encounters, I have developed a number of montaged texts that interweave our subjective experiences and understandings of textile design. The resultant 'meshes', as I have called them, resemble a 'fusion of horizons' (Gadamer 1960: 306) that offer perspectives on textile design.

Ochs and Capps (2001:6) discuss the 'polyphonic and indeterminate quality of human events and non-events' as captured by writers such as Dostoevsky and Tolstoy: although they can be hard to describe in the way that they oscillate between often conflicting perspectives in a non-linear fashion, they better resemble human experience. They encourage an understanding of narrative as 'fuzzy' and as a means for imagining possibilities, shifting mindsets and for acting from a place of uncertainty.

The way I have written the 'meshes' intentionally retains the idiosyncrasies of the speech patterns and vocabulary of the participants but are intersected and interwoven to emphasize specific commonalities and themes that arose. The effect is polyphonic: it is clear that the texts did not originate from only one individual, but it is still difficult to identify individual voices and narratives.

They are called meshes in order to highlight this interwoven character and for the metaphor it affords. Meshes filter and refine. These texts have been created to enable me to sift through the discussions and extract key concepts. Creating the meshes required iterative close reading and recall activities. As I did so, I noted down keywords and concepts that arose from each one, creating extractions of significant passages and phrases. I then reread each of the simplified transcripts and began to integrate them, creating new texts where I pasted in phrases and excerpts based around the commonalities I had discovered. This activity required me to reread transcripts and notes a large number of times – each time having to reconsider the groupings of commonalities. Some phrases are reused in several of the meshes as the complexity of meaning in certain sentences became more and more apparent with each rereading. I noted that I was developing different ways of understanding these stories, these truths.

The meshes are devised as a means of defining important characteristics of textile design. They are of course innately connected through myself and the other textile designers whose stories they are founded on. I like to consider the meshes as transparent, pliable 'supple fabrications' (Mitchell 1997), woven together (Bateson 2000) and layered up in their retelling of the narrative of textile design, piling up to become something more substantive, as described by Walter Benjamin in *The Storyteller* (1936: 92):

'That slow piling one on top of the other of thin, transparent layers which constitutes the most appropriate picture of the way in which the perfect narrative is revealed through the layers of a variety of retellings.'

Four meshes are interspersed throughout the book and they align with the main chapters retaining the spoken, conversational quality of the words. As well as the four meshes that punctuate the book I also include pieces of reflective and creative writing, both from myself and some of the contributing authors. These texts invite further interpretations, beyond those I have involved myself with at this stage.

The significance and importance of re-evaluating research is discussed by Margery Wolf in *A Thrice Told Tale*, in which she publishes three depictions of an event that took place while she was conducting anthropological field research in Taiwan in 1960. They include a piece of fiction, field notes and records of conversations and observations and an academic paper, some written at the time, others more recently: all written by her. She also provides a brief rationalized summary and commentary on each depiction. Wolf adopts a feminist critique of ethnography and asserts that the retelling of the original story in different styles to different audiences yielded different outcomes and conclusions. Wolf recognizes the requirement to be reflexive – questioning methodology and process. She states how important it was to return to her field notes when re-evaluating the fictional piece she wrote, and yet these only provide a summary, 'a partial and incomplete version of reality' (Wolf 1992: 87). They are in themselves un-self-conscious fictions.

> Stories of individuals and their relationships through time offer another way of looking, but we need ways to tell stories that are interwoven and recursive, that escape from the linearity of print to incite new metaphors. (Bateson 2000: 247)

In the preparation of this book, the meshes have been reworked again – an activity akin to securing, reinforcing, mending and repair or as Rosner might say an act of recuperation. This activity brings conversations and thoughts from the past back into focus; recognizing a lineage over time. As soon as I put these re-stories, these fabulations into words they become too fixed of course. The process of developing a publication offers critical review but the outcome is fixed in time – the time of reading often being a good while after thinking or writing. But I present them as meshes; they are a flexible tool, a substrate or a mediating material for further researchers.

Metaphor

Our ordinary conceptual system, in terms of which we both think and act, is fundamentally metaphorical in nature. The concepts that govern our thought are not just matters of the intellect. They also govern our everyday functioning, down to the most mundane details. Our concepts structure what we perceive, how we get around in the world and how we relate to other people. Our conceptual system thus plays a central role in defining our everyday realities. If we are right in suggesting that our conceptual system is largely metaphorical, then the way we think, what we experience and what we do every day is very much a matter of metaphor (Lakoff and Johnson 1980/2003: 3).

Lakoff and Johnson's classic text describes the unavoidable significance of metaphor to thinking, knowing and being: as their title points out, we 'live by' metaphors. And indeed they are fundamental to this book: abundant in the texts I have read and responded to; latent in my conversations with supervisors and textile designers; and essential to my thinking, writing and analytical processes. Andrew Ortony's revised compilation *Metaphor and Thought* (1993) provides key texts on the significance of metaphor, not only within language but also cognition. The very premise for the epistemological foundation of what I propose is set; relationality is represented by the metaphorical and feminist content of the concept of the matrixial (Ettinger 2006a). Laurel Richardson describes feminist researchers' introduction of the 'theory is story' metaphor, recognizing the importance of narrating their lived experience and how these individual and shared stories are a mode of theorizing (Richardson 2000: 927).

Donald Schön (1978: 137) focuses on 'generative metaphors', which he describes a '"carrying over" of frames of perspective from one domain of experience to another' and sets this in the contemporary context that metaphor is crucial to how people account for their personal world view, how they make sense of reality, how they set and solve problems and how they think. He asserts that metaphor can be considered as simultaneously a product (like a frame) as well as a generative process. Schön alludes to the fact that what is viewed, framed or set through a metaphor (in his example, the problematics of social policy) are also processed by it, generating new perspectives. This notion of 'framing' allows the influence of viewpoints and subjectivity on a problematic situation. Schön recognizes how storytelling invites varying viewpoints, shaping, setting or framing a problem, using metaphors as interpretive devices that invite critical analysis.

> In short, we can spell out the metaphor, elaborate the assumptions which flow from it, and examine their appropriateness in the present situation. (Schön 1978: 138)

Schön goes on to emphasize his use of the term 'problem setting' over 'problem solving' believing that the way in which an objective is framed is more important than selecting specific methods to achieve them. He says that stories have 'problem-setting potency' (Schön 1978: 150) which is sometimes derived from their underlying generative metaphor. Schön's comments set up the connection between metaphor and narrative that has become so pervasive in my research. The development and exploration of the 'textile design as female entity' involves the interaction of 'entailments' and 'reverberations' (Lakoff and Johnson 1980/2003: 140), not least the paradigm of 'design as feminine'. These entailments and reverberations act to specify the metaphor and how it may be used and understood. Metaphors can have wildly different meanings for different people based on their culture and lived experience. If we do 'live by' metaphor, I must explore the assumptions held within the generative metaphor I use here, while challenging those embodied within the established understanding of design theory and the metaphors involved.

Returning to Schön's terminology of framing, this sets up an example of 'frame awareness, frame conflict and frame restructuring' (Schön 1978: 150). In this research, the frame of understanding textile design is identified, challenged and reformed to allow a feminist critique of design theory through textile.

2

Matrixial meaning

Kyoto, Japan, 2010

Its architect, Hiroshi Hara, called it *The Matrix*. The complex curving network of steel beams of the roof of Kyoto Railway Station is evident from the main concourse. You only achieve the real sense of it when emerging up through the vast building on its seemingly endless escalators that transport you past floors and floors of retail outlets, restaurants and hotels and platforms.

The heat of the August afternoon was getting to me. My husband was off elsewhere. It was just too hot for me. The architecture of the place, although dated, was compelling. I reached the humid air of the open rooftop and stopped to take in the view of the Kyoto skyline, familiar as a metropolis but hemmed in by mountainous hills on all sides.

At that point I had already been considering the notion of nets and meshes metaphorically in relation to textiles, and the term 'matrix' struck a chord with this way of thinking. The information plaques dotted around the roof garden explained the etymological basis of the word as 'womb' or a 'place or medium where something is developed'. The building's roof forms a literal matrix in its mesh-like qualities and is womb-like in the sense that it does not entirely enclose the building. It creates a space that is at once open and closed, allowing the architectural experience to change and alter in respect to the interplay of natural and artificial light, the weather and inside/outside occurrences.

On returning home, I wanted to express the matrix-like nature of textiles in my writing, clumsily using 'matrixical' (a non-existent word of my own creation); however, some internet searching soon unearthed for me the term 'matrixial' and the theories developed by artist, theoretician, clinical psychologist and psychoanalyst Bracha Lichtenberg Ettinger. Ettinger's theory of the matrixial and associated concepts are recognized as a significant contribution to psychoanalytic theoretical discourse. Ettinger's texts are linguistically creative and challenging. With no experience in psychoanalytical texts I had to persevere but eventually an understanding began to emerge that revealed fruitful resonances.

Griselda Pollock and Judith Butler provide many critical explorations of Ettinger's written and artistic works. Pollock, in her article 'Mother trouble: the maternal-feminine in phallic and feminist theory in relation to Bracha Ettinger's elaboration of matrixial ethics' (2009) begins with an excerpt from Sylvia Plath's poem 'Love Letter', written in 1960, six months after the birth of her daughter. Pollock draws our attention to its opening line: 'Not easy to state the change you made.' She suggests that the poem is a commentary on both prenatal and postnatal maternity and an exemplar of the trans-subjectivity and co-emergence that Ettinger advocates in her theory:

> I took the intrauterine meeting as a model for human situations and processes in which non-I is not an intruder, but a partner in difference. The Matrix reflects multiple and/or partial joint strata of subjectivity whose elements recognize each other without knowing each other. (Ettinger (1993) cited in Pollock (2009: 5))

Pollock explains how Ettinger chooses to use the word 'matrix' for its literal Latin definition of 'womb' but distinctly for its definition as a complex, generating structure. Just a few weeks after our visit to Japan, I learned that I was pregnant. The coincidence of happening upon matrixial theory during my very early and as yet unknown pregnancy of course meant that I had a certain filter through which to read Ettinger's theories that helped me to understand more deeply her use of the term.

Ettinger (2006b: 219) is clear in her use of this term linked to its 'originary' mode that emerges neither as biologically nor socially gendered. She conceives of a womb/matrix as the site of human potentiality for difference-in-co-emergence and emphasizes the matrixial psychic space as concerned with severality and shareability over collectivity, community or organized-ness. Ettinger clearly states how the matrixial is not an alternative to phallic-centric theoretical models but resides and exists beyond/alongside it. It avoids setting up in opposition to the masculine or dichotomies of feminine and masculine. This very notion challenges several aspects of established psychoanalytical theory. Pollock explains that it

> [I]s not about cosy mothers and babies, symbiosis and fusion, not fantasies of return to oceanic self-loss which are so common in phallic invocations of the maternal body as subjectless otherness and origin from which the subject must be separated to be a subject at all. It invokes a dimension of subjectivity

co-existing with but shifting the phallic, in which the subject is fragile, susceptible and compassionate to the unknown other who is, nonetheless, a partner in the situation but a partner-in-difference. (Pollock 2009: 5)

Subjectivity may be, also and at the same time, for different ends and effects, encounter. (Pollock 2009: 14)

Matrixial theory supports a research approach that promotes the inclusivity of the researcher in the research project and would deny the notion that the two could be separated. In my own experience, it is undeniable that I am in a trans-subjective 'encounter' with my research. I see how my life has shaped the developments of my learning, thinking, making, teaching and writing in both explicit and implicit terms.

Portsmouth, UK, 2012

And now as I return to work after my maternity leave, the necessary completion of this project impacts on the choices my family has made in the organization of our lives to help me achieve my goals.

I have been enrolled as a research student for seven years, and during this time I have (at the very least!) travelled, taught and been taught, got married, been pregnant, given birth and become a working parent. This very piece of writing, in its content, form and how and when it was written, has been inescapably affected by all those factors, plus many more. I have always found it very difficult to find a title for my research project: of course it is tricky to capture the essence of an extended piece of writing in one or two sentences, but when viewed as a developing entity in itself in the way that matrixial theory proposes, how can it be named before it exists in its own right? Its subjectivity is 'fragile and susceptible'. Educational establishments and research councils require clear proposals, outlines, milestones and projected costings when embarking on a research project, but these schemata can never be anything more than fictions. This approach supports a binary approach to thinking with the researcher cloven of involvement in it. Taking the notion of co-emergence and the trans-subjective matrixial encounter further and exploring it in the context of the trimesters of pregnancy, my pregnancy, helps me to make sense of my actual, as opposed to proposed, research process. An experience that, as previously mentioned, is nuanced by complex personal, social and cultural issues. Pollock refers to the contrasts evident between Ettinger's view on creativity, femininity and the maternal and those of Julia Kristeva and Luce Irigaray:

> Thus, Ettinger opens up a new field that radically introduces the concept of the pre-natal/pre-maternal situation of primordial encounter as a basis for recognising another dimension of subjectivity, fantasy and thought that is not all about organs. It concerns structures, logics and affects, as well as garnered or remembered sensations, retroactively (nachträglich) caught up as the basis for both thinking ethics (relations to the other) and aesthetics (transmitted affects and transformations of/in/between the other(s). (Pollock 2009: 7)

I emphasize specific words in this quotation from Pollock as it so clearly outlines how useful the theory of the matrixial is for understanding textiles. Textiles, as designed, made objects (of material culture) are all about structure, logic (/function) and so richly concerned with affect, aesthetics, sensation, communication and relationality. What then can be said about the design (and making) process through the framework of the matrixial? How can Ettinger's textile metaphors be mirrored back to help us understand textile design? Ettinger continues where so many others have started by using textile terms as metaphors in her theories. She describes vibrating 'strings', 'threads' and 'weaving' to describe her version of co-poeisis.

> She is weaving and being woven. She bears witness in the woven textile and texture of psychic transsubjectivity. (Ettinger 2006: 196)
>
> Each psyche is a continuity of the psyche of the other in the matrixial borderspace. We thus metabolize mental imprints and traces for one another in each matrixial web whose psychic grains, virtual and affective strings and unconscious threads participate in other matrixial webs and transform them by borderlinking in metramorphosis. (Ettinger 2005: 704–5)

She describes 'metramorphosis' as 'a process of interpsychic communication and transformation that transgresses the borders of the individual subject and takes place between several entities' (Ettinger 2004: 77). 'Through this process the limits, borderlines, and thresholds conceived are continually transgressed or dissolved, thus allowing the creation of new ones' (Ettinger (1992) cited in Pollock (2009: 3)).

Thus, the matrixial sits as the epistemological framework for this study, unveiling the requirement for the use of a feminist, post-structuralist research approach for this investigation of textile design process and thinking – reflexivity, storytelling and metaphor becoming key elements in my methodology.

A New Place, 2019

Oh how true this feels. Coming back to this means a remembering – sometimes difficult, sometimes not. This thing lives now. It has made a connection to others. It exists. But now I return to it and it must take a new shape. It needs it. Things have changed. No. Things are the same, but I didn't know it then. It is both then, now and the future. This process is asymmetrical but is temporal and has flex, like the stretching and changing of shadows over the course of a day. I move around this thing with a different viewpoint, different aspects are extended and more dense. Occasionally I see the traces of a secondary shadow depending on the angle I see it from. I am putting it back out there in a different form now. The rhizome was forced to branch then but now again, it must too.

> This multiple diachronous as well as synchronous transitivity is asymmetrical, regressive, remembering and at the same time, anticipatory and projective into living futures to come. (Pollock 2009: 9)

Pollock's statement summarizes the generative aspect of the matrixial theory, the severality that Ettinger emphasizes. This facet is crucial in my application of the matrixial as a framework for both my research approach.

This act of returning described earlier in 'A New Place' also cites Ettinger's series of artworks entitled *Eurydice*, where her 'disrupted' photocopies are then painted into in an attempt to capture what was lost in the process of making (metramorphosis). In the attempted 'mending' of the image, it is altered further, resulting in a multilayered image.

> If one is to see Eurydice . . . . One must find the history of what she cannot narrate, the history of her muteness, if one is to recognise her. This is not to supply the key, to fill the gap, to fill in the story, but to find the relevant remnants that form the broken landscape that she is. (Butler 2006: xi)

In the parable of Orpheus and Eurydice, Orpheus's plaintive music provides him with an opportunity to rescue his dead wife from the underworld with the caution that he should lead the way and not look at her until they have reached the light. However, once Orpheus steps foot into the light, he is tempted and he glances around to see her. At once Eurydice sinks back to the underworld and is gone. Ettinger's Eurydice series, the parable itself and Butler's description above provide a metaphoric illustration of the aim of this research.

It would have been easier to have presented these conceptual thoughts in this book as a fait accompli but that is not the story or truth I am wishing to tell.

Actions of shedding, disruption, reworking, mending, alteration, layering and collaboration all set in its temporal contexts are important. Using Denzin and Lincoln's metaphor of pentimento extends these ideas.

Definitions of pentimento not only cover the act of 'painting out' certain aspects in an artwork and the subsequent traces of those original marks and their alterations but also describe these marks once they have been revealed. It describes emergence represented simultaneously through layering and revelation. It implicates the involvement of different individuals and their subjectivity over time, in making marks, adapting them, reading/viewing them and revealing them. Those marks, dismissed and erased, once revealed can shed new light on a subject, telling new stories, inviting alternative understandings of knowledge and meaning. Pentimento also covers the description of an act of remorse and repentance, and in this delivers an accompanying narrative that begs exploration.

The pentimento of this book is the hypothesis of alternative understandings of design. The feminization of textile design as process and object has contributed to its invisibility in the pages of design research, allowing a hegemony to develop within the academic design research community. Like Judith Butler's summary of the parable of Eurydice, I am not filling in gaps in a story but developing one by uncovering existing traces, on top of which I can find correspondence with experiences of textile design. Through this act of layering, a new narrative emerges.

3

Talking textiles

A story

I've made sure that I look right, wearing something colourful – hair big and frizzy. I knock at the door of the terraced townhouse. After some time, a woman in her late forties answers the door with a welcoming smile and I recognize her. Her sweet, bright, flat shoes and patterned tights make me like her instantly. She's wearing a vivid turquoise angora cardigan, so fluffy that it is difficult to make out her silhouette. Visually, her top half appears to diffuse into her surroundings. She invites me into the house and we go into the kitchen. Oh the kitchen! – a view onto the garden, a repainted dresser proudly displaying dozens of apothecary jars and other glass vases each holding some or other lovely flower. Her black crinkled skirt is full and reaches just below her knee. It moves and sways merrily as she walks. A beautiful short-haired grey cat slopes in through the door as she offers me a hot drink and weaves itself through her legs to its bowl. Fresh ginger tea? (Just what I need with this cold) Mug in hand I follow her down the narrow staircase, past bolts of fabrics semi-wrapped in ripped brown paper, to the studio basement. There is music playing, a radio station. The studio is so full of stuff that I don't know where to look first. I am aware that I need to take in every detail, record it somehow in my head or on paper . . . somehow? Let me try and recall it now. The décor is pretty crumby in comparison to upstairs; it's definitely a workshop. There are threads, beads and dust collecting in the corners of the skirting board. The lighting is difficult on this grey day, difficult anyway in a basement I imagine. In the far corner there are floor-to-ceiling bookshelves, filled with large, heavy books on such an unimaginable range of topics – a quick scan showing flowers to be by far being the most prominent. Pinned to the walls and in among the books, in fact, anywhere and everywhere were 'bits and pieces'. I'm not sure how else to describe them – 'objects' might be too grand a term to use to describe this collection of a dusty taxidermy monkey, samples of some kind of flooring, faded silk flowers, a bundle of old ladies headscarves, a cheap beaded coin purse emblazoned with 'Las Vegas', bones, fir cones and countless other such random paraphernalia. Paraphernalia seems much more appropriate a word to use, its meaning evolved from the phrase 'paraphernalia bona' ('paraphernal goods') from the Latin *paraherna*, 'a woman's property besides her dowry', articles of personal property, especially clothing and ornaments, which did not automatically transfer from the property of the wife to the husband by virtue of the marriage. Paraphernalia of course also means the pieces of equipment or products associated with or necessary for an activity. These items, collected by her, I know only too well are absolutely necessary to the process of designing textiles. They are about colour, texture, humour, memories, material, surface qualities, symbolism, culture and personality.

She's already coming out with great stuff that I should be recording! I'm trying to take it all in while responding to her comments. I shall just have to try and write it all down on the Tube later. As she shows me around the studio, she briefly introduces me to the three or four young women who are working hunched over tables, laptops and ironing boards, whom I have just noticed behind all the stuff. I'm unsure as to who actually works there and which ones are on work placements. She asks me where I studied. Loughborough, I said. Oh she said, Lucy went there didn't you Lucy. Lucy and I did not know one other; she was clearly much younger than me, but we gave each other a gentle smile, enough to recognize some level of sorority that seemed to please the woman I'd come to speak to about textile design. I sip my ginger tea as I walk. She begins to point out pieces of work that were framed and/or hung on the wall. She tells me that pieces like that used to be sold as designs for textiles. They were collages, craft pieces, textile doodlings, paintings onto wood. They were so far from what Lucy and the others were working on – digital designs, sublimation prints, screenprints and embroideries, scaled-down garment fronts. The studio 'tour' is soon complete and we take a seat at her desk or 'area', as there isn't really a desk to speak of, more a 'clearing' in the undergrowth of 'paraphernalia'. The conversation flows seamlessly as she asks me what I want to know. (I want to know that I'm right and not imagining all this, emperor's new clothes style – of course I don't say this, I come out with something suitably general and academic.) She starts to talk again and I have to ask her to pause briefly while I set up the digital voice recorder. She begins to speak again. But what is it, now the recorder's on, something has changed in the way she and I are speaking. It's so strange. It's become more formal within seconds. I wish I'd had the recorder on from the moment she opened the front door. But I'm not supposed to do that, am I, that's not what good researchers do. We diligently work through my questions. I try not to talk too much myself, sipping my now cool ginger tea, leaning away so as not to record my slurps. Just remembered, I should be taking notes, I start to scrawl. She starts to talk about something that I'm not that interested in and inwardly I get a little irritated, knowing that my time with her is limited. I interject, trying to steer the conversation back towards my line of questioning. She takes the lead and the conversation starts to cover some really fertile ground. I'm too drawn in to take notes at this stage; this interview has started to become a conversation. I then glance down at the recorder – no red light. No red light! Oh crap – for how long?! I'm thrown. I vocalize my observations and apologize to the textile designer but ask her to keep talking. I get the damned thing going again and I frantically scrawl down all the fascinating aspects that I think I may have missed, while also trying to take in what she's now saying. She comes to the end of her reply and there is a short pause while I just catch up . . .

Done. Ok, what's my next question again, oh yes. We're back on track now but I am so annoyed. I can now not take my eyes off the recorder and have just noticed a 'low battery' warning. Oh that's just brilliant! I will it to keep going till the end. In my distraction, I initially miss that she has asked me a question. She notices and reforms the question. A question about my job. So I reply,

> I got a job as a lecturer, which I'm still doing, because I've always wanted to go into research. I was always more experimental, nothing I ever did was very commercial . . . . I was always into the processes so . . . I got obsessed with paper making, I got obsessed by . . . . I started off my PhD in flocking, I wanted to create some innovative surfaces, flocking with metals and you, know, sort of smart textiles. But along the path, my interest in the textile process, has sort of moved toward understanding the textile design process itself.

I suppose it's come round to this for me to understand myself, really, and my own place in the textiles industry. Why do I still call myself a textile designer when I don't sell anything? I don't even make anything anymore. I feel there is a way of thinking I know I share with people like you who do sell internationally, and designing for a commercial market, and that's what I'm trying to, sort of, get at.

She has noticed that the topic of the conversation has switched sides and begins talking about herself again, but I can't get off my train of thought and continue speaking:

So, yeah. I was originally trained as a textiles designer but I'm not quite sure if . . .

Textile designer: You're not sure if you're still going down that road.

Or, kind of, which sort of position I'm in. Yeah, I just.

The battery dies. And I sense from her eyes that she feels that our conversation is coming to an end also. So I attempt some humour saying that even the recorder doesn't want to hear about me and she seems amused and a bit relieved that she's also no longer on the record. I ask her to complete the permission forms, as she does she says that she really hopes that I got what I needed. As most interviewees seem to do, she then starts to talk more candidly about her viewpoints, and again I try to make mental notes for the journey home.

She signs the forms and with an intake of breath, she looks at my rounded stomach and wishes me luck with the birth and the baby. I gather up my belongings, thank her for her time and the tea and we go back up the stairs and towards the front door, her husband comes into view from the kitchen and she quickly introduces me before he heads upstairs. As I say goodbye she tells me to pass on her best to our mutual contact and tells me to contact her again if I need to. She closes the door. I head back towards the station and feel totally incompetent of course – I'm such a rubbish researcher – I will always carry spare batteries from now on! On the other hand, however flawed the interview was, I feel that there were elements of what was said, by both of us, that offers both confirmation and further questions, and isn't that the point?

Almost two and a half years later, I reread the transcript (parts one and two!), dig out those scrappy notes I made at the back of my notebook, and remember. And I write . . .

Now seven years on again, this day is still so clear. Batteries – ha that dates it! Those questions at the end of the conversation now have an answer. Textile design research is what I am doing. I didn't know it then but those conversations are what unlocked that for me. Only through telling her story; my story; our stories, I was able to find this out. Yet, here I find myself on the frayed edges again. Not now wondering if I really am a textile designer but how I fit in as a design researcher. I am a feminist design researcher. Not making lived experience fit with the dominant ideas in all the books, but highlighting difference. I think naivety gave me courage to talk about textiles in the way I have – a troubled subjective experience. I was just doing research in the way felt right, it was later that this was legitimized by finding out about autoethnography. So I talked textiles and made research. And people read it and it rang true for them and they've used it in their own work. Such an affirmation. So now I find myself in a position which is more like a hinge, conjoining textile design with design research. I steal this metaphoric word 'hinge' from Adams, Ellis and Holman Jones (2008: 374). They describe autoethnography as a hinge – an instrument of transitivity. The point of flex and movement, the generative part, is the making of new design theory.

4

Design, thinking and textile thinking

> [T]he absence of a significant interest from the chattier academic disciplines, the task of establishing such a discourse rests quite clearly with the textile community itself.
>
> (Gale and Kaur 2002)

Questions about the nature of design began to emerge in the late 1950s as a result of research into creativity, decision-making and management as well as advances in computer technology and artificial intelligence for problem-solving. The academic discipline of 'Design Research' developed as it became accepted that design involved a very specific and distinctive type of knowledge. Bruce Archer was a leading exponent of this view and was fundamental in the inception of the *Design Studies* journal and academic design research in general. In the debut issue of the journal, published in July 1979, Archer presented a paper entitled 'Design as Discipline' and put forward these questions:

> Can design be a discipline in its own right? If so, what are its distinguishing features? (What are the kinds of features that distinguish any discipline?) To what questions should the discipline address itself – in both research and teaching? What methodology does it use? What results – what applications – should it be trying to achieve? (Archer 1979: 17)

Archer's questions were devised to encourage a rationalization of the design process and focused on industrial design. On reading these questions, it occurred to me that if I were to add 'textiles' in front of the word design as used here I would find it very difficult to find answers to them in the existing literature on design. But not only that, I wondered how the discourses of design research may have been altered over the course of the prevailing years if these questions had been addressed to the discipline of textile design.

Textile designing

If textile design is to be studied in an attempt to understand its peculiarities, then researchers should aim to systematically identify the nature of textile design and the behaviour of textile designers.

(Moxey 1999: 176)

Critical evaluations of the textile design process and the industry itself are few and infrequently published. Colin Gale and Jasbir Kaur's 2002 publication *The Textile Book* explored the range of personnel involved in textiles as designers, craftspeople and designer makers, as well as outlining the industrial, historical and global contexts for textiles, and they put forward an impassioned argument in support of textiles and its associated industries as a worthy subject for research and as a 'profession' cited at the beginning of this chapter. In their choice of words they indicate particular characteristics, and therefore differences, between design disciplines, and in doing so label textile design as quiet and unwitting (Gale and Kaur 2002).

Rachel Studd's paper 'The Textile Design Process' (Studd 2002) sets out the methods and activities textile designers carry out as they design. The paper provided different accounts of the textile design process from the viewpoint of a freelance textile designer to teams working within large corporations. Her account and the various 'summary of design processes' she develops give due regard to the variable factors that alter the experience for textile designers within different industrial contexts. She also puts forward a basic flow diagram of the structure of the textile industry and process which follows fibres, through spinning into yarns, then dyeing; weaving, knitting or non-woven construction methods; then printing and dyeing for a range of applications across apparel, furnishings, technical and medical which are then developed into products for retail or contract industries and ultimately in the hands of the consumer.

The essential structure of this diagram is simple and essentially correct, yet several aspects of the activity of textile design have been omitted: in particular, the significance of embroidery and other constructed textile and surface embellishment techniques within textile design. Since the publication of Studd's diagram in 2002, an even wider range of technical skills has become part of the repertoire of the textile design discipline. Laser-cutting and digital fabric printing methods began to be applied in creative textile design in the late 1990s. Since the early 2000s there has been a growth in interest in techniques such as rapid prototyping and 3D printing in the design and development of three-dimensional textile surfaces. Military and automotive applications could be considered under Studd's label of 'technical' textiles; however, I feel they demand some consideration for their aesthetics as well their properties. Smart textiles have also been excluded. This field covers wearable, haptic and ambient technological textiles and contrasts with the technical textiles engineered by chemists, material scientists and industrial engineers.

Figure 1 is an adaptation of Studd's diagram. I have presented it in a non-prioritized list-based format, avoiding the 'flow diagram' style that Studd has used. This allows for the tracing of multiple paths through the textile design and making process. This table serves to illustrate the basic shape of textile design activity today.

While both Studd's (2002) and my own diagram illustrate the areas in which textile design activity is taking place across a range of industries, they do not represent what the design process entails for textile designers. For this discussion it is very important to remember the breadth of the textiles industry and how textile designers' fields of activity and therefore expertise have continued to grow.

The other significant detail from the table in Figure 1 is that textile designs, particularly commercial textile designs, undergo two levels of consumption. The first which takes places within the design industry itself and the second with the end user or consumer. This fact is key to developing conceptual understandings of textile design later in this book.

Previous studies of textile design process and cognition have mainly been pedagogical, involving students of textile design in higher education. Alison Shreeve opens up the conversation about knowledge in textiles in 'Material Girls: Tacit Knowledge in Textile Crafts' (Shreeve 1997) and in doing so emphasizes the need for more extended research in this area. Shreeve directly and consistently labels textiles as 'craft' rather than as a design discipline and closely aligns it to fashion. These labels and associations are clearly derived from the context of the research, based at the London College of Fashion and published by the Crafts Council. It may also be a legacy of the progression of the art-craft-design dialectic since 1997, when the paper was written. The aim of Shreeve's paper is to emphasize the pedagogical requirement to understand and value the visual, perceptual and tacit knowledge that is intrinsic in learning how to craft textiles.

In *The Representation of Concepts in Textile Design* (2000) James Moxey also studied textile design students. His study focused on describing the outcomes of the textile design process, such as mood boards and samples. Moxey provides one of the first attempts to align textile design methods with models of design. He uses his descriptions of these methods of 'representing concepts' and attempts

	Fibres (Virgin or from Post consumer materials) Yarns Non-wovens			
	Natural / unprocessed Processed / dyed			
Textile design students Textile swatching studios Freelance textile designers In-house textile designers Designer-makers Craftspeople Own-label designers Hobbyists Research-led designers	Knitted Woven Non-woven Rapid-prototyping including 3D printing Engineered Bio engineered			
Material scientists Chemists Engineers	Fabrics Materials			
	Printed (digital & manual) Dyed Embroidery & embellishment Constructed & mixed media Laser-cut & etched Surface treatments (e.g. Washing, distressing) Smart technologies Surface pattern design Virtual technologies	Apparel Furnishing Architectural & Interior Automotive	Product for Retail Product for Contract	Consumer
Issue based transdisciplinary research e.g. sustainability, ethics, social projects		Technical & Industrial Medical & Biomedical Military Aerospace Digital technology		User
	First level consumption			Second level consumption

Figure 1 Table of textile design activity (2020). Adapted from Igoe (2013).

to match the design process he has been observing with an established design process model. The outcome of this is unconvincing, as Moxey describes an iterative, free-form process where some students are encouraged to depart from the original design brief by developing their own briefs, but then proceeds in depicting a linear design process model.

Both Shreeve and Moxey seek to gain an understanding of textile knowledge and textile design by studying the actions and outcomes of students of textile design. This is clearly an important and valid aspect of the experience of being/becoming a textile designer. However, it does highlight the requirement to extend the study of textile design to incorporate the variety of experiences and outcomes of professional textile designers at different stages in their careers. Dorst (2008) provides us with a seven-level model of expertise in the design profession. Within this model he specifies anomalies between approaches to design across the levels that help us to question the one-dimensional definition of the design process which has become so prevalent. Studd's work in 2002 gives some explanation of textile design in industrial contexts but does not deal with the cognitive aspects of textile design.

Shreeve's method is relational, adopting an ethnographic methodology, while Moxey adopts a scientific model, describing, analysing and classifying the tangible outcomes of the textile design process. Shreeve's study uses the (student) designer and their personal experience of the design process as the object of research while Moxey's study removes the designer from the research project, focusing solely on the outcome.

Pedagogical research has also been a key driver for research into textile design. In two studies exploring the relationship between textiles, engineering and technology (Kavanagh, Matthews and Tyrer 2008: 708; Kavanagh 2004: 3), the writers outline how education promotes three aspects of textile design: 'Discourse, Context and Process', simplified as 'What one wants to say, and to whom, and by what means'. They describe how education has become better at preparing students of textile design for working in textiles (the context) as a reaction to the criticism that discourse and process has long been emphasized. They go on to describe how, with greater contextual knowledge, their technical understanding of manufacturing processes has waned. In this example, 'discourse' can be read as the internal and external rhetoric as experienced by the (student) designer, the 'context' as the customer or intended market for the design and 'process' as the technical methods required for production. Kavanagh's (2004: 3) questions are directed to the textile designer and the textile design discipline for a specifically pedagogical application. This book asks similar questions but aims to engage with the entity of textile design in the context of design research theory.

The textile entity includes the textile designer and the discipline (Actor/s); the textile design object, the objective/design problem of textile design (Object); the manual and cognitive processes of textile design (Process); and the industrial, historical, political and cultural context of textile design (Context). These labels are an application of Kees Dorst's (2008: 5) argument that a focus on the process of design ignores the impact of the object, the actor and the context. I have added 'process' to this list to suggest that process is not the frame for these other aspects but rather is set in a complex relationship with them. This nexus describes the textile 'entity' I address in later chapters and correlates with an approach to the development of design thinking as 'sketched' out by Lucy Kimbell in her 2012 paper *Rethinking Design Thinking: Part II*. Kimbell facilitates a 'practice-centred' approach to design research. She suggests:

> Practice theories see the locus of the social not at the level of individuals and their minds, or in organizations and groups and their norms but as a nexus of minds, bodies, things, institutions, knowledge and processes, structure and agency. (Kimbell 2012)

And so, in asking the entity of textiles what it wants to say, to whom and by what means, the questions have a broader remit, requiring answers of a suitably epistemological slant. Studies by Rachel Studd and James Moxey (2000) both developed at UMIST, Manchester, UK, give a thorough description of the systematic design process for textiles, covering both students and professionals. However, systematic models of the design process have routinely been challenged by certain academics who emphasize the 'opportunistic' behaviour of designers in practice. Cross summarizes a range of studies that explore both systematic and opportunistic approaches to designing (Cross 2007: 109–12), highlighting the fact that the process of designing is difficult to define even though there are clear signifiers of the concept of a specific type of knowledge that design utilizes. He warns that 'the "cognitive cost" of apparently more principled, structured behaviour may actually be higher than can be reasonably sustained, or can be justified by the quality of the outcome' (Cross 2007: 116).

There are very few examples of research that have explored the phenomenon of the ill-defined problem for textile design. Moxey (2000: 53) states that in textile design 'Concepts are initially nurtured and developed at a cognitive level by searching the problem space, gathering information and stimulating the senses'. He describes the fact that the ill-defined nature of the design problem requires designers to 'import information into the problem space'. Moxey hints at how textile designers deal with ill-defined design problems when he describes concept generation for textiles as a combination of informed intuition, tacit knowledge and overt, market-rich data.

Studd (2002) provides an example of a design brief as used by a large UK-based textile company. It outlines the aims and objectives that the proposed collection must attain, including stipulations about the colours and fabrics to be utilized and the product dimensions to influence the repeat size, as well as the targeted consumer. Are these aspects merely technical and market requirements, rather than the articulation of an ill-defined design problem? Are they just setting the boundaries of the 'problem space'? Moxey and Studd focus on concept finding/ generation and representation in response to a 'trigger' (Studd 2002: 43): can this trigger be seen as the design problem? Is it a more appropriate term than 'problem'? These studies do not yet fully interrogate the notion of the ill-defined design problem for textile design. They invite further investigation into the 'trigger' for textile design and initiate an articulation of the nature of the ill-defined problems textile designers deal with (see Chapter 13).

Ongoing academic discourse on the subject of textile design, thinking and practice has been evident in individual research projects of PhD students and academics. In 2010, researchers at Loughborough University founded the DUCK *Journal for Research in Textiles and Textile Design* in an attempt to publish online material of this nature. In 2013 it was relaunched as the *Journal of Textile Design Research and Practice*. In 2010 Bye outlined a 'new direction for clothing and textile design research' contextualizing the location of clothing and textile research in design research and as a site for scholarship and providing a historical account of the situation with particular reference to North American academia. In leading design journals such as *The Design Journal* and *Design Issues* and at international conferences we are seeing more contributions from textile practitioners and researchers. Textiles Intersections and D-TEX (*The International Textile Design Conference*) are developing as international forums for design research in the field of textiles as well as interdisciplinary special interest groups of larger colloquia such as the Experiential Knowledge Special Interest Group (EKSIG) of the Design Research Society, convened by textile design researcher Nithikul Nimkulrat. Research into innovative materials and innovation strategy through textiles are a key aspect of textile design research. Anna Lottersberger's PhD from 2012 sought to define areas prime for innovation within the Italian textile market; however, a dearth of information concerned with models for textile innovation led her to develop a definition of textile practice that could be applied in B2B contexts to support design-driven innovation for this specific market. Reflecting this premise back to textile design researchers, Earley, Vuletich, Hadridge and Andersen (2016) report on the role of textile design researchers in the development of sustainability solutions for a large fashion brand asking, 'What new skills and capabilities do textile designers need to inspire sustainable design innovation in large fashion corporations?'

This research, among others including my own (Igoe 2010, 2013), began to make textiles answerable to definitions of design as well as the issues design was causing and being confronted by. But in order to do this, what was required was some articulation or clarification as to what textile design is and does as a practice.

Textile/design thinking

'Design thinking' is now a popularized and commercialized term but here should be simply understood as design cognition, the thinking associated with designing and a subject of study since the 1960s. There is, however, some agreement that the definition of 'design thinking' is now not clear and is not necessarily the most apt label for such a complex phenomenon. I refer here specifically to Peter Rowe's introduction of the term in his 1987 book *Design Thinking* in which he proposes that designers work on hunches and hypotheses and that the problem-solving action of the design process itself shapes the emergent solution (Kimbell 2011). I firmly make this distinction from 'design thinking' as a means of creative problem-solving heroicized by global innovation companies such as IDEO and which stands outside of this discussion of design theory. The co-option of the term 'design' in other spheres is problematic when not accompanied by rigorous critical interrogation potentially both on the outcomes of these processes and on the field of design itself but is beyond the scope of the publication. In this chapter, established concepts and theories of design are summarized and juxtaposed with the literature concerning 'textile thinking'. Here, I have selected to persist with the use of the term 'design thinking' to cover the embodied, cognitive activities of designers that are set in relation to their design process.

There are many good summaries of the development of design thinking as a subject of study including Lottersberger (2012: 67–70) as well as Lucy Kimbell (2011) who gives a very useful synopsis of the development and understanding of the term in her paper 'Rethinking Design Thinking: Part I'. Daniela K. Rosner's (2018: 25–40) excellent in-depth, feminist critique of the development of design research and 'thinking' in her book *Critical Fabulations* is essential reading for all design researchers. With gratitude to these authors, I can proceed here to locate and explain the development of 'textile thinking' in response to the phenomenal success of the notion of 'design thinking' beyond the world of design itself.

Textile design, in both educational and industrial contexts, is most predominantly focused on artefactual paradigms of design (Pastor and Van Patter 2011). There are clusters of research-led textile designers who are working in the field of service design and innovation – for example, Jenny Tillotson's work in 'scentsory' design. Fewer still working to bring about organizational and social transformation – Rebecca Earley and Kate Goldsworthy's work in sustainable design processes and business strategy (2017) or Anne Marr and Rebecca Hoyes practice research involving spaces, pattern and well-being (2016 and Sánchez-Aldana et al.) (2019) working with textile practice and memory. It is interesting to note that many examples of textile practice working towards social transformation or sociocultural impact are embedded within craft practice; contributing author Rose Sinclair's work (2015) on the Dorcas sewing clubs created by Caribbean women in the UK is a significant study of such impact. Textile design, in the way that design is more generally considered, is hard to place alongside positive social impact. Indeed, we are now recognizing the distinctly negative role textiles and cloth has on the environment and the people that make every aspect of them. An issue which now necessarily drives significant research in circular design methods and sustainable and responsible design, despite the industry being far slower to change.

The assertion that textile design is *design* is one of the foundational premises of this book. This may seem like stating the obvious but in the development of my doctoral thesis (Igoe 2013) I sought to find out why this notion was so difficult. In reviewing the established theories and concepts of design; the design process and cognition, what I uncovered was a theoretical canon heavily skewed by a blend of historically and socially gendered and biased factors compounded by disciplinary tenets. Scholars and theorists in and beyond design research such as Escobar (2018), Tonkinwise (2016), Kimbell (2011), Prado de O. Martens (2014) and Noel and Leitão (2018) have and are still voicing timely critique but their voice is a marginal one set in contrast to white, Western normativity. Meanwhile, the adoption of 'design methods' and most popularly 'design thinking' into organizational and innovation management frameworks expands, mutates and dilutes the general understanding of design.

Concurrently, in the UK, textile design scholars have been establishing a body of work to develop an understanding of thinking and making in a textiles context. Key texts from Anni Albers (1962) and Victoria Mitchell (1997) and later work by Sarat Maharaj (2000) as well as Janis Jefferies and Pennina Barnett in the development of the journal *Textile: Cloth and Culture* (2003–) helped to develop a forum for these academic concerns. In the mid-2010s Claire Pajaczowksa defined 'nine types of textile thinking' supported by notions of textility and characterized by the indivisible nature of thinking and making.

Design thinking and textile thinking – they sound so similar, don't they? But what lies between them are intrinsic epistemological differences set in place by historical ontologies of hierarchies of knowledge. The articulation of cognition as indivisible from the making has been the driver for the development of the term. As we know this knowledge-making is not something intrinsic only to textile practitioners (read Ingold on sawing wood), yet the way that textiles terms are so omnipresent in our lived worlds and languages; the notion is almost hiding in plain sight. The development of *textile thinking* or *textile design thinking* as a concept spans decades. Here I give a brief overview of this development principally in Europe and the UK.

In her 1962 book *On Designing* Anni Albers steers her discussion of making in general in and out of craft, design and art through her understanding of all these contexts and their relationship in the production of textiles. In doing so she establishes some of the defining traits of what has developed as textile thinking. Albers says,

'I believe that this direct work with a material, a work that in general no longer belongs to our way of doing things, is one way that might give us back a greater sense of balance, or perspective and proportion in regard to our perhaps too highly rated subjectiveness.'

She gives little credence to any distinction between crafted objects of art or mass-manufactured objects of design and offers a definition of the purpose of successful made objects as more for serving and less for expressing (Albers 1962: 64). She recognizes the collective input of makers-designers, artists, craftspeople as well as chemists and engineers in the development and production of objects but reiterates the need for all to be submissive to the materials to observe subservience in the process of producing objects. Albers metaphorizes the process of design cognition through the creation of a design outcome as a form of 'condensation' and reminds us that creativity does not exist in a limitless space but one that is compelled by rules – whether of the materials involved or those externally set.

She addresses modern forms of decoration with some apprehension, acknowledging that we sometimes seek the pleasing addition of *provocative beauty* beyond the restrained aesthetics of purpose through the application of colour and surface treatments. However, in imposing her own aesthetic, she also suggests that ornamentation and the strive for appending beauty to objects gives undue attention to the mediocre, hiding poor material choices, inciting a rivalry between objects.

In subsequent chapters, Albers outlines the significance of textile forms and their production in architecture, art and anthropology. Albers's collection of essays collated non-sequentially between 1937 and 1961 provides a foundation for my approach and the theories I propose in further chapters. Albers's contribution to writing on design as a textile maker is pioneering and erudite – diminishing notions of the heroic singular artist or designer in favour of the recognition of collaboration, commercial context and purpose. In the introduction to her later book *On Weaving* published in 1965 (Albers et al. 2017) she again sets out an invitation to others thinking and making through and with textiles and materials, saying,

'By taking up textile fundamentals and methods, I hoped to include in my audience not only weavers but also those whose work in other fields encompasses textile problems. This book, then, is an effort in that direction.'

Albers also focuses in on the goal of purpose and the conception of beauty in design and begins to question the role of the decorative alongside. The way she describes design realization as 'condensation' is poetic and relatable but certainly at odds with the concepts of the science of design that were being developed at a similar time. Without using the precise terms and learnt through her practice and own study, Albers describes hylomorphic approaches to making – the imposition of form to matter – and supports a return to privileging the connection between making, tools and materials, which has since been defined as *textility* chiefly by Victoria Mitchell and Tim Ingold.

Mitchell's essay from 1997 *Textiles, Text and Techne* proposes a textility of thought and matter represented through the etymological links of the three words that make up its title. She argues that, linguistically, we can understand the word 'textiles' not simply as an object but as a schema. And so, the construct of textiles is an approach to making knowledge manifested through the act of making itself. Be that making language, cloth or almost anything else. Ingold develops these ideas with reference to Mitchell through his lens of anthropological studies. In *The Textility of Making* (Ingold 2010) he traces the dissolution of textility in favour of the Aristotelian hylomorphic model of 'giving form to matter'. Ingold's disciplinary approach reminds us that making knowledge is world-making or more appropriately 'world-weaving'. He utilizes Deleuze and Guattari's theories of the relations between materials and forces noting that skilled makers intervene in the fields of forces and currents of material in the generation of objects. The indivisiblity of thinking, making, knowing with, in and of itself, bound up with the agency of materials themselves, becomes the premise of textile thinking. Mitchell and Ingold's development of textility permeates in the work of Dormor (2012) in her thesis concerned with art-making, philosophy and textile terms and practices. Kane and Philpott (2014) apply concepts of textile thinking to the development of sustainable materials within cross-disciplinary workshops, drawing on a range of textile processes for the purposes of fostering creative dialogue and innovation. To support this approach, they point out the application of 'textile modes of thinking' in the work of architects Frei Otto and Lars Spuybroek. Although they do not reference textility explicitly, what they discuss unearths epistemologies of textility in making and designing beyond the field of textiles.

My own doctoral thesis and an earlier article (Igoe 2010, 2013) sought to locate textile thinking in the field of design research theory. Theories of textility tended to enmesh a taciturnity with making and didn't sufficiently recognize the context of making as a practice of design in an industrial context. In one way, my work was a return to Albers's perspective but also differentially asserted the development of textiles as a design discipline with associated practices in relation to other design disciplines and not craft or art. This taciturnity was identified and explored as an obstacle to textile designers contributing to the development of the foundations of design research and theory and the zeitgeist of 'design thinking'. Through the work of Kane and Philpott, myself and Pajaczkowska (2016) who developed an understanding of textile thinking through nine examples of research praxis manifested through textile 'verbs' and drawing on etymological and linguistic links; a theoretical basis for textile design research was established and quickly became a shorthand for textile- and material-based research methods. Notable extensions of textile thinking can be found in Vuletich (2015) as she explores the role of the textile designer in industrial design contexts for sustainability goals; Marr and Hoyes (2016) who present textile thinking as an 'additional creative impulse for generic design thinking' that recognizes material agency and textile intelligence; and Valentine et al. (2017) whose work recognizes the emotive, haptic, sensory and tactile effect of *textile design process thinking* and promotes the collaborative effort required to do it. While these later examples look to evidence applied textile thinking, Lee (2020a) attends to the criticality of this as a conceptual framework. Lee, with particular interrogation to textiles in 'everyday contacts' and intimate social contexts, suggests that the essential relationality of textiles requires an ontological expansion of textile thinking into what she proposes as the *textile-sphere* – a 'mediatic environment' encompassing material and immaterial expressions of surface.

While 'textile thinking' has been a useful lever or metaphorical undercoat for emerging textile design research, through application without interrogation it often lost the etymological nuance of textility along the way. Textile thinking as a concept was established by the scholars mentioned earlier not as a justification for any lack of involvement with design academia and an invitation to carry on regardless but as a way of understanding a relational way of making knowledge through materials. Textile thinking with its roots in textility as the materialization of thought, language and expression and the agency and capacities of materials avoids addressing the context of designing. As if textiles are not objects of neoliberal commerce that exist and act in a complex socioeconomic structure. Design thinking, on the other hand, provides little recognition for designers who are material-led and for whom making is an effective way of thinking – where making is the key driver to their design process and where final outcomes and applications are routinely unknown. What was missing was a critical dialogue between these two types of thinking and in the meanwhile both terms, as is the way, have altered their meanings.

This book proposes and uses the term 'textilic practice' as an application of some of the premises of textile thinking in and beyond fabric-focused design outcomes. It is an effort to move textile thinking away from associations with design thinking and towards a more adisciplinary conception. Textilic practice in design uses a set of methodological processes or tools that focus on the materialization of creative expression through the agency and capacities of materials further explained in subsequent chapters. Materials can be understood as the 'stuff' of design – any kind of design. It is not giving form to matter but intervening between materials and 'forces'. In enforcing notions of textility rather than 'textilia', it attempts to secure an understanding of textilic practice that transcends disciplinary boundaries even manifesting in immaterial design outcomes.

Textilic design practice here is importantly contextualized epistemologically in Ettinger's concept of the matrixial (see Chapter 2). Therefore, it is a practice that is fundamentally relational, expansive and emergent.

Mesh one

'Right – I want you to imagine it's the 1940s, it's a damp smoky dark railway station, this soldier's going off to war, the girl's standing on the platform with a bedraggled bunch of flowers, waving goodbye tearfully to her.'

She wanted those flowers, you see?

It was about responding to those sorts of poetic feelings, quite chaotically at the beginning. There must be a certain amount of interpretation on my part. I must understand and interpret that poetry and make it visible – realize it, in fabric; know which colours to pull out, how would they go; translate it into textiles; make it believable.

I accumulate information related to . . . whatever . . . and then there's the process of 'tidying up' and then responding to all that and very often all those three stages merge into one, so you're looking at things as well as organizing them at the same time as making something. 'In synthesis', that would be the best explanation. I tend to consume masses of information of all sorts and sources, mostly of visual but also text-based and initially it doesn't have any particular order. I might take inspiration for colour straight from photographs or an exhibition. So being inspired by a painting and seeing how that could be a design or being inspired by the new design by BMW and how that could affect the shape of a print or swimwear. I might then make patterns almost straight from visual research. Although what we're kind of taught is really to try not to just interpret your visual research, to try and actually do a stage further; that specific way of researching primary research, secondary research, then you pick out bits and put them together to create the design, although it's still quite organic. Somehow, I always talk about it as a process of osmosis. You've looked at something so long, or worked with it for so long, that suddenly it's coming out through your fingertips. I suppose I also think it's all about looking. Because I think that the biggest tool you've got in anything is your personal way of looking at something. Working in a design team, we'd kind of build up these little kinds of stories and themes and moods and ideas. Sometimes we didn't have very much that was visual to back it up, but reading notes and things that we'd kind of written when we are Première Vision (PV) or something. We'll be like, you know, I really, really feel good about indigo dyeing or about tropical florals or about whatever it might be. Then I just need to translate them into the computer as a design or colourway.

Alternatively, sometimes my process starts with a material; I take it apart, like a kid, and then find my own way of putting it back together again. I find it's a good way to get to know the material and understand what it wants to be. I like getting people to understand the technology that is available, and how it can be used. The materials research development company I once worked for needed somebody, really, who could transfer that kind of way of talking much more easily; I suppose it's that kind of link; being able to speak to certain people in a way that kind of enables them to gain enough information and to understand what it's all about but without kind of coming across in a too much of a technological way.

Now, working for a fashion brand, much of the time, the head designer brings in books or stuff that he thinks are interesting and he'll give it to me saying, 'Okay, this is the one I want to use for this season.' So I then come back here with their fabrics and colours and themes and play for a couple of days. I'm very much about feeding off another person's requirement and twisting it around in my head. Although it just can be a terrible, terrible experience because you don't know whether you're seeing things the same way or not. And sometimes you get clients that just even when you've done it to the colours that they've given you the swatches for, it doesn't look like the colour they want. It can be very, very difficult. Although I won't ever work with somebody who says, 'I want this here.'

An example of when it gets really interesting is when I was once working for two designers the same season, and they both gave me the same picture of a little boy with a tattoo on. And so I had to find two totally different collections from this one photograph, which was exciting. And also, if you are working for, say, seven different designers a season, then you've also got to have seven different styles. Different designers are known for their handwriting. So, I will often be asked to do things that are specific to my handwriting. You have to bend your taste to theirs without losing your integrity.

Often when the design is done, I realize it is really communicating visually what I wanted to say – although I didn't realize it would have looked that way. All of a sudden, all that research was pulled into one thing, even though I didn't consciously do it; that's when I realize it's good. I realize that I have created a feeling or a sense of it being romantic; or a feeling of being jazzy; or a feeling of taking you to the 1950s; or taking you to some place. I know people might not always get my work, but if they are attracted to it for some reason – they like the imagery or something – as long as they feel something towards it, I'm happy at the end of the day. If they don't get the concept behind it, it doesn't matter.

5

Translating and transforming

Victoria Mitchell states, 'Text and textile share common association through the Latin texere, to weave. These fragile references suggest for textiles a kind of speaking and for language a kind of making' (Mitchell 1997: 7). To 'speak' is 'to express one's thoughts by words' (Oxford English Dictionary). Textiles do not have words; they speak instead through a complex synergy of visual and haptic language, semantics (Andrew 2008). Nigel Cross (2007: 25) cites the work of Hillier and Leaman from 1976 in which they described designing as 'learning an artificial "language"; a kind of code which transforms "thoughts" into "words"', and state that 'They (designers) use "codes" that translate abstract requirements into concrete objects. They use these codes to both "read" and "write" in "object languages"' (Cross 2007: 29). Tacit knowledge is embodied in these languages or codes, the details of which vary across the design disciplines, feasibly offering researchers the possibilities of exploring non-verbal 'dialects' of design object language in the pursuit of the tacit knowledge of design.

I will not digress into the agency and nature of the textile object and its materiality at this stage. I wish to explore how the textile designer creates this communicative cloth – this semantic surface. Textile designers respond, translate, interpret and tidy images, words, stories, feelings, memories and objects in the development of their textile designs.

> The qualification of a translator worth reading must be a mastery of the language he translates out of, and that he translates into; but if a deficiency be to be allowed in either, it is to be in the original, since if he be but master enough of the tongue of his author as to be master of his sense, it is possible for him to express that sense with eloquence in his own, if he have a thorough command of that. (Dryden 1680: 30)

Seventeenth-century playwright John Dryden emphasizes two key aspects that I wish to explore: mastery of language and expression of sense. To proceed in positing the textile designer as translator, I must consider what language they are translating 'out of' and 'into'? He encourages good translators to be a master of both. Textile designers respond to a varied range of visual, textual, auditory, sensory materials in their design process: a rich multimodal language. Taking Dryden's statement, the textile designer need not be a master of this multimodal language but must have a thorough command of the language of textiles in order to effectively convey what is being 'spoken of'.

Designers also describe how masses of information are collected, collated and 'consumed', some of it given to them by others and/or quickly 'vacuumed up' from visits to trade shows, exhibitions, online materials or gleaned otherwise from the visual environment. For the textile designer, the form of the original information has little significance; its inclusion is arbitrary. Direct and explicit communication is not the concern of textile design; it is precisely the expression of the 'sense', as Dryden puts it, within the language of textiles that is key.

The premise of emphasizing sensibility over content by no means belittles the textile designer as translator. The acts of vacuuming up, picking through and tidying which are part of the textile design process may not encourage deep and narrow expertise but rather a breadth of interconnected social knowledge.

Sherry Simon describes how translators must understand this connection between language and social realities. They must make decisions about cultural meaning in different languages and decide to what extent they inhibit the same significance. She adds that these decisions

> demand the exercise of a range of intelligences. In fact the process of meaning transfer has less to do with finding the cultural inscription of a term than in reconstructing its value. (Simon 1996: 138)

Hugo Friedrich's 1965 speech *On the Art of Translation* traces the history of this approach to translation to the ancient Rome of Quintilian and Pliny and describes its dominance during the European Renaissance. Friedrich also says:

> [T]he purpose of translation is to go beyond the appropriation of content to a releasing of those linguistic and aesthetic energies that heretofore had existed only as pure possibility in one's own language and had never been materialized before. . . . Its most striking hallmark is its effort to 'enrich'. (Friedrich 1965: 13)

Friedrich's speech is itself a translation by Rainer Schulte and John Biguenet, but the words used here are richly metaphorical, describing this form of translation as an act of 'releasing energies and pure possibility through materialization in the effort to enrich' an art form. This summation of translation could equally be used to describe the process of textile design. I enjoy the 'magical' qualities of this phrase, as if something ethereal has been given a form (through words or textile). What qualities does this attribute to the textile designer as translator? The textile designer doesn't just translate, she responds. The verb 'to respond' has a number of definitions and etymological historical origins (Oxford English Dictionary 2013), leading to nuanced understandings of the term. The most widely understood is 'to answer', but a more interesting one, and one which fits well with the idea of translating as 'enriching', is responding as 'to pledge back' (derived from the Latin *re-* 'back' and *spondere* 'to pledge'). If we consider that textile designers are pledging back to this multimodal language as they translate it and enrich it, a necessary level of trust is implicated.

Clive Dilnot, in his essay *The Gift*, recognizes this 'pledging back' in design as a form of gift-giving, but one outside of commerce, stating,

> [It] is the quantum of the designer's creative apperception of the conditions of human subjectivity, together with his or her ability to translate and embody this apperception into the form of the object and to offer it again to the potential user, that marks the designer/maker's 'gift' to the user. (Dilnot 1995: 154)

Dilnot skilfully triangulates the act of designing, with design as an agent of commodity and design as a subjective object. He highlights the relational properties of the act of designing as he uses the metaphor of giving gifts to explore the dynamics of design. He mentions the conative impulse designers feel – their implicit desire to make transformations in the world (transformations often driven by Western capitalist foundational structures) – and relates this to Adorno's description of gift-giving: 'Real giving had its joy in imagining the joy of the receiver. It means choosing, expending time, going out of one's way, thinking of the other as a subject: the opposite of distraction' (Adorno 1944: 42).

Dilnot is interested in how designed objects work between two people: the designer and the other. The designer takes the role of the gift-giver and the other (or consumer, first or second level – see Figure 1) is the recipient. He encourages us to momentarily rethink the connections that have been made between design and commodity. He reflects on the notion of the object as a commodity, where the gift-giver (designer) and recipient are disconnected through the capitalist structure. He argues that this scenario removes the sense of obligation from gift-giving and sets up an alternative notion of consumption.

Dilnot's concept of design as a relational act of gift-giving emphasizes the experience of pleasure as experienced by the designer and the recipient. This definition of the purpose of design is in closer alignment to Brett's (2005) definition of the pleasure-giving decorative arts and is a useful concept in distinguishing textile design from its close relatives in craft and applied arts, yet simultaneously maintains and recognizes the connection.

The notion of 'pledging back' that is developed through comparing design with translation is neatly captured in Dilnot's citation of Marx:

> I would know that I had created through my life expression immediately yours as well. Thus in my individual activity I would know my true essence, my human, common essence is contained and realised. Our production would be so many mirrors, in which our essence would be mutually illuminated. (Dilnot 1995)

This evocative passage offers a view into the pleasure, intellectual passion (Polanyi 1958) and relational mutuality involved in the design process: a process that deeply interconnects the designer with the object and user/consumer. It also allows a different reading of the innate impetus of designers – a passionate impulsion to communicate, translate and relate. 'The gift' poses an alternative definition of the character of design and the design process – one that involves the conative, cognitive and affective. In Dilnot's explanation, the gift is not the object itself but the latency of the object – a 'moment within' the object bestowed by the designer/maker. In support of this statement, he notes that most mundane objects contain this gift 'moment'. He adds that the moment is more perceptual that material. Textiles contribute to, and become embedded in, designed objects. In this scenario the gift-like moment of the textile is even more latent, as it does not constitute the gift-object in itself but contributes an essential element to it.

Dilnot (1995) differentiates between complex designed objects like computers and 'mundane' ones like 'clothes to keep us warm'. It can be understood that textiles would be categorized as 'mundane' in this context. While separating the two he also notes that mundane designed objects are no less significant than those he categorizes as complex. Interestingly, and in contrast, material culture scholar Judy Attfield (2000) called these mundane, everyday objects 'wild things'.

Dilnot affirms that the giver moves from a desire to give to an apprehension of the other's needs and desires.

> To put it in subject terms: as I anticipate the other's enjoyment and use of my object, and as I concretize those anticipated in an object that I choose/create, then I get the immediate pleasure and consciousness of having satisfied a real human need through this creative work. (Dilnot 1995: 155)

Dilnot cites Elaine Scarry's *The Body in Pain* (1985) as he describes how designed objects help to make us and 'making and designing are moments of making and designing ourselves'. He says that objects provide us 'artificially with what nature has neglected to bestow on us'. To work in this way, objects must be a convincing projection of our awareness of human existence, possibilities and limitations. Textiles, as designed objects, combining the tactile with the visual, can readily be understood as a projection of our base requirements of haptic, sensual, visual and perceptual stimulation. The designed object is a gift-like recognition of each other's base and complex needs and desires. The designer, or gift-giver, 'knows, and has understood, recognised, affirmed and sought to concretely meet our most intimate and human needs and desires' (Dilnot 1995: 155).

The notion of design as gift-giving described by Dilnot when set in context with neoliberal capitalism seems to be naive. Boehnert (2014) describes how the agency and perceptual abilities of designers towards addressing complex issues are denied by the capitalist design industry structured towards economic growth and the production of the new. White (2019) claims that the design industry in collaboration with large technology companies are creating and reordering social hierarchies.

In discussing textile design as gift-giving and as translation I focus on the cognitive acts associated with design. For textile design, due to its having first- and second-level consumers (Figure 1) within the design industry and the users themselves, this connection with social context has often been remote or lacking. However, by identifying this aspect through the development of making textile design theory we can connect design as gift-giving and translation through the notion of responding and pledging back. Both these scenarios illustrate a relational communicative act. The textile designer must, through their translation, pledge back to the original information an essence of its sense. They must also provide to the recipient a translation into cloth that meets their complex needs and desires. As discussed in reference to Dryden's comments on mastery of language, this again implies that textile designers need highly developed skills in expressing emotion and multimodal language.

To express emotion and sense requires trust. George Steiner described 'the hermeneutic motion' ('the act of elicitation and appropriative transfer of meaning') (Steiner 1975: 312) in four stages, beginning with trust. 'This confiding will, ordinarily, be instantaneous and unexamined, but it has a complex base. It is an operative convention which derives from a sequence of phenomenological assumptions about the coherence of the world, about the presence of meaning in very different, perhaps formally antithetical semantic systems, about the validity of analogy and parallel' (Steiner 1975: 312).

Claire Lerpiniere (2009) applied theories of hermeneutics to the 'inspiration' board, used widely by textile designers in the process of designing, describing how in practice these boards are used heuristically and have lacked academic and pedagogic investigation. The hermeneutic approach was applied to design by Donald Schön in 1983 when he framed it as a 'conversation with the situation' (Schön 1983: 79).

> There is initiative trust, an investment of belief, underwritten by previous experience but epistemologically exposed and psychologically hazardous, in the meaningfulness, in the 'seriousness' of the facing or, strictly speaking, adverse text. We venture a leap: we grant ab initio that there is 'something there' to be understood, that the transfer will not be void. (Steiner 1975: 312)

This initial stage relates to the notion of the 'creative' leap, the conative impulse towards making a change. Parallels between key theories of translation and established concepts of design have already been established, particularly in the research centre of Design Et Traduzione (DET) at Politecnico de Milano (Polimi), Italy. Baule and Caratti's edited volume (2017) provides a perspective on this notion from the disciplinary field of visual communication design. In this volume, Salvatore Zingale provides a detailed overview of models of translation (Baule and Caratti 2017: 71–93). He reminds us, 'The source text of design is usually an unstructured entity whose lines are blurred, open, exposed to uncertainty and incoherence, an entity striving to attain a finite structure precisely through design.'

In *Gender in Translation* (1996), Sherry Simon outlines a feminist discourse on the theory of translation. She highlights and recognizes the active agency of the translator and the participatory relationship between the translator, the text and the creation of meaning and considers Steiner's model, which, although beginning with trust, enacts itself through the perspective of masculine sexuality (Simon 1996: 29) (The other three stages of Steiner's hermeneutic model for translation are focused on aggression/penetration, incorporation/embodiment and reciprocity/restitution in the 'target' language.) Donald Schön's application of hermeneutics also utilizes interventionist metaphors, describing the designer's 'strategies' and his 'moves', likening designing to a game of chess (Schön 1983: 104). In contrast to Steiner's 'penetration' and 'entry' into the text, Gayatri Spivak describes an act of 'surrender' to the text. 'Hers is less a hermeneutical voyage into the intentionality of the text than an engagement with the sensual texture of expression' (Simon 1996: 144). Spivak goes on to describe translation as 'surrendering' and 'sensing' in the context of subjectivity, which correlates it with an understanding of tacit knowledge, using textile metaphors to help explain the scenario. She describes how, in translation, meaning 'hops into the spacy emptiness' between two languages and how the translator must attend to 'juggling the disruptive rhetoricity that breaks the surface [of the text] in not necessarily connected ways, we feel the selvedges of the language-textile give way, fray into frayages or facilitations' (Spivak 1993: 180).

> The task of the translator is to facilitate this love between the original and its shadow, a love that permits fraying, holds the agency of the translator and the demands of her imagined or actual audience at bay. (Spivak 1993: 181)

Spivak's feminist reading of the process of translation allows for an alternative subjective, relational understanding of design which contrasts with the notion of interventionist problem-solving. Spivak's mention of the love of the translator for the original text and its 'shadow' (the translation) acknowledges the subjectivity and the presence of the translator and connects with the notion of responding as pledging back (love, nurture, understanding). Spivak's use of 'frayage' or 'facilitation' invites an understanding of unravelling, disruption, entanglement as a positive and facilitative step in the creation of understanding or knowledge. Spivak's 'surrendering' is not to be misconstrued as a submission but rather as the necessity and willingness to be vulnerable to, and offer oneself up for, change and alteration in this co-emergent encounter. Michael Polanyi, in his writing on the creation of personal or tacit knowledge, captures the way in which Steiner's hermeneutics and Spivak's fraying and surrendering unite, in his concept of 'self-disposal':

> The satisfaction of gaining intellectual control over the external world is linked to a satisfaction of gaining control over ourselves. This urge towards this dual satisfaction is persistent; yet it operates by phases of self-destruction. This endeavour must occasionally operate by demolishing a hitherto accepted structure, or parts of it, in order to establish an even more rigorous and comprehensive one in its place. (Polanyi 1958: 196)

Aspects of Polanyi's theories on the tacit have been interpreted and popularized by Csíkszentmihályi as the notion of achieving 'flow' (1990). To gain control, you must lose control, so to speak. Returning to Spivak, it is a willingness to be located in the uncertain liminal spacy emptiness between.

Friedrich's notion of translation as 'releasing', Spivak's use of 'fraying' as facilitation, the translator's 'love' and the notion of tidying up echo Walter Benjamin's thinking in his 1923 essay 'The translator's task'. Benjamin emphasizes the justification of freedom (over fidelity) in translation to 'unbind' meaning from language, speech and sense and to 'liberate' and 'recuperate' it (Benjamin 1923: 82).

Transformation

Translations and translators have often been conceptualized as female and inferior in their relationship with the original text and author: the original is seen as generative, the translation as merely derivative (Simon 1996: 1). The expression 'les belles infidèles' has been used to describe translations as either faithful or beautiful, but not both (Chamberlain 1988: 455). Simon describes how feminist translation theory takes the traditionalist notion of fidelity or faithfulness to the text, author or reader in translation and redirects it to the process of writing itself. Applying questions of fidelity to an original in the process of translation towards the context of design relates to notions of unconscious and conscious variation. Philip Steadman (1979/2008) refers to Pitt-Rivers's 1884 experiments in successive copying as well as Henry Balfour's utilization of the activity as a research tool for *The Evolution of Decorative Arts* from 1893. He says,

> The origins or at least precursors of particular decorative forms were to be discovered by tracing them back through continuous series of always slightly differing copies. And as such chains of 'genetically' connected designs might begin and end with examples so widely different, that unless the intermediate links were known, it would not be imagined that they were in any way related. (Steadman 1979/2008: 99)

Following from said anthropological studies, it is widely understood that decoration has evolved through iterations of natural motifs and markings. Certain motifs have been successively copied and in doing so have changed form. Steadman sets up this copying as 'variation', which can be unconscious or conscious: either an attempt to reproduce the original as faithfully as possible or with some intent to alter or improve it. These concepts relate to approaches of translation; as such conscious variation corresponds to the feminist paradigm. Conscious variation recognizes the subjectivity of the translator/designer in this creative act: their intention and expression are key to the outcome, embodied in the mark, the stitch, the texture and the structure. A textile designer perhaps might rework or recolour a design from an archive; this is not derivation.

It contrasts newness with the comfort of familiarity – decoration as 'les belles infidèles'.

> In terms of pattern, individual motifs are totally transformed within the pattern as a whole, by the chance swaying of a dress or curtain. Pattern eludes, evades and troubles our gaze. (Graves 2002: 52)

A feminist reading of translation invites an exploration into the translator herself. Bogusia Temple describes how translators 'are often women paid for discrete pieces of work where they are not even acknowledged or named in the final written text (see also the invisibility of the translator by Venuti 1994). Their structural/social position informs their translation through the words that they choose to convey concepts but their influence on the text is marginalized and often ignored' (Temple 2005: 5.4). This situation is also synonymous with the role of the textile designer, often female, paid for the rights to one-off samples that go on to be incorporated into another design product, the input seldom credited and the impact often ignored. The correlation between the female translator and the female textile designer is significant in the development of a new understanding of textile design. The translator is further characterized by José Ortega y Gasset in his 1937 essay *The Misery and Splendour of Translation* (Ortega y Gasset 1937: 94), which views translation as a Utopian endeavour:

> To write well is to make continual excursions into grammar, into established usage, and into accepted linguistic norms. It is an act of permanent rebellion against the social environs, a subversion. To write well is to employ a certain radical courage. Fine, but the translator is usually a shy character. Because of his humility, he has chosen such an insignificant occupation. He finds himself facing an enormous controlling apparatus, composed of grammar and common usage. What will he do with the rebellious text? Isn't it too much to ask that he also be rebellious, particularly since the text is someone else's. He will be ruled by cowardice, so instead of resisting grammatical restraints he will do just the opposite: he will place the translated author in the prison of normal expression; that is, he will betray him. Traduttore, traditore.

Ortega y Gasset's depiction portrays a shy, humble person (as translator) full of courage, intention and aspiration yet 'marching toward failure' and betrayal (Ortega y Gasset 1937: 94). This characterization only holds true if fidelity in translation is held as its defining role. If the translator adopts the sense of freedom encouraged by writers such as Benjamin, Ortega y Gasset's character can be rewritten as a quietly courageous pioneer, a rebellious bricoleur, a humble subversive, a feminist? Simon (1996: 83) provides several historical examples of how translation has been used by female writers to find a voice, socially, politically and artistically. In regard to this, she describes translation as an 'intensely relational act, one which establishes connections between text and culture, between author and reader'.

In the integration of the metaphor of design as translation, notions of suspension and surrender to liminality in translation/design and the translator/designer as rebellious bricoleur is the concept of a simultaneous movement towards and beckoning forth to the possibility of transformation. It requires the designer to imagine, embody and translate new possibilities, each of these activities involving the adoption of relational liminality: being between and at once in two situations.

In their contributing chapter, Elena Caratti and Daniela Calabi respond to and collaborate in the development of 'the translation paradigm for design culture'. Delving into their previous research developed from within the fields of visual communication design and architecture, Caratti and Calabi explore 'texture design' which they state clearly is texture including and beyond the textile. Texture design as a translatory mediator of place, territory, skill and cultural identity. For them, design (particularly involving textures) is a communicative act which makes memories accessible.

6

The translation paradigm for design culture

Elena Caratti and Daniela Calabi

Defined 'topologically', a culture is a sequence of translations and transformations of constants ('translation' always tends to 'transformation').

(George Steiner, 1975: 426)

Design and translation have a lot of affinities on multiple levels: not only for their conceptual foundations, values and principles but also and in particular in terms of processes of cultural transfer. The same evolution of the meanings associated to the word *translation* confirms the fact that this activity can be central in disciplines that go beyond the concept of translation in its literal sense (transposition of a text from a natural language to another).

We would like to assert here that translation is very close to the cultural, communicative, dialogic and creative dimension of the design discipline in all its declensions.

Indeed 'design is more than a socio-technical system. Design is a "cultural system" that, in producing and spreading innovation, . . . realizes a sort of *semiosfera*' (Penati 2013: 15); in other words, design produces multiple 'texts' (with an internal structure and a series of cultural external connections) that can be translated through different codes (visual, verbal, auditory, etc.). Design transfers ideas, cultures, philosophies, visions, experiences, images and imaginary of an epoch, of a context, producing, sharing and therefore 'translating' new meanings, new attitudes, new visions of the world.

To understand the concept of translation and its sense for design discipline, it is useful to take in consideration its meanings from the perspective of Translation Studies.

We have different declinations of the concept of translation: as Osimo observes (2015: 1–3), to translate, for ancient Greeks, is linked to the verbs *metafero* (to transport), *me-tafrazo* (to paraphrase) and *metagrafo* (to transcript).

In Latin we have further interpretations of the same term: the verbs *vorto* (to copy), *scribo* (to trace, to create, to compose) and *exprimo* (to model) are connected to a creative activity that promotes cultural and linguistic innovation. Instead, *converto, transverto* and *imitor* refer explicitly to the narrative translation that is finalized to the production of a readable text, without a faithful connection with the original one. In this case the problem of comprehension and content accessibility is central: a text (in all its forms) needs to be finalized to a specific receiving culture and entails a process of mediation between the cultures and sensibilities of the author and the receiver.

The use of the Latin verb *traducere* (and the substantives traductio, traductor) is relatively more recent (with Leonardo Bruni's work 'De Interpretazione recta', 1420) and includes three different categories of translation: the imitation or emulation (*metre en romanz, romançar, riducere*), the conversion or the explanation (*to turn, to deduce, to transmute*) and the re-expression or to render (*translater, transladar, transferir, to translate*). The same English word *translation* originates from the Latin *transfero, translatum*; basically it assumes a 'transit' between two levels of discourse, but over the time, the concept of translation has become more specific and it has assumed different and ramified meanings aimed at underlining its transformative, cultural, relational, cognitive, innovative potential.

The proximity between translation and design is particularly evident not only in communication design (Baule and Caratti 2017: 14) but also in other areas of design where immaterial and communicative qualities sustain and integrate with technological or functional properties translating social and cultural meanings. We can recognize in Translation Studies theories some principles and procedural criteria that can support design in its essence and cultural pluralism.

'Design is translation' starting from the *design process*: Torop's concept of 'total translation' (1995) is useful to find some analogies between the different stages of *translation process* with those of design process. The theorist, inspired from Jackobson's studies, defined the *translation process* in term of 'whatever transfer from a *prototext* (text of the sender's culture) to a *metatext* (text of the receiver's culture)' (Torop 1995). The steps, independently from the implied codes or transfer typologies, can be described as follows (see Osimo 2014, Kindle 65–8):

1. prototext analysis and elaboration of translation strategy;
2. content transposition;
3. formal re-codification;
4. metatextual management of translation residual;
5. translation critics.

This sophisticated model has many points in common with design process (Jones 1992: 61–73):

a. The first *analytical and divergent stage* of design process is finalized to de-structure the original brief (the prototext) to find not only criticalities but also design strategies and alternative ideas.
b. *Design transformation*, as Jones affirms (1992: 66), is finalized to impose a pattern that is precise enough to permit convergence to the single design. It is characterized by a series of transpositions that Torop describes in term of *interlinguistic, intersemiotic, intralinguistic translations* (according to Jackobson's definitions, 1959: 260–6) and moreover *metatextual, intertextual, intratextual translations*. In other words, as designers we realize a multiplicity of translational passages: from an idea to a concept, from function to forms, from contents to expression, from language to language, from techniques to techniques, from support to support (Baule and Caratti 2017: 269).
c. *Re-codification* process is a sort of a subcategory of design transformation and consists in the passage from a semiotic system to another (e.g. from verbal to visual).
d. *Design convergence* is the stage after the problem has been defined and the objectives have been agreed (Jones 1992: 68): the designer's aim is to reduce the secondary uncertainties (the semiotic noise or the residual) progressively until only one of many possible alternative designs is left as the final solution to be launched into the world.
e. *Design evaluation* (or translation critics) intervenes at the end of the design process; it contemplates the critic or the revision of the previous stages according to shared criteria.

The parallelism between translation process and design process allows us to outline some general principles that reinforce our assertions; design can be defined in terms of translation for different reasons:

- For the *attention to languages, their codes and translation models* (in all their declinations) that open unexpected possibilities of innovation and transformation. From this perspective new paths and new methods for design practice can emerge.
- Design, as the translation, is strictly connected to a process of *interpretation* and *negotiation*: all its components and variables are not constant but they can be interpreted and negotiated under the logic of 'pertinence', starting from spatial, temporal, perceptive or semantic delimitations. This is strictly

connected to the effort of the designer to find the best final solution through a series of trials and attempts that can be only a compromise.
- Design very often proceeds, in parallel to translation, through the categories of *imitation, selection, reduction* or *complementarity*, to express the relationship between the *prototext* (text of the sender's culture) and the *metatext* (the final output or text of the receiver's culture).
- In the same terms of translation, design projects need to have an *internal coherence* and *cohesion* at syntactic, semantic and pragmatic level.
- Like translation, design is *target-oriented*: the cultural, geographical, historical contest of the receiver is at the core of the project. The designer and at the same time the translator put themselves in the position of the final users to comprehend their norms, point of view and sensibilities. The designer needs to predict a model of the possible final user who should be able to interpret his choices.
- The principle of *translator invisibility* has, in some cases, a direct counterpart in the *invisibility of the designer*, in his or her anonymity (Baule and Caratti 2017: 19).
- Similarly to translated literature, design is a system that *plays intertextually* with other systems and domains: from this perspective the project is not an ended and closed product; it's a work in progress connected with other projects, with other codes, with the society, the history not in a deterministic way but citational (Barthes 1991: 181).
- In parallel to translation, design is developing its *metalanguage* as capability to comprehend the meaning and the sense of its transfer practices. To face various levels of complexity, designers must be equipped with theoretical concepts that enable them to circulate productively. They also need a methodology by which they can access meta-view points on various perspectives including their own point (Morin 1977: 179).
- Through the translation paradigm design reinforces its *reflexive vocation*: 'every translation is an act of critical interpretation' (Neergard 2013: Kindle 439); at the same time, design through the translation paradigm can adopt further analytical filters to reinforce its capability to critic culture, society, the political system, against prejudices, conventions, stereotypes and manipulations (Baule and Caratti 2017: 272).

The different modes of conceiving the translating activity in design can be resumed in three main points (Zingale 2017: 89–90):

1. It consists in the ability to say explicitly something that had not had the possibility of being expressed before, but which is nonetheless present

in the common conscience as content looking for a form of expression: in this case, the designer invents and elaborates the proper form of expression that was lacking or inadequate before.
2. The translating activity in design presents itself as the ability to say clearly what was obscure and would have no other possibility of being comprehended. In this case, the designer is an interpreter of semiotically undefined contents and invents or elaborates a form of expression that makes those contents more accessible.
3. Design is an act of translation because it tries to say differently something already expressed, but that is semiotically weakened by the changing cultural contexts (or by historical, ethnical, geographical ones), but which could gain more strength if renewed and reformulated through techniques and instruments enhancing its expressive effectiveness.

This argumentation about the strict relationship between design and translation hasn't the presumption to be exhaustive; it's part of a wider and ongoing research that is finalized to the progressive construction of a gaze, of a design attitude able to conjugate linguistic and semiotic competences with the multiple complexities of design.

Texture design, too, is ascribable to a translation system where the combining principle implies the process of decodifying traces and the isolation of alphabet signs, the multiplication and succession of modularities within the principles of series and segmentation.

The meaning of the term 'texture' is related to the idea of a narrative plot which is *also* textile, but it's not the only acceptation. Every surface traced by signs, identifiable as a narrative of texture, gives back significant values, legible and interpretable as imprints on the skin of things.

In fact, it is possible to identify a closeness of meaning of the word 'text' (through which narration emerges) in the etymological and structural sense deriving from the Latin *tèxtus*, past participle of the verb *texere*, to the meaning of the word 'texture' and to the consequent concepts of 'narration' and 'communication', which are at the base of communication design.

Texture design manifests itself both as an ancient discipline and as a symbolic frame dense with traditions, as it belongs to vast historical and design contexts. Certainly, the art of textile processing has expressed, over the centuries, the full mastery of a very diverse heritage of languages, which is articulated in different times and places with formal variations, intertwinings, contaminations and overlapping of symbols between different cultures (see Gombrich [1979] 2000).

However, through the recognition of writing and the richness of the meanings of the various textures, as well as through the observation of their diffusion and variety of design, it is possible to observe as follows. The intertwining of the signs on the surfaces (modular, chromatic and tactile) as well as the use of different materials and technologies affirm the evolution and transmission of the cultural identities of human civilization. Texture design is thus affirmed, from the earliest times, as an *instrument of communication of identities* (see Ciarrocchi and Calabi 2017: 23–32).

The use of textures is then transversal to the arts, and the study of texture itself has been approached from different points of view; today the contaminations between perception, design, historical, artistic and semiotic disciplines are evident. Thus, through texture, design reveals the interesting vocation to become an educational tool for creative disciplines.

The creative skills in the definition of the weaves and their variants build the semantic value of a texture: both when the textures are interpreted and reproduced through the most diverse printing technologies, with the use of analogue or digital languages, and when they decode meanings and symbolic perceptive characters. Once the domain of decorative art, texture has therefore played a unifying role in the visual arts.

Concerning the signs used in the fabrics, it can be noted that their combination is similar to the calligraphic compositions, both for the visual impact of the intertwining composition and for the symbolic force of the meanings. Consider, for example, the pages traced with the gothic typographic font 'textur', used in the printing of the J. Gutemberg '42 lines' Bible.

Textures, like calligraphy, are therefore material traces, which originate from sequences of gestures: from the hand that weaves the weft and the warp and the hand that generates writing. Roland Barthes (see Barthes [1994] 1999: 63) poetically reminds us how the hands, which in the prehistory of civilizations were mainly engaged in the locomotor function, were finally released from that task thanks to the evolutionary passage of the human being to the erect status, assuming then the fundamental commitment to *free words*. A liberation of the gesture, which however 'imprisons' the reader in the interweaving of the plot.

Barthes writes,

> Epistemologically, the concept of intertext is what brings to the theory of the text the volume of sociality: it is all the language, anterior and contemporary, which comes to the text, not according to the path of a detectable filiation, of a voluntary imitation, but according to that of a dissemination – an image which assures the text of the status, not of a reproduction, but of a productivity. These

principal concepts, which are the articulations of the theory, all agree, in short, with the image suggested by the very etymology of the word 'text': it is a tissue; but whereas previously criticism (the only known form in France of a theory of literature) unanimously emphasized the finite 'fabric' (the text being a 'veil' behind which it was necessary to fetch the truth, the real message, meaning), the current theory of the text turns away from the text-veil and seeks to perceive the fabric in its texture, in the interweaving of the codes, the formulas, the signifiers, in which the subject is placed and defeated, like a spider that dissolves itself in its web. The neologism lover could therefore define the theory of the text as a 'hyphology' (hyphos is the fabric, the veil and the spider's web). (Barthes [1974] 1999: 6)

The textures therefore define a (meta) tactile/visual language that parallels the symbolic one traced by writing. The weft and warp design, which belongs to the material due to that transposition activity which is the *translation*, is 'texus': a narrative plot. This is because a translation from a tactile language to a visual language is possible, changing the support or the matter of the support, as it is possible to transfer the symbols from one composition to another, generating new meanings and involving the different forms of visual narration. Textures are therefore translations, with all the implications of meaning that this creative action entails.

The modular elements that make up a texture are mainly the result of combinatorial variations that create the appearance of the whole. The textures therefore make the *morphogenesis of the field* possible, a design of weaves that generates infinite variations of textures on the surfaces.

These weaves are made up of signs, calligraphies, colours, shapes and are essentially *micro-graphie* (Gaur 1997); they are figurative writings of a 'non-linguistic' semiotic space. A space where the carefully designed signs, then decomposed and recomposed, create interactions to form a 'text-image'.

In the design of surfaces, composition is therefore a special form of writing on the *skin* of things, where material values are added to the functional, meaning and perceptive aspects.

Texture design articulates two fundamental *perceptual forms of knowledge*: first, managing the interpretation of objects with the visual investigation of their surface, at a distance; second, returning an interpretation of the substance, of the interiority of objects, with contact and haptic perception (Panofsky 1989: 179 tr.it.). Panofsky uses the word 'haptic' with the meaning of 'tangible': touch is extended to the perception of forms and space through the whole body and no longer exclusively through the hands.

In texture design, perceptive modalities interact and influence each other: 'synaesthesic perception is the rule' (Merleau Ponty 1945: 309 tr.it.). Therefore, it is possible to consider the *reader's* gaze as a sort of 'touch' at a distance. Because the layer of visible substance prepares for the haptic understanding of things. Because it carries out an action of mediation with those that can be defined as 'surface landscapes' (see Bruno 2014) able to offer perception the symbolic *translated* worlds composed of series of signs. Therefore, texture has a translative-*predictive* role as it anticipates and prepares to the understanding of meanings; it also has a role of *mediation*-translation, relating observer and object.

In textures, the possibility of experimentation in the field of visual cultures is constantly renewed. Therefore, from the point of view of studies on perception, texture design lends itself well to educational exercise; the study of the compositional process is particularly functional to basic design (see Calabi 2016).

The experiences of schools such as the Bauhaus, the School of Ulm and, in the United States, the experience with William Huff and his studies on tessellations in the plan (see Huff 1984: 36) reveal the fundamental importance of texture design for the development of *compositional skills*. Furthermore, the design of signs and the composition of the page combine well with the concept of *learning by doing*, typical of *basic design*, which is carried out with preparatory value within the principle of seriality (see Marcolli 1975: 98–107).

It is understood that the skills acquired through the study of textures are not only instrumental to technical exercise and visual grammar. The design practice aimed at composition (through the applied study of perceptive, formal and chromatic effects) activates, in the case of visual communication, the development of an appropriate *culture of the gaze*. It is no coincidence that the compositional choice of serial repetition is a widespread solution in graphics and, in general, in communication design. It's important to note, for example, how the profitable season of the 1960s brought out the linguistic abilities of the *form in succession*, with results of strong visual impact, catalysts of attention.

Among the great theorists and masters of basic design there is the Italian Attilio Marcolli who in his 'Field Theory' (see Marcolli 1971) highlights the value of segmentation of the field in the logic of seriality. In the signs arranged in a planar grid, the organization's methodological processes are recognized in reading hierarchies, consistent with the *Gestaltpsychologie*. Texture design, as summation of signs, generates unitary formal meanings which are different each time, as a result of discrete units that emerge from the background according to the rules known to the studies on perception. The generative principle of texture design presents recursive syntax, due to its ability to generate infinite 'visual phrases' (see Chomsky [1966] 1978).

At the same time, it is rooted in studies on the organization of the perceptual field and the phenomenal units: seriality, modular composition, succession, perception, *deconstruction* (see Derrida [1967] 1998). Whenever a text is deconstructed, the structure of alternations and relationships generates new perceptual values, in order to adapt the result to the original expression. In other words, a *translation* of meanings takes place, the result of which is a 'metatext', a product that is semantically unchanged compared to the original text (see Popovič 1975) and therefore linked, from one or more pertinent levels, to the starting form.

The textures are *disassembly and reassembly*; they are born from a generative evolution of material form and meanings, which can take place by virtue of the translation principle and of that principle of segmentation of the field that allows reproducibility. The correspondence in meaning of alphabetic translations is shared by this form of visual writing. Textures are therefore abstract configurations of a narrative told through images (Veca 2007: 191), in which a 'morphogenetic' type of writing, whose form is in potential transformation arising from the relationships between the plots, dominates. Texture design invites the creation of a text-writing whose body is made of graphic (type) modules; it produces narrative and graphic text; it connects texts and hypertexts; in the page, it relates semantic writing and image. The textures are poietic design (from the Greek *poiein* which means *to do*) and estesìa (sensitivity, perception).

Texture is therefore a means, an interface, a medium whose value is often rooted in the cultures and territory of origin. The recurrent motifs, the shapes and the colours make it possible to identify the traditional, geographical and cultural origins expressed in the symbols. They charge the modularity of *sinsemantic meanings* that can be interpreted completely within the value of the whole. When the form of writing enters the memory it is translated into identity and sense of belonging. In this case, the design of surfaces makes immaterial traditions accessible. Through colours and signs, the textures reveal the artistic influences, the history and the origins to the expert. Like a story, texture is open to the interpretation of those who know the symbolic language. Signs that translate signs, therefore, in accordance with the concept of 'unlimited semiosis' by Charles S. Peirce (Peirce [1931–58] 1989), reconfirming the analogy between translation requests and design instances.

In this particular translating passage that is being proposed, the sensitivity of the texture designer (see Baule 2017) expresses itself as a careful care in proposing transposition and identifying translatability. Many forms of craftsmanship knowledge of the Mediterranean Basin express this design sensitivity through texture design, a translative point of view of tradition and culture. Therefore, through the study of constants and differences between signs, it is possible to interpret the intrinsic identity inherent in surfaces. With the assumption that every translation derives from a 'prototext', meaning from an initial text, the original reference here are the artistic cultures of the places where they are rooted.

While the material and workmanship return a global identity also linked to the common historical, morphological, geographical and geological features of the Mediterranean countries, the 'aesthetic' – and therefore perceptive – elements of the surfaces define those 'immediate identities' typical of local cultures. The whole set of signs that characterizes surfaces often translates local aesthetic characters; it explicits the belonging to a specific place thanks to these immediately perceptible aspects that offer codes for decoding. Texture design lends itself to these intersemiotic passages, without losing the semantic connotations of the context and the environment that generated them. Texture design, therefore, intended as the *design of cultural translations*.

As in the translation process, design also identifies a practice in the transition from one language to another, from one morphology to another, from one world of meaning to another. By translational analogy, it is the intersemiotic and, in general, perceptive passage to a visual language – found, for example, in the narratives that migrate between cultures and media, which tell of techniques and technologies, pigments, styles and historical roots.

It can be said that the design of surfaces of artisanal artefacts translates into visual forms from the anthropological space. The surfaces become the space of communication and exchange between worlds that express cultural characters with different signs. Texture, therefore, is intended as a decisive passage that spreads the character of identity and belonging, expliciting it in the process and sometimes hybridizing and stratifying signs of different origins.

In this case the textures are intended as 'cultural fabrics', as forms of writing born of design and historical crafts that respond to the traditions of the places where they are rooted, which make the memories accessible. Therefore, texture design represents a means of mediation between languages that express themselves with different forms of writing: on the one hand that of the territory and its traditions, skills and manual techniques that give rise to artistic crafts; on the other, that of ornamentation as an interpreter of local cultural identities.

These reflections lead texture design to translation design (see Torop [1995] 2009) – a translation that, from an interdisciplinary point of view, identifies a nucleus of theoretical principles and consolidates itself as a *communicative act*, as a linguistic transposition with translation rules and norms.

Notes

The concept of semiosphere was introduced by the Russian semiologist Jurij Lotman in 1984. As Osimo asserts, referring to Lotman, semiosphere can be conceived in terms of a universe of signification in which the various spheres (from the individual to the continent) communicate with each other through membranes embodying the culture of boundaries or cultural differences (Osimo 2015: 11).

Jackobson (1959: 260–6) extended the concept of translation beyond the common sense of *interlinguistic transfer* between two natural language systems. He expressed two additional categories: *intralinguistic translation* or reformulation: interpretation of verbal signs through other sign of the same language (and same code); *intersemiotic translation* or transmutation: interpretation of verbal signs through non-verbal signs (the two systems differ in term of code).

Mesh two

People respond to textiles quite badly, I think. Even at college it seemed to be quite a 'low down' course. I say to people I do textiles – oh what do you sew, do you make clothes, and it's like, no . . . I actually explain to people textiles is really broad and quite sculptural and it's quite three dimensional and you can use, you know . . . doesn't have to be fabric, it can be metal, plastic and what have you. People just don't get it. I remember a few of the experiences where you're presenting work to an audience that the majority of them are engineers, textile engineers and it goes completely over their heads, they're looking at you like you only do pretty things. They see us as people who make things look pretty. It seems like a fluffy subject. Once you say 'textiles' people get all these different stereotypical images in their mind and it's hard to get them to understand what you're about. 'Yeah, you've got big jewellery on, you must be a textile designer.' But you can't really define a textile designer.

Textiles is moving to technology to try and rid that idea, which I applaud. It makes an awful lot of sense, obviously. But the whole making of beautiful fabrics isn't a fluffy thing. It's really not. And it's that that we've got to sell/explain.

It's the whole male/female thing, it's like textiles is predominantly female and then, generally, like product design is mostly male and they'll design something like a textile, big panels that kind of fit together, and they're like look, they're textiles and I looked at it and think, god, it's a bit crap, and we could have done it millions of years ago, kind of thing, and yet it's awarded 'best use of textiles' and it's just . . . shocking. It really drives me up the wall. People don't seem to, kind of, seek out textiles. If it's done by some male industrial designer who's, you know, great or whatever then it's fantastic. Textiles is not thought of that highly. Textiles isn't obviously completely forgotten but I do think it is up to us, the textile people, to really push forward our ideas and our techniques and really kind of get ourselves out there, I think. We all know what textiles is, whereas most of the other disciplines, it seems to me, are constantly evolving, whereas textiles seem to be, kind of, stuck. It's like, we're textiles . . . shitty textiles . . . which doesn't really help.

It's the making that I like. I like the whole process. A lot of my decisions are made on the loom, although I design, but things change on the loom and I don't think I could ever get to the point where I could ask somebody else to take on what I'm doing. I like the process. I think I like the structure of weaving because it takes some of the variables away. Like painting is pretty scary on a blank canvas. I like to push that structure, work within a structure like that. I don't think I'm an artist. I'm a designer and I'm a designer craftsman and designer maker. I don't know exactly which. It changes. I just love fabric and materials.

And when you've been working with something for so long it becomes less deliberate and somehow the work for me takes on more of a life and I know when to stop something too, because I know then it's just becoming . . . . I can't sort of describe the process but I seem to be thinking something in my head but what I'm doing I kind of later realize that, oh, it's kind of linked but it's not on purpose.

I didn't really appreciate, maybe . . . didn't appreciate my creativity until you come into the environment of a different discipline like this. I realized that the way that I think is completely different to how they think. Actually my input is very important in terms of that.

Dealing with people who probably know little about textile designing – they're mainly fashion designers so they don't know what's feasible to print, particularly – they'll buy something that fits in with their look, their style, their direction. There's an appreciation of the beauty of it but no understanding of the work involved. Textile design in the textile studios, in the way it's working now, is the most daft situation – you do the stuff in the way that a fine artist does stuff, and then you go out and you say: 'What do you think – do you want to buy it? Is it right for you or is it not?' So it's a very bizarre situation . . .

I don't particularly like going to trade fairs. I hate it, it's reactive. I like to ring someone up and make an appointment and go and see them. It's a private thing. As a studio we generally just don't do particularly well in the trade fairs but you have to go because you have to show your face and get new customers. I'm not a hard-sell salesperson. I'm not a salesperson at all, you know. I'll try and persuade people that they want things but basically if it's right, it's right and if it isn't, it isn't – they'll come and buy it. I hadn't realized how good you had to be at selling as a designer in that scenario, that was a new one on me. Maybe that's related again to the idea that we're behind everything and that we need to sell ourselves to these other fields of design in order for our work to go anywhere. Textile designers are shy people, they don't like to be on stage, they prefer to stay behind the scenes. But you have to be utterly convinced that what you're doing is great and right. But that whole thing of convincing people to kind of place their budgets on something that you feel is the right thing is . . . quite an interesting twist on events.

You're always working on two seasons because somebody is always looking for something different . . . and you're trying to show them new designs all the time or a new enough look that convinces them. it's good to put your work in different contexts. It's just like working for a client really, I suppose.

Really early on, I worked with a fashion designer, creating key embroideries for his collection. And yet I haven't even got a seat, I'm standing at the back. And on the piece of paper on the chair it often says, 'Thanks to so and so and so and so for the hair. Thanks to so and so for the tie.' And at the bottom it says, if I'm lucky, 'Thanks to me for the embroidery or textile.' But never my full name. 'Cause they don't want somebody else to come along and use you.

I did challenge it with the company. They said, 'They want to buy this label, I'd be a fool to diffuse it with your name and you'd be a fool to diffuse your name with my name, because they would buy less, because they want me, you know?' So yeah, fine. Let's carry on, because you can't buck it, you can't fight it. Because that was it. But I would really love textile designers to have people backing them to say, 'No, your name must be on it.'

And I think that when you get textile designers who've actually done well, whose names are really well known, they are people with either fantastic business backing or have that character of showmanship. I often think that textile designers work like this, and fashion designers work like that. We all get off on that little mark, and we're really happy if we've done that nice mark, we'll go to bed really happy. Still, there are some people that say, 'Oh, don't you think it's a shame that you're not the name?' Sometimes yes of course I feel like that, but often I'd hate to be that name and I'm happy with what I do and where I am.

I think us textile designers tend to be, I don't know whether it's we're the type of people or whether it's the kind of, the history of it, but we tend not to be nearly as confident about what we do as other design disciplines. There's that whole kind of side of fashion which is about showing off and about being, you know, a bit more theatrical or a bit more, you know, kind of, look at me, I suppose. I feel that we're quieter people, it's not all about me, me, me, working with fashion people, they are a bit pushy, more pushy. Textile's kind of quietly working away, kind of, coming up with these things. There's a very different . . . it's a different characteristic, it's a different kind of person that wants to do that. It's a different kind of person that wants to, you know. . . . My students describe how when collaborating with individuals from other design fields they kind of feel that they're producing cloth for them and that it's an unequal partnership, if you like, and that . . . they seemed to be kind of resigned to that; that's kind of just how it is. But that doesn't surprise me, somehow. I think historically textiles, as a subject area, has always been seen as a bit of an underdog and I think it's because, it's kind of, it's almost because it's so related to the every-day that we're kind of so used to it and it almost, you know, stems back to lots of domestic practice and people hand-knitting and those sorts of things. And because it is, in a sense, a supplier to other industries. It is, you know, the stuff they use, so because it's not the ultimate end result, you know, there isn't the same starriness or star designer sort of thing associated with the textile designer because it always then gets developed or moved on into the product or into another kind of area. I think it is seen by others as a service industry, especially the fashion industry – shouldn't say that at all. With my career this is one of the real bugbears. It shouldn't really be like that but it is, because fashion's demands are so much different to ours and the hierarchy and the politics behind it are so complicated, you know. It's incredible. We're a service provider for all of those different design disciplines, and so it, you know, it affects how all of those different areas work. You do end up being the slightly lower down one. You have to just be prepared for that.

For me, here, it's all about . . .it's not about trying to surprise so much, it's about trying to fit in with what someone else's idea is. It's trying to give her what she feels. You must recognize what's needed for who you're working for. I'm closely informed about what they need in the collection and what's going on in the collection so I can fit with their themes. I don't as such have my own range. I work across all teams. It's quite unique but it also means I don't actually get involved in kind of the selection process. That's what the garment designer does. So at the end of the day they are kind of more accountable for the range as such. I'm just kind of a tool for them really to put it together, I'm like a resource.

7

A story of hard and soft

Modernism and textiles as design

Pennina Barnett provides an alternative understanding of the phenomenon of metramorphosis as developed by Ettinger. She describes 'soft logics' in reference to Michel Serres's concept of 'sack thinking' (Barnett 1999: 183). For Barnett, this paradigm sits beside the binary ideology (Serres's hard, box thinking) of 'either/or' and invites multiple possibilities, encouraging 'and/and', permitting 'the opportunity to be oneself in a new way'. Serres (1985) talks about the liminal threshold between hardness and softness, how one gives way to another. Soft logics and their significance to an understanding of textile design thinking require considered analysis, which I will certainly address in Chapter 13, *Making, problems and pleasures*, but for now I wish to use Serres's concept of a relationality between hard and soft to explore a narrative providing a metaphor for the socio-historical context of these ideas.

I am going to take Paul Scheerbart's 1914 novel *The Gray Cloth* (Scheerbart 1914) as a reflection of the contradiction between textiles design as the ideal medium/tool for the modernist message and how its associated thinking was marginalized within the universalism of the movement. This is inextricably paralleled with the prevailing position of the feminine and feminism in modernist thought (Sparke 1995).

I first came across Scheerbart's name in Richard Weston's introduction to the fourth edition of Niklaus Pevsner's *Pioneers of Modern Design* (Pevsner 2005: 9). Weston critiques Pevsner's original text, commenting that no account of early modernist architecture would now ignore the expressionist circle of Bruno Taut and Paul Scheerbart. A few internet searches later unearthed a review of Scheerbart's novel by prominent design historian Victor Margolin (2003). Margolin's review describes the plot in detail, and I quickly became intrigued by its narrative of the relationship between coloured glass and grey fabric, architecture and clothing, male and female, hard and soft.

Conceived and written as an expressionist novel, at the dawn of theoretical modernism, the novel is set forty years later, at the watershed of what would become popular modernism. It begins by introducing the hero-architect and coloured glass enthusiast, Edgar Krug, seemingly loosely based on Scheerbart's friend and collaborator, Bruno Taut. We meet Edgar, and his impulsive and immovable opinions, at a showcase of silver sculpture, in an exhibition hall of coloured glass and iron near Chicago which he had designed. The characterization of Edgar is accompanied by the sound of the organ, expertly and passionately played by his future wife, Clara Weber. Edgar is annoyed by the fashions of the women attending the event, feeling that their clothing choices showed a lack of respect for his coloured glass walls. When he eventually meets Clara, the talented musician who had created the phonic atmosphere that had amplified the effect of his architecture, Edgar notices that she is wearing an outfit of grey fabric (with 10 per cent white), which he feels is the most complementary clothing to be worn within his colourful glass buildings. Almost immediately he proposes marriage, with a clause that Clara should only ever wear this combination of grey and white. She instantly accepts, and they are married that night. The novel then travels with Edgar and Clara on their glass airship as they visit his various architectural projects around the globe. Throughout the novel, Clara is encouraged by other women to break the marriage terms or at the very least subvert them in some way. While the novel focuses on Clara's clothing, it is not her clothing style that Edgar is concerned with but the cloth from which it is made – its colouration, patterning and textures. Edgar Krug not only stipulates that Clara must wear grey cloth with 10 per cent white but that her clothing should not be made from velvet or silk (Scheerbart 1914: 10).

The *Gray Cloth* was the first of Scheerbart's novels to be translated into English, in 2001. Reiterating Weston's comment (Pevsner 2005: 9), John Stuart (Stuart 1999: 61) describes how architectural historian and theoretician Reyner Banham lamented Scheerbart's exclusion from the canon of literature on modernist architecture, despite being a key influence in the avant-garde art and architectural correspondence circle The Crystal Chain, active in 1920, which included Walter Gropius and Taut (Stuart 1999). Walter Benjamin expressed his esteem for Scheerbart's writing, and Scheerbart's 1913 novel *Lesabéndio* directly influenced Benjamin's the Arcades Project, 1927–40 (Morse 2011; Morse 2013; Stuart 1999: 68). Stuart (1999: 61) groups Scheerbart's work with the writing of Jean-François De Bastide, William Morris, George Bernard Shaw, Ayn Rand and Umberto Eco for its influence on architectural design.

Written within the German expressionist oeuvre, Scheerbart's fantastical, science-fiction-based story about modern architecture was characteristic of the utopian thinking associated with the movement and typified in the glass architecture of Bruno Taut. The onset of the First World War and its economic and psychological impact on the German people, and also the wider global population, provided the backdrop of disillusionment that saw the utopian emphasis on self within expressionism evolve into the concept of universal truth of modernism.

The novel's influence on architectural theory is certain, although arguably understated; however, its treatment of clothing, fabric and colour has certainly been ignored. Reading this story as a textile designer, it elicited frustration in me. The textiles were being denied their decorative, pleasure-giving role by virtue of the dominating concepts of architecture. At play is Scheerbart's humorous and ironic tone, often rejected or overlooked by many (including Benjamin) (Stuart 1999). As John Stuart states, in his introduction to his translation of *The Gray Cloth*, Scheerbart courts the discussion about the relationship between architecture and textiles initiated by Gottfried Semper some sixty years earlier.

> He was, moreover, able to relish the rich irony of these antagonistic positions by proposing in *The Gray Cloth* that contemporary women's outfits be fixed and unchanging – and thereby modern – while architecture was colourful, vibrant, and expressive – and thereby fashionable. (Scheerbart 1914: xxxvi)

Interestingly, in his paper *Unweaving Narrative Fabric: Bruno Taut, Walter Benjamin, and Paul Scheerbart's The Gray Cloth*, Stuart uses textile metaphors to describe his own analysis of the novel and likens Scheerbart, as storyteller and thinker, to a weaver:

> Rather, I would argue, Scheerbart wove a narrative fabric . . . . Moreover, in the process of unweaving this fabric, we gain knowledge not only of the culture that produced it, but through its interpretation of the architecture culture of which we are a part today. (Stuart 1999: 69)

He also notes Scheerbart's interest, at the time of writing *The Gray Cloth*, in 'interactions and negotiations between fantasy and reality'. Statements such as these invite comparisons between the means of conception and creation of *The Gray Cloth* as a text (specifically as narrative) and that of cloth itself.

John Stuart deftly summarizes the relevance of *The Gray Cloth* to the themes of this book in terms of its topic, context and storytelling methodology: 'Scheerbart's *The Gray Cloth* provides ample evidence of the importance of narrative as a mediator between utopian ideals and the constructed realities of gender, fashion, materials, human interaction, and architectural experience at the basis of twentieth-century modernity' (Stuart 1999: 69).

And so as I explore the literal story, considering how soft materials (textiles) are suppressed in favour of the hard (glass architecture) in this imagined version of the modernist world, I also apply it as a metaphor. This allows me to explore the interrelationship of Clara and Edgar; Clara as a representative for textiles as feminine/matrixial and for feminism in the modernist context and Edgar represents the domination of the modernist notion of universalism and the metaphorical patriarchal guardian of the hierarchy of the arts.

The *Gray Cloth* illustrates perfectly how the aesthetics and design of textiles and female clothing were subjugated to architecture within the modernist movement. Stuart states that by the time the novel was written, several leading Germanic architects (Van de Velde, Hoffmann and Behrens) were designing women's garments as part of a complete design environment (Scheerbart 1914: xxxv), or 'Gesamtkunstwerk'. Gesamtkunstwerk can be understood as meaning 'the total work of art': it is a term that was used prominently by composer Richard Wagner and applied to modernist architectural theory in the teachings of the Bauhaus. Textile design was considered to be an ideal medium for developing the concept, due to its ability to be mechanized and its versatility as a creative medium.

> Modernist textiles – because they functioned on so many levels . . . were inherently engaged in modern life, they occupied actual space in the gallery, home and showroom, they transformed the human body, and they changed the face of industry. As such they constituted a vital element in developing conceptions of the total work of art. (Gardner Troy 2006: 16)

Gardner Troy (2006: 13) describes how the concept of Gesamtkunstwerk permeated all aspects of textiles – its design, theory, production, marketing and consumption – which situated textiles at the heart of the modernist movement, allowing artists, designers and theoreticians to explore gender roles, primitivism, abstraction, constructivism, new technologies and materials and consumerism. Some might say that the very permeation of the ideology of Gesamtkunstwerk into textile design both highlighted and subjugated some of the defining characteristics of the discipline. Its functional characteristics – adaptability, transferability and versatility – were exploited, while the typical aesthetic concerns of textiles – colour, motif, decoration and haptics – were marginalized in favour of the unified style. It is well known that despite its manifesto for equality, the Bauhaus functioned on patriarchal principles, the majority of women students were directed into weaving workshop, so much so that they became known as the 'women's workshop' (*Anni Albers: A Life in Thread* 2019). Gardner Troy (2006: 15) describes textiles as an 'object of neglect' within modernist theory and attributes this to two main reasons. The long association of textiles with the work of women in the domestic sphere, societal gender roles and a lack of access to education for women has seriously impacted on the inclusion of textiles in historical and theoretical inquiries. Gardner Troy also explains how the ambiguity of the textile medium itself has been detrimental to the development of an understanding of its significance in the history of art, design and craft. Textile design employs so many varied techniques and skills and is so commonly is given an auxiliary role, surreptitiously used to form other designed objects, that it is difficult to categorize and easy to overlook. In *The Gray Cloth*, the highly talented Clara subjectively experiences or exhibits these phenomena, and as such I attribute to her the entity of textiles at the time of modernism.

> I came to the Bauhaus at its 'period of saints'. Many around me, a lost and bewildered newcomer, were oddly enough, in white – not a professional white or the white of summer – here it was the vestal white. But far from being awesome, the baggy white dresses and saggy white suits had a rather familiar homemade touch. Clearly this was a place of groping and fumbling, of experimenting and taking chances. (Anni Albers in 1947; Albers 1962: 36)

Albers's description of the chaste 'uniform' of the Bauhaus relates well to Clara's grey garb. Both examples implicate that too much colour, pattern and texture in clothing is sullying and immodest, an obstacle for the eye and mind in its search for the modernist 'truth'. Albers remarks that she found this scene initially odd but accepted it. Clara, through her modest clothing, serves as a vehicle for her husband's version of Gesamtkunstwerk. Rather ironically, it is the lack of colour in her dress, its rejection of 'fashion', that encourages her husband's clients to accept more colours in their building. Edgar is adamant that his architectural concepts should not be overshadowed by the immediacy and sensuality of the textiles of fashionable clothing.

> The clothing must step aside for the architecture. Under no condition is it to compete with the architecture. Only gray fabric is allowed. (Scheerbart 1914: 9)

Clara asks her friend Amanda Schmidt:

> Do you think he just wants to possess me as an aesthetic contrast? (Scheerbart 1914: 17)

Stuart states, 'The dichotomy between fashion and architecture in *The Gray Cloth* may be seen, though, as opposed to the ideology of the Gesamtkunstwerk' (Scheerbart 1914: xxxvi).

Clara's acceptance of Edgar's marriage terms can be read as a metaphor for the acceptance by the textiles discipline of the hierarchical nature of the modernist movement, favouring architecture over textiles, with architecture governing the design and application of textiles in clothing and interiors. Ironically, Edgar's beloved glass is in fact strengthened by a textile structure: a strong mesh reinforces some of his buildings:

> Between the two sheets of glass lies a thick wire mesh and the whole thing is melted together. (Scheerbart 1914: 24)

An expression of Semper's theory of the textile origins of building in Scheerbart's notably ironic style, perhaps? Rebecca Houze (2006) argues that it is precisely Gottfried Semper's theory of cloth as a symbolic building material, and principally his concept of 'Bekelidungsprinzip' – the notion that a building's significance depends on its 'dressing' – which influenced this move to consider cloth and clothing as essential to a complete and modern architectural space, or Gesamtkunstwerk. Mallgrave (Semper 1851: 1) suggests that Semper's vision of Gesamtkunstwerk was one where 'architectural masses became enlivened and shaped, as it were, by ornament, colour, and a host of painted and plastic forms'. Houze (2006) identifies the architectural designer and cultural commentator Adolf Loos as another follower of Semper's theories. His critiques of 'ladies' fashion' and ornament can be read as an expression of his personal interpretation of 'Bekelidungsprinzip'.

In her essay *The Textile as a Structural Framework* Houze takes Semper's concept of textiles as architecturally structurally 'significatory' (Houze 2006: 298) and uses textiles as a conceptual structural framework to develop an understanding of the cultural life of Vienna in 1900. Here, I am examining *The Gray Cloth* by considering textiles as primarily significant to both the architectural narrative of the story as well as its conceptual framework in the expressionist roots of modernism.

It is revealed later that Edgar's own workrooms at his home at Isola Grande were not walled by glass, but by reinforced concrete, lit from above and applied with all manner of textiles, decoration and natural materials. Clara's friend Käte Bandel remarks,

> I find the wall covering of the darker room very interesting. Especially the dark linoleum with niello-like painted ornament on the walls. I also like the embroidered

silk on the walls. Fur I like less on the walls. The colourful hummingbird feathers are also interesting on the solid wall. (Scheerbart 1914: 107)

This information aligns Edgar Krug with that of modernist architect Adolf Loos. Loos's ascetic exteriors belied the interior spaces, which were 'dressed' with various textile and material surfaces (Houze 2006).

> It is better to have a colourful house than colourful clothing. The former makes all of life colourful, while the latter only serves vanity and makes away with money that should be for building houses. Edgar was right about The Gray Cloth. (Clara Krug, in The Gray Cloth. Scheerbart 1914: 86)

This excerpt emphasizes the notion of textiles and clothing as commercial, trivial items, while architecture aspires to higher objectives. Andreas Huyssen (1986) states that modernity classified high culture as masculine and popular or mass culture as feminine. Clara's acceptance can be seen as metaphorical of both the submission of textiles to the modernist tenet and, more broadly, of textiles as feminine, submitting to the patriarchal structure of the design world. It appears that it was the very practitioners of textile design, being predominantly female, who prevented textiles from being the ideal, modernist design practice.

If we consider the female characters in the book, we can see that Scheerbart generally develops them as talented and artistic. One of the focuses of Scheerbart's novel is on Clara's communicative skills, both discursive and musical. A large proportion of the text is given over to Clara's telegrams to and from her friends. Her organ playing 'roars with stormy rhythm' (Scheerbart 1914: 4) and she is able to subtly influence Edgar's clients' design choices. She is venerated wherever she goes and makes friends easily, eventually becoming famous in her own right. The points at which Clara subverts the marriage contract correspond with her playing music and her meetings with groups of other women, specifically in the painters' colony of Makartland, briefly in Japan and in the animal park in India. In India, a colossal towering organ is constructed especially for Clara.

> And she played such that the wild animals stopped their roaring and looked in astonishment at the sky above. (Scheerbart 1914: 53)

At that moment, Clara's excitement is increased with the news of the arrival of colourful silks from Japan. Clara allows herself to be dressed in these fabrics and feverishly plays music almost throughout the night – 'often it sounded suddenly like wild, waltz music' (Scheerbart 1914: 53).

It is at this point that the tables are turned for just a moment, the soft usurping the hard. Clara becomes world famous for her concerts in India, while

Edgar comes to know rejection and compromise. Textiles, cloth, frivolity and sensuality momentarily take over the novel, represented by Clara's expressive music, the sumptuous Japanese silks and the eighty-five-strong female entourage sent to dress her. Simultaneously, Edgar is wrangling with engineers in Ceylon, who suggest that he consider using a textile, a wire mesh structure spread with coloured glues, in his construction to better achieve his aims. He does not accept this as a viable substitute for coloured glass. Embittered, Edgar sends a rather cynical congratulatory note, warning Clara of the uncomfortable 'curse of fame' (Scheerbart 1914: 56). Almost immediately, Clara rejects coloured clothing, rejects the possibility of equality and starts to shy away from invitations to play large concerts, setting out to find her husband and support him more fully in his architectural projects, committed to wearing grey cloth with 10 per cent white. Conceptually, this moment in the novel serves as a brief foray into Semper's theories, with feminine, relational textiles (represented by Clara) as the symbolic and structural essence of architecture. However, the power balance is quickly and tacitly redressed in favour of the status quo of patriarchy.

Ideological adaptability and plurality is a thread throughout the novel. Clara is perplexed by Edgar's seemingly inappropriate yet fixed vision for glass architecture in the polar setting of Makartland. Her clothing adapts to the conditions, thanks to a skilful seamstress who interprets the 10 per cent white to commonly include fur, suitable for the climate. Käte Bandel, a painter and close companion of Clara, takes up this topic again. She talks about how the wooden architecture that already exists in Makartland supplies both the qualities of functionalism and sensualism – noise reduction and 'coziness' (Scheerbart 1914: 33). The culturally indiscriminate nature of the principles of modernism is particularly evident during their visits to fictional locations in Japan, India and Arabia, where Clara's grey clothing is heavily criticized and subverted. In Japan, the Marquise Fi-Boh challenges Edgar about his wife's grey cloth, branding it repugnant (Scheerbart 1914: 41).

> As he entered the cabin, Herr Krug wondered more than just slightly how his wife could adjust so well to each situation. (Scheerbart 1914: 27)

Clara's behaviour throughout the novel is symbolically textile-like in its relational, matrixial qualities. She adapts well to the customs and conditions of each location, forging relationships quickly and easily. Creatively, she is expressive and instinctual. She can be both questioning and seductive. Throughout, Clara's interactions with others shape both her and her experiences: she responds to situations, whereas Edgar largely remains firm.

The dynamic between Clara and Edgar is echoed in the relationships of modernists such as Sonia and Robert Delaunay, Anni and Josef Albers and, later, Jacqueline and Jacques Groag and Charles and Ray Eames. The female is no less of a creative leader but societally bound to the quieter, 'softer' design fields of textiles, clothing and costume often disregarding their training. Gardner Troy (2006: 15) comments on how many of the leading textile designers of the era adopted textiles as their primary discipline through necessity, as a means of developing a sense of autonomy in their relationships with their famous husbands.

> Sonia Delaunay . . . is noted by historians for her 'instinctive' feeling for colour, whereas her husband, Robert, is attributed as having formulated a colour theory. Robert Delaunay embodies the male stereotype as logical and intellectual, Sonia embodies the female stereotype as instinctive and emotional. (Buckley 1986: 238)

Whitney Chadwick, in her commentary on the Delaunays's relationship, describes how much of art history is happy to portray this relationship as 'untroubled (by) relations of dominance and subordination' (Chadwick 1993: 32).

She outlines the standard depiction of their characters within the literature, where Sonia is painted as

> [A] Russian Jewish expatriate, all warmth and generosity, quietly adjusted herself to his needs, setting aside her own career as a painter and instead devoting herself to applying his esthetic theories to the decorative arts, and the creation of a welcoming environment for the couple's many friends. (Chadwick 1993: 32)

However, Chadwick proceeds to delve deeper into an understanding of the synergy of their marriage, focusing on the concept of 'simultaneity' (a theory of colour, abstraction and expression), traditionally attributed to Robert, but which seemingly was developed in tandem and with mutable emphasis in the work of both Robert and Sonia. At the same time that Scheerbart was writing *The Gray Cloth*, Sonia Delaunay began making 'simultaneous' dresses and fabrics, arguably a key development in their joint concept which freed colour and form from the static canvas to the physical body. Chadwick quotes a poem by Blaise Cendrars written about Sonia's new work:

> colours undress you through contrast; On her dress she wears her body

This powerful statement hints at the continuing legacy of Sonia's ideas in their impact on textiles, clothing, style and identity. In relation to *The Gray Cloth*, it points to the power of colour within the expressionist origins of modernism and the notion that Clara's femininity and individuality is literally hidden behind the fabric of her clothes.

Buckley's 1986 paper *Made in Patriarchy* encouraged a feminist analysis of the history of women in design and explains many of the reasons for the gendering of design disciplines, as well as the marginalization of those associated with the feminine. Andreas Huyssen (1986) takes the concept further, positioning and exposing the feminization of mass culture and its resulting denigration quite specifically at the dawn of modernist thought. David Brett (2005: 184–214) provides a detailed exploration of the subjugation of the decorative in modernist ideology and its implications to consumption and gender.

Thinking about the place of textiles in the modernist movement highlights several points of discussion. The idealism of modernism opened up the design discipline of textiles to a wider range of creative practitioners, with many artists and architects working in or with textiles, or with 'truthful' materiality in mind. However, it was still women who largely populated the discipline. If we proceed to consider the feminine aligned to the postmodern paradigm due to its relational, matrixial characteristics, and textiles as gendered in femininity, this reveals the contradiction of textiles as the ideal medium of modernism. Textiles had been appropriated by the concept of Gesamtkunstwerk and was paradoxically marginalized by it: the feminine cloaked in the masculine.

A version of this liberal feminism is illustrated when Clara commits herself to further the acceptance of colourful glass architecture and gleefully remarks how her voluntary appearance in grey, with 10 per cent white, helped her husband close a deal with a client in Cyprus (Scheerbart 1914: 77). She disregards her own persona to become more 'equal' in partnership with her husband and 'works' to develop his business.

In 2012, Leah Armstrong curated a digital resource to accompany the exhibition 'Portraits: Women Designers' at the Fashion and Textiles Museum, London. Eight out of the thirteen women designers featured in Armstrong's collection were textile designers working in post-war Britain. The images gathered by Armstrong from the photographic library of the Council of Industrial Design are products of their time, and I do not wish to become too heavily involved in visual analysis here but rather to use them as an illustration of the problematic of the gendered role of the textile designer and its effect on the status and knowledge of textile design. As Armstrong summarizes in her commentary (2012), Lucienne Day is depicted seemingly working at the kitchen table at home, wearing a neat cricket jumper with rolled-up sleeves. A jug, a teacup and saucer are in front of her on the table – is she designing for them or are they part of her home? Beyond a pen and a roll of tape there are no other obvious textile design 'tools'. Behind her are lever arch folders and a set square and her demeanour in the image is awkward. Dr Marianne Straub is casually dressed, leaning forward as if listening, while fondling some fabric swatches. Shirley Craven appears to be naked in a model-like profile shot, sitting in front of her designs. Althea McNish seems to be just a stylish young woman selecting patterns for her interior decoration from a swatch book. These highly successful, prolific and pioneering designers are depicted primarily as women, with their role as a designer hidden from view, simplistically represented or intentionally misrepresented, emphasizing their femininity and/or domesticity rather than their profession.

Although writing closer to the time of their births, there are uncanny comparisons between Scheerbart's story and the relationships of other designer couples working at the later stages of modernism – for example, textile designer Hilde Pilke who changed her name to Jacqueline Groag on her marriage to architect Jacques Groag (Armstrong 2012). There are particular parallels also to Charles and Ray Eames. Neuhart and Neuhart's lengthy double volume on the Eames's (2010) makes pains to suggest that Ray Eames's credits to the commercial and creative success of the Eames Studio has been exaggerated, perpetuated publicly (but not privately) by Charles Eames himself. They state that although Ray did creatively contribute that her main role was 'first and foremost Mrs Charles Eames' (Neuhart 2010) and that she was unendingly devoted to this role, cemented by an alleged pact for no children. In the same breath Neuhart and Neuhart are less than complimentary about her personality – her incapability of making decisions and maddening unprofessionalism – and indeed, rather unnecessarily, her physique. In their biographical account of her, often drawn from personal experiences the authors having been Eames Office employees, they focus on her painstaking choices in clothing, her own and that which she selected for Charles – more parallels with *The Gray Cloth*. They mention Ray's abilities in interior design and presentation, her sensitivity to colour and form – her decorative sensibilities. In the late 1940s she created several textile designs for the Eames Office as well as magazine covers which utilized her painterly abilities. After this period, she created very little work of her own and dedicated herself to being the architect of the Eames image and reputation. Her background, which financially enabled the Eames Office existence as well as her own talents as an artist (not a designer), was sidelined. Neuhart and Neuhart's book suggests that Ray Eames made this choice and was steadfast in this role throughout the difficulties of their marriage; nonetheless the patriarchal influence on women in this era would have been overbearing.

Indeed in his review of Scheerbart's book, Victor Margolin decides that Clara's voluntary donning of the grey cloth does not come about by patriarchal coercion, and that in doing so she does not compromise her artistic power (Margolin 2003: 94). I disagree. Although it is unclear from the novel why exactly Clara makes this decision, I believe this act symbolizes societal suppression and her fear of her own power. The argument of whether women's clothing detracted from architectural design was never her own. She is 'assimilated into its protocols' and ultimately becomes its scapegoat as she negotiates the notoriety and fame her grey clothing generates. There is a clear correlation between the point at which Clara begins to voluntarily accept her grey clothing, the rejection of her own fame and her yearning for domestic life, pleading with Edgar for their extended air-bound honeymoon to come to an end. Edgar tells her that he plans to build an extension to his house at Isola Grande especially for her:

> the room is not that large and there is a harmonium in it. When you play, one hears it best in the large dining room. While playing you cannot be seen at all from the deep-set room. You can also read and write there. You will like it.

She expresses her desire for it to be coloured in grey tones:

> 'Oh' shouted Frau Clara, 'that is indeed wonderful'. (Scheerbart 1914: 96)
>
> You cannot imagine . . .how much I long for quiet domesticity and how happy I am about my gray room in which my harmonium is placed. Yes! (Scheerbart 1914: 100)

Here again, we can draw parallels between Sonia Delaunay's real life and Clara's fictional one. At the height of Sonia's commercial success and Robert's downturn, Sonia talks of how 'success literally assailed me', 'I was capable of being a woman manager, but I had other purposes in life' (Delaunay n.d. in Chadwick 1993: 47). It was at the point when the worldwide recession affected sales of her work that the tables turned again and it was once again Robert's moment in the light.

I feel that Clara decides to adopt the grey cloth voluntarily as a way of settling rumours, negating speculation and to show acceptance of her marital status, situation and domestic life. Scheerbart tells us quite directly that Clara starts to turn away from her music. Once installed in Isola Grande, Clara is compelled to spend her time not in the grey room but in an emerald room, shining with amethyst ornament, housing orchids which she meticulously cares for under the supervision of the gardener, abandoning her organ playing in favour of their cultivation (Scheerbart 1914: 118). She literally becomes quiet. She is hidden away from view. Cloaked in grey. No longer on view. This notion is addressed by Iris Marion Young in her interpretation of the writing of Luce Irigaray and Simone de Beauvoir:

> To fix and keep hold of his identity, man makes a house, put things in it, and confines there his woman who reflects his identity to him. The price she pays for supporting his subjectivity, however, is dereliction, having no self of her own. (Young 1990: 124)

I propose that *The Gray Cloth* provides a metaphor for the paradox of textiles in the modernist design context. Clara's narrative epitomizes the subjugation of textile design practices into modernist ideology. This story prompts a consideration of the disciplinary entities of design and their role in the development of design research and, consequentially, design history. It instantiates the dichotomy of architectonic and textile practices (Ingold 2010). Hierarchies of accepted knowledge production established through a hylomorphic ontology and historically gendered-making practices collaborate to suppress varied approaches and understandings of design. This suppression persists and therefore requires a pluralist, intersectional feminist critique to highlight abandoned or influenced contributions to design history and research.

8

The gendered textile design discipline

Disciplinarity

A 'discipline', in the religious rather than academic sense, is a phenomenon that is simultaneously a collective and a dispersion. A 'discipline' requires disciples; individuals who feel drawn to a particular set of teachings tacitly learn and adopt the rules and rituals associated with the discipline allowing them to guide their thoughts and behaviours. Disciples follow and embrace the teachings, which may be explicit and written down or implicitly communicated. They will take comfort in knowing they share their fundamental beliefs, thoughts and behaviours with others. Essentially the disciple has a tacit relationship with the discipline, which is both internal and personal and external in relation to other disciples across time and location:

> [A] heuristic vision which is accepted for the sake of its unresolvable tension. It is like an obsession with a problem known to be insoluble, which yet, unswervingly, the heuristic commands; 'Look at the unknown!' Christianity sedulously fosters, and in a sense permanently satisfies, man's craving for mental dissatisfaction by offering him the comfort of a crucified God. (Polanyi 1958: 212)

Using Polanyi's religious analogy for man's craving for mental dissatisfaction and applying it to the shared knowledge and purpose of designers allows us to reconsider the notion of the design 'discipline'. It helps to explain and describe the collective and permanent mental dissatisfaction that drives individuals who call themselves 'designers'. There is a shared vision of an all-encompassing unsolvable problem: a compelling intellectual passion, easily triggered.

Salustri and Rogers's (2008) paper offers several definitions of the term and considers its various meanings in reference to design. Salustri and Rogers (2008: 299/7) state,

Once we have learned to do something in a certain way, we will tend to do that thing the same way forever, or until a 'better' way presents itself (and sometimes, not even then). In this way, we will tend to not try other ways to do a thing because we have learned one way of doing it.

Design has been traditionally categorized into disciplines, which include many sub-disciplines that become specialisms for specific designers: for instance, fashion design includes specialists in knitwear, tailoring and underwear, among others. The boundaries between disciplines are becoming less clear, with many polymath designers producing a range of successful design outcomes. For example, Hella Jongerius's signature style has been incorporated into designs for furniture, ceramics, lighting and footwear. This approach supports the notion that the design process is a consistent and transferable practice or procedure, which can be applied with relevance and success in all fields of design.

Any 'model' of the design process, with no specificity in regard to specialism, separates the design process from the particular making, manufacturing processes and techniques that are integral to designing. It assumes that the specialist knowledge required to design different kinds of objects effectively has little or no bearing on how a designer might approach designing in the first place. When making is removed from the process for the sake of constructing a generalized model, it may not adequately cover the range of versions of the design process that will be experienced by designers working in all sectors of the field. For an area such as textile design, one that reaches into craft and applied arts, such a model is problematic. If, however, we accept that the procedures associated with designing are transferable and universally intrinsic, then we must also ask why most designers specialize within one area or sub-discipline of design.

Wang and Ilhan (2009: 5) 'propose a sociological distinctiveness to the design professions which is really their key distinguishing signature'. They oppose the notion that individual design professions hold specific knowledge and that there are social, historical and market-led reasons for this concept being maintained in academic writing. They describe a 'sociological wrapping' around the 'creative act' and proceed in their investigation by questioning what a profession is; they do not assume that different design professions possess a specific knowledge, but rather that they are all centred round the creative act. They present this as a circular diagram with the centre of the shape taken up by the 'creative act' (design process) with two concentric circles encompassing it. The concentric areas represent first the non-domain-specific knowledge they propose and second the sociological wrapping of disciplines or professions. Wang and Ilhan advise that in order to define a design profession one must decipher what it does '(with any general knowledge that assists in the creative act) in a sociological process of defining itself to the larger culture' (Wang and Ilhan 2009: 7). The authors use architecture, interior design and industrial design as examples of three professions at different stages of defining a professional identity. They consider that, of the three, industrial design is the 'least professionalized by sociological standards'. This statement seems to be based on the number of US designers subscribing to membership of professional organizations. They argue that although all three professions vary in regard to organized and structured professional standards, what they share is the fact that the knowledge they possess is not 'domain-specific'. Wang and Ilhan conclude by questioning the difference between 'discipline' and 'profession', referencing an online discussion topic started by Ken Friedman on the subject in 2007. Wang and Ilhan state regularly in their paper that the ideas they propose are counter to the common discourse, and that they challenge concepts developed by leading academics in the field of design research.

The discipline or profession of textiles has not been as rigorously professionalized as areas such as architecture but there are several accounts exploring and purporting to explore the specificities of textile knowledge, in both design literature and material culture studies. As such, it remains a worthwhile activity to find a location for textiles knowledge in the wider field of design precisely because it may yield new insights into the creative act for textile designers and/or designers in general. The notion of 'sociological wrapping' is of importance and one which, whether in agreement with Wang and Ilhan's proposals against domain-specific knowledge or not, is something that many in the field of design may readily recognize.

Textile design appears to attract a broad range of 'disciples'. As shown in Figure 1, the term 'textile practitioner' can at once describe students, artists, craftspeople, hobbyists and designers of various levels of expertise, approaches and experience, all with markedly different approaches to following and embracing the 'teachings' of the discipline. Textile design encompasses teachings from the broader disciplines of design, art and craft, indicating that textile design disciples have formed a tacit understanding of a specific blend of design knowledge (although contested by Wang and Ilhan). This knowledge is considered to be embodied in the designed outcomes of textile design and exhibited in the textile designer's approach to design thinking and the behaviours and activities they undertake within their design process. The textile design discipline has particular protocols for presenting design ideas (Moxey 2000) that are not shared with any other sub-discipline of design, while even commonly used systems for recording design thinking and process, such as sketchbooks, will be used in subtly differing ways. It would be extraneous for me here to provide a potted history of the development of the textile design discipline or the textile design industry, and in any case this has been the concern of many design and industrial historians. Here I focus on the idiosyncrasies of the textile design discipline and the specific characteristics of textile designers, asking what behaviours or methods they share which combine to define textile knowledge and the textile design discipline? What Wang and Ilhan propose invites me to consider the sociological wrapping of textile design. How has the discipline developed, and how is it perceived? How does it operate and present itself? As Buckley (1986) implies, textile design has been (and is) sociologically gendered (also see Mesh Two and the preceding chapter). The gendered wrapping of textile design and its delay in professionalizing itself has affected its ability to have an impact on the non-domain-specific knowledge that Wang and Ilhan propose. This is emphasized in the way I have used the persona of Clara Krug in Paul Scheerbart's novel *The Gray Cloth* as a representation of textiles as an entity, incorporating yet shifting between the nexus of the textile designer, the textile discipline, the textile design process and the textile design as embodied outcome. I shall call this entity Textiles (with a capital T). I wish to push these characterizations into conceptualizations of textile design practice.

The textile entity

I am a fresh graduate and prize winner, sitting in my own stand, one of hundreds, at an event that was then called 'Indigo' which took place at the Première Vision trade fair in Paris in 2001. I was surrounded by the varied textile design samples I had produced as a student, pinned to the wall behind me and laid out on the table in front, my name emblazoned across the top of the stand. Trade show visitors nonchalantly walked past or came for an idle rifle through the mounted samples: I could only find out who they were if I caught a glimpse of their name badge. Some people came and spoke with me, introducing themselves as fashion designers, and I enthusiastically explained my work. Often, it quickly became clear that all they wanted to know was whether the textile sample could be mass-produced and how much it would cost to buy. I had carefully prepared for that moment in my life, cataloguing and labelling each piece of work, fully expecting to sell my work. I did sell a few pieces, and many people seemed interested in my work, but soon realized that what I was offering in terms of textile design was not appropriate for that forum. I felt quite exposed, misled and misunderstood after this experience. Why had I been invited to show and sell my work there? Had I not sold it well enough? Should I have done something differently? How could I do better next time? I realized that I would be nothing if I did not please these people. I embodied my textile designs; they were full of my creativity. At the time of designing and making them I did not think about whom I would sell them to. I was concerned with the process and developing creative outcomes, but my design discipline required me to 'put it on show'.

There is an interesting dynamic between the role of the textile designer as artistic, creative and skilled and their requirement to produce work that others will enjoy and pay for. They have independency and licence in their creative endeavours, but the outcomes of their activity are destined for a supporting role in another designed product.

I progress here with the notion of textiles as an entity, gendered through social constructs as feminine, though the discipline naturally encompasses designers of all genders. The textile entity's attributes, skills and persona as a commodity prompts parallels in my mind with the life of a geisha. A muted female, highly skilled and committed to the cultivation of those skills, but regarded more simply for the pleasure and beauty their skills provide and resigned to her requirement to trade on her skills. The process by which a textile design for sale was created was of little importance, but it should be viable and must always be 'beautiful'. How it functions, be it in a classic woven form or incorporating innovative smart systems or new materials, is often of secondary importance to its decorative sensibilities. If it doesn't excel on both counts, it does succeed.

Textiles is decorative and female. Textiles must use all its performative and sublimely seductive characteristics in order to communicate possible applications to potential partners and patrons in a world which is hidden. Partners and patrons are courted, flattered and pleasured, ritually and continuously. Textiles enigmatically seduces the senses with its artistry, in a modest and submissive way. Textiles surrenders itself, allowing the partner or patron to momentarily own it.

Textiles is a geisha.

The role of the geisha is commonly misunderstood due to the secrecy of the community itself and its unique cultural and historical significance to Japan. Comparing the textile entity to a geisha highlights the dichotomy experienced by the textile designer and echoes the position it holds between art, craft and design. A geisha must master several artistic practices, such as dance or music, and develop her ability to a high level, but the development of these skills is just an element of her entity that must ultimately express modesty and stylized traditional/historicized/cultural notions of beauty. The development of her skill is boundaried by the transaction that occurs which commissions their performance. The appearance of a geisha is highly ornate and decorated, excessively feminine, using motifs and symbols in hair and make-up to highlight this. The vast quantity of rich fabrics that their bodies are swaddled in is all part of the performance. Lesley Downer describes Koito, a geisha, as she dresses for work:

> She had become a compilation of markers of femininity – woman embodied. As she put on her make-up, her persona too began to change. She was stepping into the role, like an actor does, whereas she had been down to earth and straightforward, she became coquettish, speaking in a coy girly voice .... A geisha has to be expert at choosing the right kimono for the right season and the occasion. (Downer 2006: 236)

Viewing textiles-as-entity-as-geisha, applying Downer's quote, illustrates the acceptance of a subjugated (female) role as described by the textile designers. A geisha's persona is consumed by the textiles and the make-up it is swathed in, yet is indelibly marked by it. Textile designers are anonymous, yet have a distinct handwriting they are valued for, and their ability to produce designs that are just 'right' for the 'mood' or season marks their commercial success.

Once hired by a patron, a geisha's primary role is to flatter, cosset, listen, entertain and amuse them, all against an implicit backdrop of a sexual encounter: the promise of pleasure. She serves drinks, performs dances and promises the potential of pleasure. She surrenders her subjectivity to her encounter with the patron in return for his enjoyment and fulfilment. Her interior world is concealed and unspoken. Each geisha develops her own approach to this given role, which she must adapt for each patron, but the goal of providing a promise of pleasure for financial return is the overarching goal. Textile designers provide what is needed. When the brief is known in advance, they must design something that speaks of that sensation. When it is unknown, they must be able to make judgements on global aesthetic concerns and translate this into textiles, trying to capture a 'feeling'. A textile designer often must surrender their subjective aesthetic in order to serve up what is needed at that point. A textile studio must serve her patrons and encourage them to make a transaction if she is to continue in the commercial sector. It is the textile design as object that sells itself; it shares all those feminine characteristics embodied by the geisha: modesty, sensuality, decoration, beauty, intrigue and availability.

If you visit a textile trade show, you are likely to see the typical scenario of a textile designer's sales pitch (the 'daft situation' as a famous textile designer once called it). The textile designer (or textile studio agent) is standing up behind a table in the studio's stand (see Figure 2). Two or three people (fashion designers, interior designers, buyers, perhaps) are seated on the other side. The textile designer slowly but swiftly presents sample after sample to the seated people whose gaze is fixed steadily on the numerous beautiful and skilful designs that are moving quickly in front of their eyes. Occasionally, one of the pair reaches out to touch a sample or puts it to one side for further consideration. They know what they are looking for (they think), or at least they will know when they find it. They might make a purchase or they might walk away. The seated trio comment among themselves; the textile designer usually maintains silence while they look (Figure 2).

In this situation, textiles-as-entity is rendered mute. Judged solely on appearance, how it elicits sensation. This state is curiously liminal. The textile swatch/sample is a designed object, but it has not yet fulfilled its role. It seeks a transformation into something else, assimilation into something else, beyond just being a textile. The seated pair in the scenario above might purchase one or two samples to be developed into their fashion range. At the point of sale, most often there will be no indication of how the textile will be applied. Even

Figure 2 Press image from Première Vision trade fair, February 2019. Textile designers (standing) showing and selling their designs to buyers (seated).

if purchased or commissioned, a textile design may go no further than the boardroom table. And what of the textile samples that are dismissed, those that are never purchased? These fully worked examples of design, these 'samples', do not achieve any transformation. They are consigned to the archive, perhaps to be retrieved and reworked when the moment 'feels' right again.

Textiles is considered simple and uncomplicated not forthcoming or interested in articulating what makes it special or unique. Its muteness has impeded its relationship with other areas of design. Textiles may be specifically chosen or even commissioned but equally may never be sold or be put into production, leaving its potential unrealized. Textiles is on the shelf. Textiles needs a suitor.

Textiles is a maiden aunt.

The notion that a designer will produce a large quantity of fully worked designs for an unknown brief, only for a fraction of them to be purchased or put into production, is unique to textile design. It occurs for both textile design studios as well as designers working 'in house' for a large company. While commenting on this 'daft situation' there is a sense it also often affords textile designers a creative autonomy. Textile designers are accepting of this status quo: perhaps it allows them the opportunity to explore a wide range of designs and processes. Textiles in sample form, when in exhibitions or displayed for commercial sales are often better understood in these circumstances when incorporated into a mock product – often seen at textile trade shows as 'garment fronts'. Friedman (2003: 513–14) offers a viewpoint which contextualizes this situation in design theory:

> On occasion, the intuitive practice of design produces unpredictable desirable results that can be seized retrospectively as the useable result of muddling through. Far more often, however, muddling through produces failures of two kinds. The first kind of failure involves proposals that fail in the early stages of conception or development. This is a good time for failure, since failure in conception or development eliminates potentially wasteful efforts. The second kind of failure involves completed attempts at solutions in which the designers believe that they have solved the problem even though they have not done so. This is far more costly in every sense. One of the central aspects of this kind of failure is the fact that some designers never learn that they have actually failed to meet client needs, customer needs, or end-user needs. This is because designers often end their involvement with the project before the failures arise and the clients of most failures do not return to the original designer for repair work.

Friedman's observations illustrate several things. The first to note at the outset is Friedman's derogatory tone in relation to more intuitive design practices, those aligned with the applied arts, such as textiles; they 'muddle' through producing 'failures', which certainly frames this viewpoint. Nonetheless, the second thing it highlights is the very nature of the 'daft situation'; the production of all these 'possible' design solutions is costly and wasteful in terms of time and materials for the designer or company. The third point it captures is the sheltered position this situation creates for the designer. For textile designers, selling designs to other designers at the first level of consumption (Figure 1), their position is quite unique, their relationship with the ultimate end user can be distant, yet the impact of their work is crucial. Exposed is a deeply problematic, irrational system and unsustainable trading model. Despite this continuing as the mainstream vehicle for textile design commerce, recent and ongoing research into circular design models is challenging this in the face of the need for sustainable business models (Goldsworthy and Earley 2018; Vuletich 2015).

In relating textiles to the stereotypical maiden aunt, it exposes the often taciturn nature of the textile design discipline, uninterested in participating in the wider discourse of design research and naïve to what it might contribute. Textiles is the quiet girl sitting in the back row. 'Maiden aunt' is a somewhat quainter and kinder label for a woman who could equally be called a 'spinster'. A spinster, a female spinner of thread or a female who remains unmarried beyond the normal age, emphasizes the often negative socially constructed feminine gendering of textile practice. The maiden aunt/spinster metaphor also speaks of the unfulfilled textile design sample/swatch, complete and beautiful but consigned to the shelf and never put into production. These forgotten 'virgins' of textile design practice invite a closer investigation into the historical, social and economic factors that affected the development of trading and other business systems in commercial textile design and other related industries. In other words, how did the 'daft situation' described above come to be common practice, when models of commissioning, pitching or licensing for design work might be a more appropriate system?

The textile design that is put into production and applied to a garment or a sofa – how can this scenario be conceptualized? In a sense it undergoes an adverse state change from designed object to component or raw material for the purposes of being applied within a subsequent designed product. It allows a new product to come into being. The presence of the textile design may be obvious and integral to the new product.

Textiles enables other designed products to come into existence. It is a fertile ground allowing others potential to be realized. Textiles (and materials) are adaptable and giving to the cause of design. Textiles provides. Textiles offers. Textiles supports. Textiles soaks up sweat, tears, blood. Textiles' role as the 'giver of life' in the chain of design always requires a partner.

Textiles is a mother.

It is no new concept to find parallels with material and motherhood; they are etymologically linked. What I seek to do in coming to this metaphor is to consider how it affects our conception of the design process. Textile designs become raw materials or components for other types of designers, putting a level between textiles and wood, plastic and animal skin (all of which can be surface-designed in the manner of a textile, too, but nonetheless are natural or engineered substances). It reminds me of a quote from William Morris, discussing decoration and ornamentation:

> ... in many or most cases we have got so used to this ornament that we look upon it as if had grown of itself, and note it of no more than mosses on the dry sticks with which we light our fires. (Morris 1877)

This state change places textiles in the peculiar position of being a designed object that comes first, allowing others to come into being but is marginalized. The feminine entity of 'textiles' brings other designed objects into existence by communicating potential and translating pleasure at the same time as being marginalized and ignored. The perception of textile design as a raw material, seen as natural, may actually speak of the cultural significance and sensorial power of textiles. Textiles are surrendered to the subsequent product. But what if we were to envisage this situation as a version of Ettinger's metramorphosis, in a trans-subjective matrixial encounter, with textiles-as-mother where each participant are partners-in-difference, their experiences changed and linked? This places textiles in a synergistic relationship.

By characterizing textiles as an entity aligned with the social construct of the feminine, I have incited three contentious metaphors. Metaphor, of course, is often used a key device for the marginalization, subjugation and trivialization of women and their lives, and feminists have both challenged and utilized metaphor as a means of emphasizing their argument.

> Translations
>
> You show me the poems of some woman my age, or younger,
> translated from your language
> Certain words occur: enemy, oven, sorrow
> enough to let me know she's a woman of my time
>
> obsessed
>
> with Love, our subject: we've trained it like ivy to our walls
> baked it like bread in our ovens

worn it like lead on our ankles
watched it through binoculars as if
it were a helicopter
bringing food to our famine
or the satellite of a hostile power

I begin to see that woman doing things:
stirring rice
ironing a skirt
typing a manuscript till dawn

trying to make a call
from a phonebooth

The phone rings endlessly
in a man's bedroom
she hears him telling someone else
Never mind. She'll get tired.
hears him telling her story to her sister

who becomes her enemy
and will in her own way
light her own way to sorrow
ignorant of the fact this way of grief
is shared, unnecessary
and political

In its first few lines, *Translations*, by poet Adrienne Rich (1972), indicates the endurance of metaphors in shaping and limiting female lives. The line I find particularly powerful is '. . . hears him telling her story to her sister'. It captures the crucial importance of narrative feminist qualitative research methodologies as well as the requirement of a feminist critique of design research. Rich's metaphors of the female obsession with love as gardening and baking initially seem steeped in the domestic, but this is quickly countered by the inference of a military context: women's passions held hostage. This sudden reframing of the metaphor at this point in the poem positions women not as cosy housewives but as political prisoners.

Metaphor as 'frame restructuring' is what Lakoff labels 'a cross-domain mapping in the conceptual system' (Lakoff 1993: 203). He goes on to emphasize that metaphors are not propositional, but rather that they are mappings, 'sets of conceptual correspondences' (Lakoff 1993: 207). In the way that I have utilized metaphor, I have conceptually mapped the characteristics of textiles and femininity onto one another, identifying those 'correspondences' within the context of design.

In using the archetypes of geisha, spinster and mother, I do not wish to communicate a reciprocation of these patriarchal labels but point to how the textiles entity has both tacitly subscribed and been held to these roles. The labels of geisha, mother and maiden aunt or spinster have some correlation with notions of the neopaganist concept of the 'triple goddess' of maiden, mother and crone, as well as Jungian archetypes, though I do not want to present them in this way. The specificity of the labels chosen enact the feminist activity of 'naming' and reclaiming terms so that alternative scenarios are provided. Delving into the geisha, spinster and mother metaphors for textiles allows a feminist reading of its position in the design hierarchy and how its character as an entity, embodied in the nexus of the textile design, the textile design process, the textile industry and the textile designer, has contributed to its taciturnity in relation to design research.

Exposing these metaphors of the entity of textile design appears to play to gender binarisms, forgoing concepts of the post-gender cyborg (Haraway 2006) of feminist technoscience. Indeed, in the following chapter Marion Lean extends the metaphoric archetypes through her applied research into innovative textiles. The Mother, the Father, the Spinster, the Sportsperson, the Geisha and the Soldier serve here as narrative mechanisms to expose the need to challenge the phallogocentrism of theories of design research and I explore Ettinger's matrixiality as a framework for this. Daniela Rosner (2018) uses the backdrop of feminist technoscience to develop her critical fabulations of and as design. Kathrin Thiele (2014) provides a reading of differentiation and diffraction in the work of posthumanist scholars Karen Barad, Donna Haraway and Vicki Kirby as a lens for the notion of difference in the work of Bracha Ettinger. Thiele (2014: 208) calls this 'diffracting (new) feminist materialisms with matrixiality'. Thiele underlines that Ettinger's feminine metaphoracity is not to be taken as any biological binarism or prioritization of motherhood or pregnancy but instead matrixiality is an 'apparatus for conductible affectivity, which gives voice to the affected body-psyche co-emerging with the other and the world' (Pollock 2012 in Thiele 2014).

For an author of textile design theory, it is simultaneously unsurprising, awkward and useful that Ettinger uses (as Thiele puts it) the 'theoretico-aesthetical imagery' of weaving and knitting when explaining the entanglements of co-emergence. It provides proof in point that the thinking used in the process of making textilic structures is innately relational and set in a co-emergent encounter with their context. Thiele attempts to reconcile the approaches from the feminist theorists she explores and suggests an ethos where it is recognized that '"we" are always/already entangled with-in everything' (Thiele 2014: 213). 'We' does not point to fixed embodied subjectivities but a woven textile/texture subjective 'encounter-event' (Ettinger 2006a).

Applying the matrixial framework to the archetypes recognizes and implicates the social constructs of the Mother, Spinster and Geisha archetypes of textiles in their own weaving and in the weaving of the concept of the textile design discipline and thus the weaving of theories of design. This entangled agency means 'we' (as above) are already in design research but the ethos of diffraction that Thiele discusses has not been activated within the development of design research.

> With diffraction – both as concept and as apparatus via which we envision difference differently – we witness a change in attitude: an opening up of the whole engagement with difference(s) and differentiality as 'a mapping of interference, not of replication, reflection or reproduction.' (Thiele quoting Haraway 2014: 204)

Taking on textile thinking

Marion Lean

In my final degree year of textile design at Duncan of Jordanstone College of Art in 2011, fellow students perfected their repeat floral prints, applied for internships at Timorous Beasties, pulled all-nighters in the knit room and pulled hair in the queue for the laser cutter. I had begun to think about problems which were outside of the print room. I felt burdened by a high level of practical textile design ability (print) but minimal ideas of how to apply this to social challenges. I set myself a design challenge to address health awareness, in particular smoking, through textile design.

My final undergraduate collection *Alter Mind, Trigger Behaviour* used the textile technique 'devoré' (from French, literally to devour, also known as burn out) to represent the slow but deadly deterioration of the body in response to smoking. Conceptualizing the body as material, the destructive breakdown of the body through smoking, was mimicked by deterioration of fabric. Though a beautiful and well-produced collection of prints and fabric manipulation, my passion lay not in the finished material outcome but in the new information I'd collected about issues in other fields (public health, social science, activism), now embedded in a textile collection. In a 2011 blog post I described my work as 'embracing and contesting perceived textile design thinking methodology'. A drive which was misunderstood/confused by attendees at New Designers graduate design exhibition who were not expecting to be finding delicate bodysuits with blacked-out lungs.

As friends went off to design internships at trend forecasting agencies and high-street chain head offices, I joined the MA in critical practice at Goldsmiths, University of London. The intention was to establish a means to apply my practical textiles and material skills to address wider design challenges. Arriving at Goldsmiths, I registered, visited the library then, next stop, the textiles print room. I was however informed that since I was studying *design*, I could not access the (art) textiles department. Many years on, I might have handled that conversation differently, but being a newly arrived Scot in London I thought I best *ca canny*.

During my MA, I found ways that I could apply my textile knowledge in the briefs set. Through a textiles lens (expanded on later in Lean 2020), yet not limited to the textile medium, I developed new ideas, tried new technologies and collaborated with designers from a range of disciplines, including interaction design, branding and architecture, to create outputs including films, projection mapping and public installation. The themes I explored included lack of tangibility in online social-media relationships, perception of the body and time travel. Textile thinking in this experience led to projects which though textile oriented were ultimately undisciplined, new and exciting. This work led to professional experience developing wearable technology that connects people across continents using haptic feedback. Observations about tactile sensibility developed into my hunch that the discipline of textiles which centres around the sense of touch has the potential to critique the practices of technology and data, which are typically screen-based, untouchable and immaterial.

I enrolled for a practice-based PhD at the Royal College of Art (RCA) in 2016, compelled to return to my interests surrounding body and health messaging, this time bringing experience in Internet of Things (IOT), wearable technology and consumer electronics. I aimed to use textile thinking to address body representation and experience using technology such as sensors, fitness trackers and so forth. To begin with I worried I wasn't a 'real' textile designer; I didn't create metres of beautiful fabric or collaborate with product and fashion designers or create new materials. During my master's course, my early textile training was complimented by opportunities to learn from others through collaboration outside of the textile design discipline and the development of my design methodology which is motivated by emerging concerns and criticisms about technologies. In my varied creative practice, whether developing an installation or in my facilitation of others, I not only bring an interest in the material object but additionally in bringing people together in a physical space to have an experience and together create an atmosphere to create and debate ideas. Rather than limiting my approach to developing physical textile and material outcomes I was keen to explore how textile thinking approaches applied in design research could lead to insights and innovation which may be useful beyond the field of design.

I began to read about textile thinking. To me, textile thinking was 'how textile designers think'. You know – engaging the senses (touching stuff!), drawing, prototyping, collaging and moodboarding to create patterns and identify themes, collaborating, asking questions, engaging others and experimenting with technology to explore new mediums and dimensions for design. *The Tacit-Turn: Textile Design in Design Research* (Igoe 2010) and *In Textasis: Matrixial Narratives of Textile Design* (Igoe 2013) became key reading for understanding examples of textile thinking. Igoe's work aimed to widen the scope of the field of textiles so that it might be understood as design and freed from the boundaries of 'craft' labelling. However, I felt there were some areas that needed additions if it was to align with my experience of design and thinking in textiles. In particular within atypical environments outside the studio, using 'materials' as a loose term encompassing people, data, insights and outcomes which could be described as experiences and experiments rather than samples or swatches.

I began to develop a series of hypotheses to 'take on' textile thinking – experiments which might identify and test the concept of textile thinking. The aim being to expand our epistemological understanding of textile thinking and reveal the potential impact of textile design practice and research applied in wider multidisciplinary engagements.

Igoe's work (2013 and this volume) aims to reveal the embodied, tacit nature of textile cognition, argues for recognition of intricate, enigmatic, non-linear design methods and for these practices to be integrated into and acknowledged in design research. The tacit knowledge and intuition embedded in the thinking and making of textile practice methodologies have rarely been documented. For textile practitioners, regularly collaborating in other fields means they often work in non-linear ways, to build sensitivities, nuances and understandings of new fields and develop tacit knowledge through interdisciplinary working. From clothing to cars, the role of the textile designer is integrated across an expansive range of industries. However, textiles' input is often shrouded by the other disciplines or seen as mere decoration, regarded as an addition instead of recognizing textiles' 'designerly' contribution to the whole. More recently, textile design-led approaches which enable others by facilitating interaction and engagement are being explored in different settings and contexts. Use of textile design-like activities in projects addressing loneliness (Nevay 2017) and supporting those living with dementia (Robertson 2019) show how textile thinking functioning outside of the textiles domain can produce or contribute to knowledge generation. Researchers in the area of textiles and sustainability, in particular textile recycling (Hall and Earley 2019) and the disruption of fast fashion habits through textile design intervention (Ballie 2014, 2020), emphasize the responsibility of textile designers *as* designers and the requirement for textile thinking to address issues beyond the textile studio, embracing design activism. However, textile designing and thinking as a valued form and process of knowledge generation in design still struggles to be acknowledged; this has been noted by Ballie (2014; Philpott and Kane (2013, 2016) and Valentine et al. (2017).

Igoe identifies key characteristics of the textile design process and textile thinking, both tacit and explicit, and places them within the context of design research. Textiles is presented as a collective 'entity' that draws together designers, objects and processes and is given three identities as mother, geisha and spinster. She uses metaphor in labelling to communicate and decipher intangible or inherent understandings held within the disciplinary field of textiles. The three entities adequately and artfully cover the scope of decorative aesthetics in textile design practice. The 'Mother', often behind the scenes, or in the synergies, resonates with Igoe's interview findings with textile designers describing their experiential relationships with industry – for example, developing textile designs for fashion products. The 'Geisha' represents textiles' aesthetic qualities performing to engage and enhance experience. The 'Spinster', however, is curious and pushes boundaries.

I believe that the three entities described by Igoe are at risk of further pigeonholing a mystical 'textiley' nature of practice and that they should be expanded into other roles to support emerging textile practices. I explore here additional attributes which could represent the emerging role of textile designers within multidisciplinary working environments in particular where collaboration with technologies is concerned.

In order to explore a 'new' or expanded version of textile thinking for these emerging fields I named additional 'entities' that I identified through my own research – textile thinking behaviours which are based on interaction, decision-making and resilience. I employed Igoe's entities in two experiments. First, in Testing Textile Thinking 1, as a tool for analysis, looking at where textile thinking could be identified in the development of smart textile prototypes, a key field of growth for textile practice. And second, in Testing Textile Thinking 2, as an interactive data collection tool where designers from all disciplines could explore textile thinking aspects in their own practices.

Testing Textile Thinking 1

Textile thinking as a tool for analysis was tested at the Smart Textiles Salon in 2017. The Smart Textile Salon is an interactive exhibition and presentation that takes place as part of the annual International Conference on Intelligent Textiles and Mass Customisation (ITMC). Responding to the fact that smart textiles and 'wearable intelligence' are facing integration and expansion into other disciplinary fields and marketplaces, the event invites designers and researchers to present recent prototypes as an indication of current research in this space. Using the salon as a selection of the most up-to-date examples, I examined the objective and subjective attributes of a range of smart textiles and wearable technology innovations with applications in personal use for health and well-being, environment, construction and transport. After an initial survey, it was clear that Igoe's original 'entities' could not sufficiently cater for all the textile technology collaborations on show at the event. This three-part entity concept represents the role of the textile designer in design agendas where empathy, emotion and expressivity are collectively considered. However, when it is applied to design of wearable technologies, or in a smart textile context, this concept tended to miss some qualities, in particular, attributes which link to current technological applications and collaborative methodologies, so I added further attributes.

The exhibition at the salon featured twenty-nine exhibitors from academic research labs, independent research centres and small business owners in Europe, the United States and North Africa. Prototypes and demonstrations were exhibited as working samples or systems and each exhibitor also gave a short introductory presentation. Some of the prototypes were created in order to showcase a technology. Others were samples of materials without application, at an early stage or looking for collaborative partners to develop the work further. The event was an opportunity to meet with researchers in the fields of materials and smart materials to understand the processes and challenges of the research stage and gain perspective into the trajectories of collaboration involved in applied research and market opportunities. The prototypes and short descriptions were collated in a catalogue which was used to support my analysis. I reviewed aspects of the development processes for smart materials and products displayed and created an analysis tool to input 'data' from each exhibited prototype. The tool was a form with three categories to identify types of projects:

- Object – including material, system and sensors used
- Innovation – including information about the team, the collaboration methods, funding drivers, the destined industry and if the innovation was 'sustaining, breakout or disruptive'
- Textile thinking – which looked for elements of Igoe's three textile entities and later included the addition of a further three 'new textile thinking' entities

Of the twenty-nine exhibits, most of the prototypes were designed for personal use (sixteen) or for use on the body, with environment (nine) and portable (four) applications the remaining. The potential industries served by the range of smart textile prototypes featured were health/sport/well-being (sixteen), outdoor/construction (three), automotive (two) and clothing/safety/art (eight). The majority of the examples took the form of a technical inquiry (twelve), alongside materials inquiry (ten) and social and design-led inquiry (five). Particular evidence of textile thinking present in the examples included consideration of physical intimacy; need to be close to the body/skin, supportive; the use of traditional construction techniques; and to provide 'alternative readings of a situation' such as metaphor. Other significant additional attributes in the prototypes included being strong, durable or resilient – concerned with measurement and quantifying and the role of the textile itself as a way of disguising technology.

The results showed that of the projects analysed, four aligned solely with the characteristics of the original textile entities and one used solely additional or 'new' textile thinking characteristics as described earlier. The remaining twenty-four examples showed a balanced mixture of characteristics.

In Figure 3, I outline Igoe's classification of textiles as three entities and show the additional attributes evident in the emerging field of smart textiles and wearable technologies. I classified these as Sportsperson, Soldier and Father to encompass 'new' textile thinking characteristics.

The focus of my investigation in Testing Textile Thinking 1 was not solely on 'textile' outcomes or objects but in areas where textile designers and researchers have contributed to social or technological solutions where the outcome is not easily identifiable as textiles, such as service design ideation in the design of a wearable technology product. For example, Martijn ten Bhömer (2016) used models to explore experience in his study of the use of prototypes for 'embodied sense making'. Physical objects helped stakeholders develop ideas about immaterial concepts such as services. Ten Bhömer found that physical prototypes could be used at the design meeting stage to imagine the product in use, to illustrate the product in relation to the body and to propose intangible design features and smart textile services, including digital functionality or sound.

I added characteristics to the textile entities which, inherent to textile thinking and design practice, enable collaboration and interdisciplinary knowledge exchange in the context of the experience of wearable technologies and smart

TEXTILE ENTITIES		
Mother	Geisha	Spinster
Enable other objects to come into existence/becoming Invites (and requires) partners to participate in realizing new creations Relates, adapts Communicates Gives Physical	Indigenous social perspective provides alternative readings of a situation (metaphor) Performative Decorative Seductive Exquisite Patron receives a particular level of control over the behaviour (Potential of) sensory pleasure	Simple, uncomplicated Muteness, inability to forge relationships Overlooked by those looking only for beauty Academic Pursues own interests (curious)

NEW TEXTILE THINKING ENTITIES		
Sportsperson	Soldier	Father
Measurement, quantify Competitive Communication Dedication, motivation, focus Strength Discipline, commitment Confidence, optimist	Fighting, courage, strong, Endurance Functional Teamwork, loyalty Decisiveness, judgement, initiative Knowledge, awareness Selfless service	Provider Leader, verbally expressive (compared to Mother seen as less visible) To be seen, role model Dependable Immediate Resilient Protector Teacher Disciplinarian

Figure 3 Expanded textile thinking entities (adapted from Lean 2017/2020).

materials. The addition of the further three entities was intended to incorporate functional aspects of a designed textile prototype as a way of studying an object using a specific lens and enabled a guided interrogation. The Mother and the Father are the same but different. The textile designer-facilitator does not solely contribute to aesthetics yet performs all the tasks required of her, interlacing several entities into one. Having established that the characteristics could be used as a tool to analyse designed prototypes, they were then used to explore ways of analysing design practice.

Testing Textile Thinking 2

To test the characteristics of the entities in Figure 3 and to see if they feature in other fields of practice, I created an interactive exhibit as a platform for others to describe their practice based on the key characteristics. In 2018, during an interim 'Work in Progress' student show at the RCA, visitors were invited to map the characteristics of their practice using the list of descriptions and icons shown in Figure 4.

The icons and descriptions of characteristics (Figure 4) were displayed on a sandwich board in the form of a spectrum–like clock face (Figure 5). The tool was designed so that visitors could engage with the characteristics by first reading the description to learn what each entailed and then choosing on a scale from 1 (a little) to 5 (a lot) how much they felt each characteristic featured in their own practice. Numbered nails (1–5) and coloured builder's line allowed exhibition visitors to trace out aspects of their practice. Visitors chose a coloured line according to their identified practice – designer, non-designer or textile designer. Their responses created patterns and the visitors interacted with an exhibition piece to create a data 'materialisation' (Lean 2020) in a visual, tactile and tangibly sociable way. The results showed that the textile thinking characteristics I'd illustrated and arranged in numbered scale (1–5 for how relevant each characteristic was) could be used to describe elements of practice by both textile designers and other designers. This showed how textile thinking characteristics could be used to analyse design practice and outcomes. This exercise enabled dialogue between the participants and myself about the concept of textile thinking; how textile designers think and the characteristics

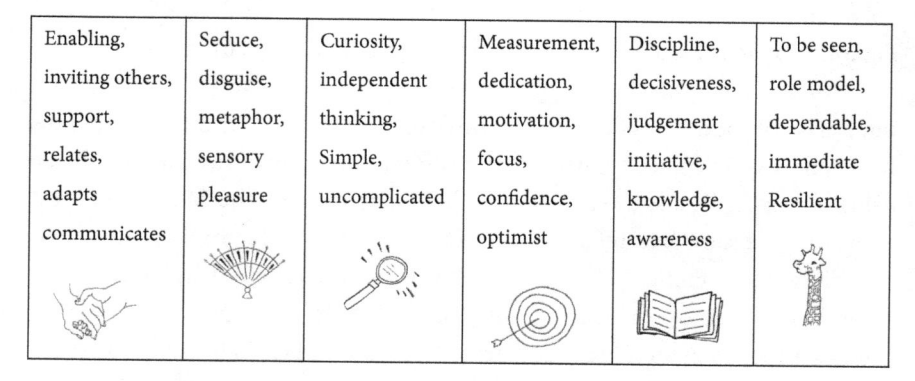

Enabling, inviting others, support, relates, adapts communicates	Seduce, disguise, metaphor, sensory pleasure	Curiosity, independent thinking, Simple, uncomplicated	Measurement, dedication, motivation, focus, confidence, optimist	Discipline, decisiveness, judgement initiative, knowledge, awareness	To be seen, role model, dependable, immediate Resilient

Figure 4 Expanded textile thinking characteristics, attributes and icons used in an interactive exhibit at the Royal College of Art (Lean 2018).

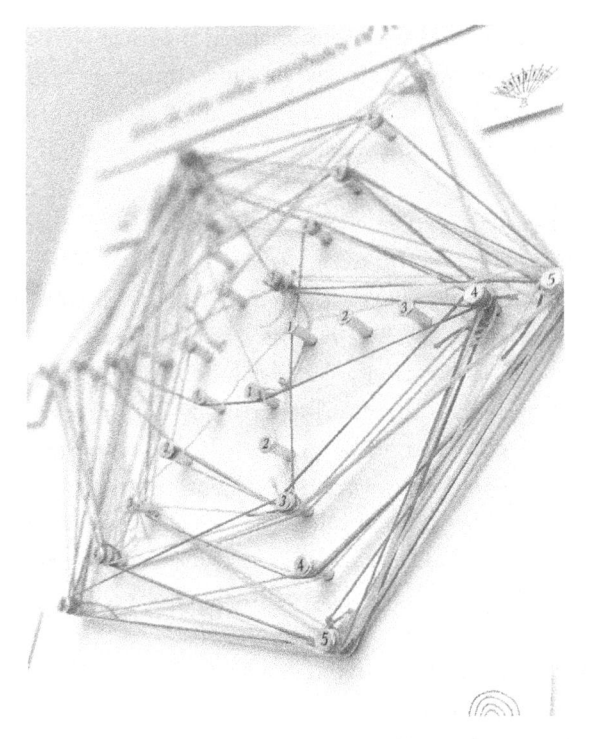

Figure 5 Textile thinking interactive exhibit at the Royal College of Art, London, UK (2018).

of that practice; and initiated discussions on the transferability of textile approaches in other domains. By applying human, relational characteristics to activities and outcomes of design practice, data in the form of designed objects and individual behaviours and design decisions were analysed using metaphors of human relations, emotions and entities (Mother, Geisha, Spinster, Sportsperson, Soldier, Father). Observations from these experiments suggested potential for the expansion of the repertoire of textile design approaches and activities particularly with regard to technology-oriented textile outcomes but also in some design activities that do not produce a 'traditional' textile (material) outcome.

Textile thinking in practice

My own textile design research developed to explore the potential of applied textile thinking as a practice in design research, described in my doctoral thesis 'Materialising Data Experience through Textile Thinking' (2020). This has focused in particular on the use of material practices as tools for research but where the 'final' outcome may well be quite 'immaterial', for example, the design of a service, system or interaction. In this, I developed a formal set of qualities which are presented as a visual methodology map for textile thinking as a research practice (Lean 2020). This map as a practice-based research contribution is useful for textile design researchers as a tool to aid collaboration in multidisciplinary settings – for example, to communicate one's approach. This is also relevant to textile design practitioners and researchers who can use this as a framework to identify and find value in aspects of their existing practices. I continue to carry out design activities and lead research encounters which, while previously could be seen as atypical for textile design, can now be identified, against the work of others *as* textile design which crosses boundaries, fosters relationships and enables new ways of designing in research.

Further to this I propose seven criteria for textile design research: applying tacit knowledge; affect and being in the synergies; experimenting with materialities; problem setting; engaging technology as a research tool; inspiring new practices; building relationships and knowledge exchange (Lean 2020). I used these criteria to identify where textile thinking as a practice contributed to both exploratory and applied research within community-based, educational and policy environments. A contextual review led to identification of existing textile thinking in practice by researchers and practitioners, enabled coherent reporting on my own practice and resulted in a methodology which supports the position of textile design as a research platform in other fields.

To test the application of the established characteristics of textile thinking in my own practice under real-world conditions I undertook a policy placement with the UK government's telecoms organization, Building Digital UK (BDUK). This setting provided the context for knowledge exchange using textile thinking approaches, which were used to engage people in research activities. The aim was to learn about the experiences of living with a high-speed internet connection. The outcomes of the research are insights about the impact of gigabit-capable connectivity which were presented to stakeholders and will inform the development of future interventions for demand stimulation – to encourage the uptake of fibre internet connections. The results (collected insights and a model for data collection) show how textile thinking approaches can be used to develop embodied methods for use in data collection. The methods included technology demonstrations, face-to-face conversation, physical mapping activities and creative research collaboration with illustrator Mitch Miller to capture the research activities and insights revealed in a hand-drawn data materialization.

Engaging novel approaches for data collection raises concerns about validity, especially when experimental methods are employed. The approach taken in this example of applied textile thinking relied on the ability to communicate some of the tacit knowledge of textile design in ways which aimed to avoid confusion and dismantle barriers. This required a level of trust between me and the stakeholders at BDUK in the application of particular methods in the study. For example, the notion of an ethnography workshop for data collection was more easily communicated than that of a 'textile workshop'. Through this experience I learned that capturing experience and developing data representations which offer tangible understandings of the methodology are useful for communicating the process and findings relevant to the research context. To support experimental design research, communicating the approach through which insights and findings materialize is valuable when entering and participating in new domains and research settings.

In another example of creating criteria to analyse design research, Sanders and Stappers (2008) categorized 'traditional' design disciplines which suggest focus on design of products, against 'emerging' design disciplines which focus on designing for a purpose. For example, 'traditional' includes visual communication design, whereas emerging design contains 'design for experiencing'. Sanders and Stappers proposed that

> design will become synonymous with research to create new landscapes of opportunity for designers and researchers. The 'fuzzy front end' will become populated with hybrid design researchers and research designers. (Sanders and Stappers 2008: 2)

They write that 'new disciplines will spin out and people will begin to explore the new design spaces on the emerging landscape' (Sanders and Stappers 2008: 13). In my research, which is based in a 'traditional' design discipline, I propose exploring and supporting how we perceive 'design for purpose'. Rather than the creation of a new discipline, I argue that the 'traditional' fields support applied approaches as a practice for research by providing a lens to conduct enquiries.

Textile designers cross dimensions and domains. Today I'd recommend to my twenty-two-year-old self, that restless textile screen printer, to continue experimenting with materials and metaphors, colours and collecting but also to build bridges and cross boundaries, sign up for unusual events, persuade illustrators to animate your patterns and apply for policy placements. Within the 'traditional' design disciplines there are already valuable examples of processes and tools to 'design for purpose' such as contemporary textile design researchers who are redefining 'purpose' for practice-based research. This includes practices which inform new research methods, and lead to sociocultural insights which are purposeful and useful for innovation in other domains, as well as (and instead of) material innovation.

Applied textile thinking is not a new discipline, or a hybrid, but instead a platform, a largely untapped 'landscape of opportunity' for design and research. It is this grounding that enables daring explorations into new areas. What may be required is a reframing and recognition of the ways traditional fields can and do contribute to wider sociocultural agendas and wicked problems. In turn, this will act as an invitation for 'traditional' practitioners and designers to perform 'research' – exploring topical and timely issues through their own mediums and techniques which may lead to insights and innovation in both print rooms and policymaking.

10

Tracing back to trace forwards
What does it mean/take to be a Black textile designer

Rose Sinclair

The individual is both site and subject of these discursive struggles for identity and for remaking memory. Because individuals are subject to multiple and competing discourses in many realms, their subjectivity is shifting and contradictory, not stable, fixed, rigid.

(Richardson 2000: 929)

'On my daily walk home, I stop at a large newsagent's chain, as usual before approaching the location of the daily newspapers, I take the opportunity to browse the bulging rack of the latest crafting, knitting and sewing magazines, I regard this as my guilty pleasure. I avidly look amongst the magazines, many are wrapped in plastic covers, holding in paper patterns, fabrics, yarns, notions, free give always. I have a professional interest. This area of design is my life and at the time I am writing for the last seven years my doctoral research focus has been on the crafting practices of Black British women. I am particularly interested in the relationships between networks established in the Caribbean and re-established through migration, in textiles networks such as Dorcas clubs, on arrival in post-war England. It is these traces, exploring roots and routes through both amateur and professional practices that offer points of "tracing".

What is it about these magazines? Well, they offer me, the professional, an opportunity to understand the latest consumer trends but also to continue to see if anything new has emerged as the latest "in thing" or , just to immerse myself in the place of craft. But there is one thing, I continue to notice, one thing; just as on my numerous previous visits, there is not one person on the front cover, on closer inspection of those magazines not covered in plastic wrappers, that there are no persons who are part of the editorial or contributors' teams who look like *me. A practitioner, designer, academic of over twenty years in the making, yet the practice space in which I dwell, and inhabit as a person of colour, as Black woman; I am invisible in the crafting space.' A space, often liminal, (Barnes 2006) within the pages of text, allows for the reader a construction of creative methods through which they understand portrayal of self and by extension representation.*

I was aware that people of colour were not visibly prominent in these liminal spaces – were not the faces on or in the magazines. However, not to see *any* people of colour raises unexpected concerns and responses, questions are asked of me in the spaces I inhabit within institutions, such as 'Don't Black women knit? Why would you need to knit in a hot country?' (Hamilton-Brown 2017) to 'Black women don't quilt' (Patel 2019). From this perspective the invisibility of women and people of colour in this specific space represents our real hypervisibility in the wider crafting spaces, which straddles both the spaces of the amateur and professional.

Claiming your traces

Kyra Hicks (2003) in her seminal book *Black Threads: An African American Quilting Sourcebook* identifies that it is the invisibility of the Black women from the dialogue of crafting in both the profession and amateur space that leads to her highlighting the textual existence of the past, present and future legacies of quilting as a craft practice by women of colour. Black American feminist writer bell hooks (2007) highlights the absence of naming Black women in the displays of their work in museums or art gallery events, highlights their hyperinvisibility, and it is now that there needs to be a stance towards the claiming of rights to our culture through naming work of Black makers. A stance highlighted by textile artist Faith Ringgold (Ringgold and Obrist 2019) who highlights the importance of Black makers in writing their own stories as if they are written by others, they tell the stories from their own perspectives not your own personal truth. Notably, Ringgold refashions her text as textile, a woven fabric, constructed with warp and weft threads, so providing a reading as well as creating material for a construction of identity both as tracer of her place as textile designer and her place as a Black woman telling her creative story.

What is both present in the dialogue of Hicks, hooks and Ringgold is the need to present the values, heritage and an aesthetic of Blackness, amidst a crafting dialogue that does not see Blackness. bell hooks (2007) calls into question the spaces of Black women's creativity identifying the movement between creative spaces, for example, the church space to the home space to the professional space. It is the movement between these spaces where the identity of the creative is formed and developed, but in that movement, it can become lost. While from the UK perspective there are postcolonial dialogues related to masculinity in the fashion textiles space (Checinska 2017b), still to be discussed: and the migratory factors that surround the development of the aesthetics of fashion and textiles crafts practices of a postcolonial legacy (Tulloch 2017; Sinclair 2015, 2019). Authors of postmodern aesthetics such as Cheryl Buckley (1986, 2009) and Johnson (2018) point out failure to recognize the place of the female, the marginalized and those for whom crafting and textiles have the possibility to create new futures. Hicks (2003) believes that what fuels the practice are the networks of practice that emerge both online and in physical spaces (Gauntlett 2011; Thomas 2018). Patel (2019, 2020) explores this through the professional practice of Black, Asian & Minority Ethnic (BAME) women and their craft and textile practice in the social space. All this seeks to ask – where are the places where Black women as textile designers can find spaces to connect through new geographies of space, which in turn allow them to create those 'tracers'?

I wish to focus on the question of tracing practice and routes through tracing, an issue that is also discussed in Igoe (2013).

What is it therefore that fuels the tracing of crafting practice when it is invisible or when it becomes the site of 'discursive struggles for identity' (Richardson 2000:929)? Hicks seeks to define this tracing as being fuelled by following three areas:

1. The growth of specific textile exhibitions that showcase the 'Black experience' through the textile craft.
2. The growth of online spaces that connect makers.
3. The ongoing spaces and professional bodies that facilitate face-to-face connections and exchange.

Hicks (2003: 9) and hooks (2007: 317) assert that it is essential to trace the practices of Black women, in order to do the following:

- Meet heritage and cultural needs.
- Preserve Black histories.
- Create a context for collecting and preserving the specific textiles practices of all people not just a few, thus assigning values, cultural heritage.
- It will encourage current and future cultural engagement and assist in future development and tracing of cultural capital.

Elizabeth Robinson (2012) readily acknowledges that research on women of colour in the UK concerning their crafting practices and their approaches to making is lacking; the work of Jo Turney (2009) identifies that crafts join communities of makers through process and practice but again this research has remained firmly focused on white women and their crafting practices.

The UK census (2011) identified that just over four million women identified as BAME, while just over one million identify as Black. Available industry figures currently estimate that over 4 million women in the UK knit, with 1.5 million women knitting on a regular basis; this figure however does not delineate between race and ethnicity in its figures. Recent UK Arts Council and Creative Skills research publications have highlighted that while there has been a distinct rise in the number of BAME people undertaking fashion-related practice, the figures related to BAME participation in craft, which includes the practice of textiles, are often so small that it is not actively recorded.

Tracing back to look forward

Tracing your own practice and how you come to dwell in the textiles space is an important dialogue that all professional designers go through. Igoe (2013) starts this process by questioning her own textiles' journey and traces her approach to practice and has an ongoing reflexive dialogue with herself about the design process and practice. This results in critical dialogues, dissecting the design and creative process in textiles practice.

Reflecting on this, questions began to emerge for me based on my own approach as a practitioner researcher and are broken down in to the following areas:

- Textiles practice as composed of traces and layers and systems – a palimpsest of interconnecting parts that have to be retraced.
- Discussion around traces; textile as traces; what can be traced can also be retraced: (Igoe 2013: 52) providing a multilayered and layered/layers/palimpsest. The difficulties encountered in tracing (Igoe 2013: 51).
- How to trace back the possibilities attributed to tracing back (Igoe 2013: 104,161,185), that is, uncovering traces.
- Traces and imprints as traces (Igoe 2013: 19).
- Where our traces are painted out, what happens? Painting out traces. Painting the absences (Igoe 2013: 25).

Visibility and hyperinvisibility through a feminist lens

Both Igoe (2013: 33) and Cheryl Buckley (2009) comment on the invisible role of the designer, especially if they are female. Elinor, Richardson, Scott, Thomas and Walker (1987) in their book *Women and Craft* highlight how homeworkers act in design-as-translation (Igoe 2013) with the professional designer makers, yet are also makers at home in their own right though, but due to the prevailing social conditions they inhabit are not duly recognized as part of a wider community of practice.

> Here I can position my own biography, my mother while training to be a nurse in the early 1970s was also an outworker for a local garment company. In this work, her professionalism as a 'dressmaker' is done through the use of her skills to further support her family. it is also the point at which as a young girl I also learnt to help my mother, I would also be sewing, adding buttons to garments, using the overlocker, I learned really quickly to make by seeing, and make by doing, knowing that every mistake would mean a reduced pay packet, the aim each week was to meet the Friday evening, Saturday morning deadline pick up, from the foreman.

The use of a Black autoethnnographical perspective offers the opportunity to further provide a voice for the often multilayered complex experiences that form us as Black makers, crafters and designers. Thus, for me the fashion industry held no illusion, between who designed the clothes and who made the clothes that were sold in the shops; at this level there is no interaction with the designer, just interaction in the system of manufacture.

Through this intersectionality of fashion and dress through race, Carol Tulloch (1998: 360) reflects on the complex nature histories of fashion, that is,

> predominantly Eurocentric, with a notable concentration on Britain and Paris. Like its fellow subdiscipline, design history, published works have mainly concentrated on the 'heroes' of dress or design – again European-based and white. Race has rarely impacted on dress history.

Tulloch (2016) further highlighted this in fashion and design. Thus, the role that race plays in fashion and design can often marginalize the Black designer and maker who does not see themself even in the histories of the subject they inhabit. Tulloch (2016) identifies the role that race plays in fashion and design, which can often marginalize the designer and maker making a clear distinction about the continuing hyperinvisibility of the Black people in the 'fashion space'.

the issue of the invisibility of black people has long been discussed in, for example, postcolonial studies. Despite their extensive range of activities in the public gaze that has snowballed over the centuries, the issue of invisibility remains a caustic point in need of address in the twenty-first century. (Tulloch 2016: 283)

Tracing self. Tracing our roots

Who does what practice? How do you come to be a professional in the textiles space and do what you do? Why do we need to trace our roles, our positions and our points of professional practice at all as people of colour? hooks (2007) describes this as a form of coming out, making visible the unknown. Contemporary textile designers such as Bisa Butler draw heavily on this notion of tracing in their work, not only through the act of making but also by subverting the process through the use of 'fabulating' (Warren 2020) tales, applying an expanded Black design palette to develop new possibilities. This allows new tracers, creating new narratives of both Black textile artists and designers as well as the Black experience and placing these, as Warren states, in an 'interstitial space between fact and fiction'. Where our traces are painted out, what happens? As Black designers we find routes to re-painting in our traces, and re-painting the absences, by filling in the voids (Igoe 2013: 25).

The question I am often asked as a textiles practitioner and designer is, 'How did you get into textiles?' For me personally this was not an unusual space to be or to place myself in, as I grew up surrounded by makers. My own mother was part of the Windrush Generation arriving in the UK in 1960. My mother came from the small island of Jamaica to the much larger island of England in 1960. My mother was a professional dressmaker (Buckley 2007: 131–2) but was only able to use these skills effectively among those in her community and the local women of the church she attended. Her skills however remained in her community, as she would go on to train as a nurse and work for the National Health Service (NHS). Together with the women from her church they often used the front room (McMillan 2008) as the making space for their local 'Dorcas Club' meetings (Sinclair 2015). Making and crafting through cloth would continue to play an important part in my mother's life, as she engaged in it through community projects. This meant that the world of making was a space that was situated for me. Growing up I was surrounded by Black women who made things, whether baked, sewed, knitted, or woven; making and crafting was a normal activity and formed an essential part of my upbringing. Making with purpose for the community was the norm, as was the exchange of knowledge within a communal setting of co-collaboration and the retention of authenticity (Twigger-Holroyd 2018).

Tracing our roots: How do I dwell in this space, what brought me to this point?

I can define I am a Black British woman who is passionate about textiles both as practice and process and everything in between.

In *Ways of Knowing, Being and Doing: A Theoretical Framework and Methods for Indigenous and Indigenist Research*, Karen Martin and Booran Mirraboopa (2003) offer a framework for this approach that I apply in the following text to define textiles practice through the tracing of (my)self and retaining ones' authenticity:

'Where I From'

I am claiming

I am declaring my genealogy, my heritage, my culture

I am positioning (because I can)

WHY?

To locate myself as a Black British woman of Caribbean heritage

As a Textile Designer/Practitioner

As researcher (in an academic space)

WHY?

This allows others to locate me

This allows others to determine the types of relations/ships that might exist.

WHY?

In providing these details I am also

Identifying

Defining

Describing

The elements of **'Where I From'**

and

> **Locating my research**
> **Locating my practice**
> **Positioning myself**
> **Claiming my space**

This reiteration of the words of bell hooks (2007), as previously discussed, call on processes of self-identification of creative spaces for Black women. Through this dialogue, the issues of agency emerge through the textile design praxis and therefore a move towards the overlap of design discourses, which lead to a reconfiguration of the spaces occupied, and how Black women are seen and negotiate institutional spaces of praxis.

It is the movement between these liminal spaces (Barnes 2013) where the identity of the creative is formed and developed, but in that movement it can become lost. It is however a contentious space, one where the designer or creative can increasingly go unrecognized as their work emerges in a 'new art' or 'professional space' and the maker or designer's identity and specificity, as hooks (2007: 327) maintains; in archives and museum spaces identities remain concealed with the title applied too often 'Maker Unknown'. In this unknown space the professional maker of colour has to negotiate vagaries of gender and race.

Tracing further: Crafting the professional space

The complexity of the design process and the critique through feminist understandings continue to create difficulties in navigating the terrain of Black design crafting practice. In 2017, Thick/er Black Lines, a research-led art collective, presented the work *We Are Sorry for the Delay to Your Journey* which sought to clarify how the work of Black female creatives' past, present and potential futures can be explored and discussed through the linear graphics of the modern underground map (Hand, Mhondoro and Ove 2019). While this chapter focusses on predominantly female practitioners, I must acknowledge that Black male textile designers exploring craft culture and heritage are far less reviewed or researched in either the professional or personal spaces of textile making.

Tracing back to trace forwards

Althea McNish is held up as the foremost Black textile designer of the twentieth century. She arrived in England from Trinidad in 1951 and by 1957 had graduated from the RCA as its first Black graduate of textiles. A formidable creative woman, she paved a trail in the world of textiles, art and design (Checinska 2017a, 2018; Sellers 2017) winning both national and international acclaim (Mendes and Hinchcliffe 1983; Hlaváčková 2019). She would create textile work for the leading textiles and fashion houses of the time such as Ascher, Hull Traders, Liberty's and Tootals (Jackson 2005, 2009; Walmsley 1992). Michael Webber (1968) writes, 'Textile designers are also doing well in Europe. Althea McNish regularly visits Italy, Switzerland, France and Scandinavia, and is also visited every year in her London studio by buyers from overseas manufacturers.'

McNish was also one of the leading artists of the Caribbean Artists Movement (CAM) which emerged in the 1960s to give voice to a rising Black creative aesthetic seeking to create and locate their own tradition in face of the dominant tradition (Harris, White and Beezmohun 2009; Walmsley 1992), Althea would go on to dominate this design space for over sixty years and the legacy of her research and work stills lives on.

Figure 6, which is taken from a collection of Women Designers curated by Leah Armstrong in 2012, shows textile designer Althea McNish at work reviewing wallpaper samples (also discussed in Chapter 7). For Igoe, this is linked primarily to the issues of gendering and perceived professional status of textiles for females in wider society. For me, as a designer reviewing these images, and writing this text, the story extends beyond what the picture reveals; Althea had extended her design expertise beyond just fabrics and was involved in designing 'interior spaces' and by this time also designing for major wallpaper companies such as Wallpaper Manufactures Limited. By the time this image was taken, what is considered one of McNish's most successful textile designs and

Figure 6 Portrait of textile designer Althea McNish, 1960.

one of the most iconic textiles of the era 'Golden Harvest' had been printed by Hull Traders.

John Berger (2013) identifies the key traits that tell us how to read photographs not only through the visual evidence they present but also in the other information they present us with about the time. Berger emphasizes that 'a photograph celebrates neither the event itself nor the faculty of sight in itself. A photograph is already a message about the events it records . . . at its simplest the message decoded means: I have decided that seeing this is worth recording' (John Berger 2013).

For McNish, her role is significant and worthy of seeing and recording not only because of her professional status and gender but also her race. In addition to the issues of gender and reading femininity, the image also presents the issue of tracing the role of race, or rather women of colour, specifically seeing Black women in the professional textiles design space. McNish was herself constantly described by her geographical origin as in (Figure 7) 'the girl from Trinidad' or as a 'West Indian' with subsequent text having connotations or perceptions of geographical imaginations, of how she is perceived to use or apply colour through the design praxis through the creation of a space the making of 'a calypso room with lazing in mind' (Hislop 1966).

Figure 7 Althea McNish in her design studio featured in Hislop (1966) 'Bachelor Girls Room', Ideal Home Exhibition, London, UK.

The subsequent picture (Figure 7) is always mistaken for being taken at the Ideal Home Exhibition in 1966 but actually highlights McNish in her own design studio of the same period. What the image does show is the transition that McNish made professionally from designing fabrics to designing spaces, as well as showcasing her design space as a freelance designer, and not being shoehorned into a single design practice. What is also notable is that this was the first Ideal Home Exhibition to be filmed and featured on the BBC in colour.

The image (Figure 7) is supplied with the headline: 'My Ideal Room by a Bachelor Girl, . . . Colour, colour . . . and nothing costing more than £49.10s. Those were the principles Althea McNish worked on as she designed her strictly "66" bachelor girl's room.' The image showcases McNish in her design space, her design studio that she inhabited to make her work happen, highlighting the tools and the space where her work comes to life. What is intriguing is that this picture is often used without the adjoining article written by the author Vivien Hislop, which is used to describe McNish's ideal room and for the ideal young twenty-six-year-old 'bachelor' girl about town.

The *Daily Mail* Ideal Home Exhibition was described by Buckley (2007: 141) as the place to portray 'the ideal home, its conception and its construction . . . based on the ideas and opinions of women'. Here Althea McNish in her role as a textile designer informs these 'ideal homes'. As a Black woman, the importance lay in tracing a new space forward in identifying the needs of a wider migrant demographic that was now settling in Britain. At the same time McNish was making waves at the Ideal Home Show, she would be working on making new 'traces' with the CAM, who were seeking to establish a new 'voice' and creative agency for emerging Black artists and creatives who now found themselves needing to have a voice. And so, this image superimposes the rise of the new agency and creative voice of the Black female textile professional emerging from a post-war 'British empire'.

I argue here that traces identify pathways to which you can assign a link to a particular approach to designing and making.

I am a textile designer, and I continue to wear multiple hats as academic, practitioner and researcher; storytelling through textiles allows me to use 'tracers'. I revise 'Where our traces are painted out, what happens? Painting out traces. Painting the absences' (Ettinger cited in Igoe 2013: 25) but reframe this as 'Painting in the traces, and Painting in the absences'. My work now not only embodies textiles practice but also connects to politics such as in Windrush Arrivals 1948 (Goldsmiths Jan 2019–Feb 2019 and V&A London Design

Weekend Sept 2019). I create spaces that explore the Black female creative experience through textiles, set up as immersive in person or remote experiences such as in the 'Caribbean Front Room' installation in collaboration with the Broadway Theatre, based in Catford, South East London, England.

In developing their practice, the textile designer makes decisions about their pathways of practice and this although often modelled as a cyclo-linear one, it is not. Issues of race and gender are interlinked and integral to the construct of textiles practice and its profession, yet this is an area that is not yet thoroughly explored and cannot be in such a small space as I have here.

We must shed light onto the spaces where the professional designer's roles need further unpicking. Although increased figures of BAME designers employed in the fashion sector is a point of excitement, the numbers of those participating in the crafts, including the textiles sector, are diminishing. This gives rise to concerns over the growing invisibility of BAME individuals working in textiles.

Notes

1. An Arts Council report, Creative Media Survey (2012: 38) highlighted that BAME made up 17 per cent of the fashion and textiles workforce but had limited information on further breakdown of data and clear representation across the fashion and textiles industry.
2. Between 2011 and 2014, there was a 126 per cent increase in BAME in the design industry which includes fashion, products and graphics; however, textiles is not included in this definition. Between 2011 and 2014, the number of BAME in the area of crafts was considered too small to be sampled. Taken from *Creative Diversity: The State of Diversity in the UK's Creative Industries, and What We Can Do about It* from the Creative Industries Federation, 2015 and *Creative Industries: Focus on Employment*, 30 June 2015 – a report from the Department of Culture, Media and Sport, UK Government.
3. Golden Harvest was a textile design based on a combination of English fields and flowers and sugar cane fields of Trinidad designed by Althea McNish and manufactured in 1959 by Hull Traders Ltd.

Mesh three

I like to inlay the idea of the story or a memory in a fabric. So, there's quite a narrative that runs through my work, by collecting old things and looking at imagery of old lace and things that kind of hold some kind of history. I go to car boots all the time, so I have so many sources of inspiration here buying things like these; I collect old ladies' headscarves. 'Cause the colours are so fantastic. I just collect images I like or collect photos, buttons for colours, I don't know. I collect feathers, things for my own pleasure that I like. Just things that catch your eye; everyday, really simple, simple things, quite random really. Just lots of different feelings, different scraps basically. Rusty and cracked, just scraps of different things. The scraps of embroidery and things I pick up at car boots and things; they are valuable to me. The process is very spontaneous, I keep collecting. And I tend to notice that whatever's around you sort of develops your work without you even realizing it. So at that moment whatever's present around me, I keep picking from that and putting it together.

As a team we might kind of go through drawers and drawers and drawers of vintage things, sort of old swatches that we have to see whether there is anything there that we could kind of reuse, re-colour or develop something from, use as inspiration. Or we would go out. Maybe we'd have like half a day . . . so little time to do anything, but maybe we'd have half a day to go to some local kind of vintage shops to go and have a look at stuff.

Textile designers like stuff. At college, the big thing we all had in common was that we collected weird things and I thought that was just me then I realized it was a textile thing. I don't know other people, like my friends, who are interaction designers or moving image designers or even fashion – they don't collect things like we do.

I used to just make things, like, I just used to have lots of fabric and needles and things on my table and I just used to make objects and just play with materials and sew materials together and stitch into materials. Studying textiles was really freeing because there was no outcome, so it was just about playing with materials. When I started my MA they pulled me apart completely. It was very painful. So I started playing with material, I had been thinking too much before.

I'm sort of fascinated by characteristics of materials within textiles and normally what I do is take a material, take it apart, like a kid, and then find my own way of putting it back together again. I'm kind of just looking at what I can do with them. The nice thing about fabric is you can keep doing things to it. I do also just love pattern which is odd because I don't wear any pattern or really have any or surround myself with pattern in my home. But there's something about creating it that I really love. It was literally in my final year of school when I started textiles when I just loved it. I can't really, I can't describe it; nothing has kind of had that effect on me before or since. And I don't really know how I chose textiles but that was the area that I went into and then really enjoyed it. I think it was a lot of the, just constructing, playing with little things, making stuff, and colour and loads of different materials. Just experimenting that I really liked. So I think it is all about the playing with materials and wanting to use different materials and work with different techniques and having lots of little things on the go, I think.

I draw on all sorts of influences; theatre, film, you name it; paintings, ceramics, sculpture, nature; the senses and music. I take a lot of pictures and then try to sort of play with it, a bit like a pick and mix. Simply, whatever I did in my end process was something that I pulled together as a textile; as a textile design as such, but to me it was a series of forms which fitted together or flowed to make a rhythmic pattern over a surface which would then appear as if it was going to be part of a continuum. My work relates to how I'm feeling at that moment in time and if it feels like it's an important shape even if it's just like, you know, a crappy little heart or something . . .it's kind of more how I'm feeling and how the shape relates to my mindset at that time.

I'm a bit childish. As soon as I know something's supposed to be a trend I kind of lose interest a little bit or I feel like I'm not really . . . or I haven't got much ownership over my work so I just sort of follow my own gut instinct. I'm just the kind of person that works so much, likes doing lots of different things, I'm very just kind of get straight into it and not kind of take a step back and reflect on what I'm doing.

I think all textile designers are very playful. When you look at a textile designer looking at a product or a garment, we're very childlike. There is an understanding of materiality and we all tend to be extremely tactile, so very often it's not so much a material but the potential of that material that makes us excited. That wonderful thing about warp and weft crossing and creating that third colour. That's what excites me! And if we like something it's not only visual. We put a finger into it! And we all get off on that little mark, we're really happy if we've done that nice mark, we'll go to bed really happy.

For me, a lot of the attraction to textiles, working with textiles, is that you're kind of making things for yourself. It does seem very self-indulgent that you do stuff and you don't really know what it's for. I'm not sure if I'm too worried about what other people think but I have to feel in tune with it. I never feel I have to accommodate something that is not of my liking. I just need to find it fulfilling.

I guess when you're actually designing for a company, the biggest thing is you stop being a designer for yourself. So what you actually create no longer really is your own. Although it continues to be very personal there's a kind of, a little bit of a cut-off, I suppose and you have to be prepared to kind of do things you may not choose to do necessarily.

I'm feeling quite sad after that – cause I'm not making any more.

No, I'm fine with it. I shall go back to it at some point, but . . .

11

Paraphernalia and playing for design

The notion of collecting 'stuff' for the purposes of inspiration and as objects to inspire through colour, material and form is a recognized feature of textile design (Igoe 2013). Kimbell (2012) describes how most designers are 'entangled' with the objects they use and create and explains how designers 'reconfigure the socio-material world' in different ways.

Textile designers commonly use the word 'collecting' to describe this activity of accumulation, but philosophical explorations of collecting such as Baudrillard's (1968) pose further questions about the nature of this type of activity and its place within the context of designing.

The types of objects that textile designers sometimes 'collect' – buttons, old headscarves, bags, stuffed animals, feathers, scraps, car booty – are everyday objects, and it appears that the criteria for inclusion into a textile designer's collection are hugely broad. These 'collections' are seemingly random, items selected for aesthetic or culturally symbolic reasons. The objects are not carefully or proudly conserved, classified or displayed; they are items of use, of purpose. They are things, stuff, trappings, bits and pieces, accoutrements, paraphernalia. I like the term 'paraphernalia' most of all in describing the nature of these 'collected' items, because it at once gives an explanation of the collective worth of these disparate items and provides an understanding of them as items of use.

Steven Connor (2011: 11) explains the etymology of the word 'paraphernalia' as a woman's personal property exempt from the marriage dowry, typically clothing and jewellery, and as such is bestowed a sense of triviality, but is simultaneously used to denote equipment and apparatus in certain professions. He describes how paraphernalia constitutes the items and equipment one might need for a specific occupation. The historical, gendered definition of the term is important in my application of 'paraphernalia' within the occupational process of designing textiles. In Connor's exploration of the term, paraphernalia is at once unnecessary and indispensable. So, by calling the items gathered by textile designers' 'paraphernalia', we can begin to understand their complex nature and roles: often decorative and assumed to be of no exchange value (explained by their exclusion from the dowry) but yet recognized by law as important personal property. In Tongan culture, *koloa* meaning 'treasures' or 'prestigious objects' (Veys 2017: 141) are decorative objects such as woven mats and barkcloth textiles made and presented ceremonially only by women, and associated with women's 'generative powers' (Addo 2013 cited in Veys 2017: 139). These objects are highly valued in Tongan culture precisely because of their association with high-ranking women and their *mana* or supernatural potency. They are essential in ceremonies for wrapping bodies and such but are also customarily exchanged, gifted and inherited in veneration of their value, often in great quantities within royal or high-ranking families. Early missionaries in Tonga perceived these objects as merely decorative, encouraging their production as suitable women's work (although Veys points out that the items considered as *koloa* are not solely made by females but they can only be valued as such by such associations). The missionaries in their Western Christian normativity neither saw nor understood the significance of these decorative textile items in protecting the matriarchal culture of embodied *mana*. When wrapped in barkcloth *koloa*, people's bodies gave physical form to abstract notions of divinity (Veys 2017: 128). The missionaries thought they were just dressing up.

Decolonizing both our understanding of creating decoration as well as the roles of decorative objects in world-making is required to fully understand textiles as design. Textiles as a form of design in copoiesis with craft and art but contextualized within the commodification of products or services.

These items – decorative in themselves or used in the process of designing the decorative – can be legitimately recognized as the necessary equipment for a textile designer to carry out her occupation and professional activities. However, the gendered slant of the word will always carry with it this idea of excessive equipment, almost as if too much 'stuff' has been packed, insinuating that the task at hand is unknown and therefore the person must equip themselves with a variety of things 'just in case' – Aha – I have just the thing! – that the person is clueless about what might arise in the situation or activity they must engage in. This notion very neatly helps to explain the absolute necessity of these items to textile designers as they design. The historically female-gendered definition of the term helps to explain why these items aren't given a level of value and recognized purpose in design research literature.

After identifying these items as paraphernalia, can we continue to see the gathering of these items as an act of 'collecting'? Baudrillard describes collected items as 'loved objects' (Baudrillard 1968: 48), whereas Connor talks of 'magical things' that seem to say, 'play with me: try to make out what I might be good for'. Connor's 'magical things', or paraphernalia, are very much everyday items, and this type of item is not excluded by Baudrillard from his concept of 'loved objects'. Also, Baudrillard defines collecting as 'qualitative in its essence and quantitative in its practice' and suggests that collecting centres on both the feeling of possession and on the activities of 'searching, ordering, playing and assembling' (Baudrillard 1968: 50).

I find that textiles designers' 'collecting' for designing and studio or workshop 'collections' do not sit easily within Baudrillard's concept of collecting. Baudrillard's version involves the type of avid fanatic who creates an 'intimate series' with which they experience 'serial intimacy'. The textile designer's definition of collecting does seem more like an accumulation or a gathering of equipment and materials, principally because the aim of gathering these objects is purposeful.

A textile designer's paraphernalia is gathered with the rationale of providing for and nourishing an ongoing activity. Without making any facile connections to the archetypal prehistoric female gatherer, considering this type of collecting as some form of 'foraging' does help to explain its nature. The act of foraging originates from a need to deal with immediate requirements but also to cater for future needs and minimize the potential for deprivation. It connects with the notion of purposeful accumulation and hoarding. Foraging is adaptive. It takes place in rainforests and rubbish dumps and requires an understanding of the given environment, planning and timing, and often great skill, tenacity and courage. Foragers take and use only what they need from what is available in the act of satisfying essential needs. Foraging can be a singular or collective activity. Foraged items are often not enough in themselves but require some level of processing in order to make them useful: disassembly, and/or re-assemblage, in combination with other items (like cooking). Tom Fisher likens it to 'composting' in his chapter which explores some of his personal objects and their playful roles in the patterns of his life as a maker, designer, researcher and more.

The difficulty in extrapolating some definition of the act of gathering stuff for the purpose of textile design is that it seems to sit somewhere between Baudrillard's notion of collecting and that of foraging. Baudrillard makes the distinction between collecting and accumulating, saying that accumulation is an inferior stage of collecting and that it only starts when the collector discerns and discriminates between objects, in recognition of the objects' cultural meaning (Baudrillard 1968: 58). He also says that at some point a collection is called upon to take part in some form of exigency whereby it exerts its meaning, its message. Baudrillard asks, 'can man ever use objects to set up a language that is more than a discourse addressed to himself?' (Baudrillard 1968: 60).

It is this last question that explains the connection between collecting and foraging through the notion of paraphernalia. Collecting is a personal activity, and yet collections may hold other types and levels of meaning and value in a wider discourse and context. Foraged objects are by definition essential items with clear meaning and value. The term 'paraphernalia' allows objects to inhabit both of these of these scenarios. The exigency Baudrillard speaks of could be seen as the assemblage, processing or use of collected or foraged paraphernalia within the textile design process.

Playing with paraphernalia

Textile designers often describe how they play with materials, objects, paraphernalia in the act of designing. I wish to explore detailed definitions of playing and connect them with the ideas of gathering paraphernalia for textile design.

Johan Huizinga's 1938 (translated 1949) book *Homo Ludens* is the classic study of the play instinct and Huizinga's perceptions and definitions of play go some way in developing alternative understandings of playing as designing. Huizinga characterizes play as an activity which 'lies outside the reasonableness of practical life; has nothing to do with necessity or utility, duty or truth' (Huizinga 1949: 158), and yet it takes place within set boundaries and rules, intensely and utterly absorbing the player (Huizinga 1949: 32).

In 2008, I created a piece of work whose aim was to express the playful, interconnectivity of my creative thinking and my research process (see Figure 8). It references the House of Cards, a game designed for children by the Eames Office in 1952. The game is constituted of a number of slotted cards, each featuring imagery 'from the animal, vegetable and mineral kingdoms' (Eames Gallery n.d.).

The player can build a range of different structures by interlocking the cards as well as responding to the visual imagery on each card.

Figure 8 House of cards. Exhibited at Royal College of Art Work in Progress show (2008).

This combination of the visual and dimensional through play helps to visualize and make tangible the connection-making that is so much a part of the design thinking. The cards can be repositioned, forming different relationships and utilizing varying amounts of space. Often, the player will choose their favourite card first and subsequently that card goes on to become the foundation for the burgeoning structure.

In my version of the *House of Cards*, each card featured visual material that had been pivotal at different stages within my research at that stage. The house of cards was intentionally presented on a trestle table not unlike those used in a design studio or workshop. It served as a method for me to draw together, in a visual way, the different conceptual strands I had followed, and also for me to visualize the various types and areas of knowledge I had covered. The house of cards displayed the heuristics of my research process in a simple, visual way and is representative of the methodological bricolage approach I was utilizing. What are the benefits of using a game, something you play with, as a metaphor for cognitive structures formed during the process of design research and thinking? My house of cards, a generative structure, stands as a three-dimensional model of my experience of matrixial thinking. It is fragile, relies on interaction, and requires the player to think in three dimensions. The way the printed cards interlock and splice enmeshes the concepts in whichever way the player or viewer chooses. Presenting my research practice and thinking as a game allows others to literally play with my ideas, to build a new structure from them, to make alternative meaning from them. I referred to my own experience of playfulness in the early stages of designing and researching; in making this model I reflected this opportunity and encouraged it in others. The pleasure and success of building a house of cards is something that you can experience over and over again, although differently each time. Build it up, knock it down, build it up, knock it down.

> The satisfaction of gaining intellectual control over the external world is linked to a satisfaction of gaining control over ourselves. This urge towards this dual satisfaction is persistent; yet it operates by phases of self-destruction. This endeavour must occasionally operate by demolishing a hitherto accepted structure, or parts of it, in order to establish an even more rigorous and comprehensive one in its place. (Polanyi 1958: 196)

In the same sense that Huizinga describes play as something beyond necessity, Michael Polanyi, in his classic text *Personal Knowledge* (1958), talks about 'bursting the bounds of disciplined thought' (Polanyi 1958: 196) and relates this to seeking excitement through playfulness. He mentions a 'craving for mental dissatisfaction' (Polanyi 1958: 196) as a component of creativity, correlating with Huizinga's notion of tension in play. 'Baby reaching for a toy . . . to achieve something difficult, to end a tension' (Huizinga 1949: 29). Combining Polanyi's explanation of the compulsion towards playing for creative purposes and Huizinga's definition of play as characteristically voluntary and free, outside of and disinterested in ordinary life but simultaneously and necessarily limited and orderly (Huizinga 1949: 26–9), conjures up an image of an emotive, tacit, absorbing yet episodic activity that closely resembles the act of designing.

In the process of design, designers routinely manage an internal dialogue between their inner instinctual playfulness (the affective) and their disciplined thoughts; their understanding of the context for design encompassing technical, economic and other boundaries (the cognitive) is all driven by the conative.

The quote above connects Polanyi's work with Schumpeter's theory of creative destruction. In his 1942 book *Capitalism, Socialism and Democracy*, economist Joseph Schumpeter famously described the phenomenon of 'the perennial gale of creative destruction' to define the dynamics of industrial change and the transformation that often follows innovation. He depicts capitalism as a process that continuously reforms its own structure, 'incessantly destroying the old one, incessantly creating a new one' (Schumpeter 1942: 83). He also describes the agents of this creative destruction in the original text as 'Unternehmergeist' which refers to 'fiery souls' or 'spirits'. Creative destruction is a useful concept when exploring design cognition, as it places intellectual passions into a social, economic and industrial context. It describes the creative individual (as agent of capitalism) as one who craves newness and achieves it through destructive behaviour.

Baudrillard makes the connection between playing and collecting, describing how for children collecting is like a passionate game, a way of mastering the world, of arranging, classifying and manipulating (Baudrillard 1968: 48). Huizinga expands this notion of mastery by defining the function of play in two related ways. He describes it as a contest for something or a representation of something.

> These two functions can unite in such a way that the game 'represents' a contest, or else becomes a contest for the best representation of something. (Huizinga 1949: 32)

If play is an essential aspect of design methods, Huizinga's unified definition of play allows the existence of two versions of the design process. One of these is playing as contest, representative of the masculine transactional paradigm oriented towards design as solving problems; a second version focuses on representing, understanding and communicating in the most effective way: this would represent a feminine relational concept. Both design 'contests' are judged internally and externally to the designer, but in the first design contest the emphasis is on internal judgement. I feel that this design provides the best solution to the problem; I will offer this idea to the client. The second design contest places more emphasis on external judgement. All these designs could provide what is required. The client can select which of these designs works best for their needs. This second scenario is more closely aligned with the textile design process. Textiles seek to represent narratives, memories, emotion. Huizinga describes a child using representation as play:

> The child is making an image of something different, something more beautiful, or more sublime, or more dangerous than what he usually is . . . . His representation is not so much a sham-reality as a realization in appearance: 'imagination' in the original sense of the word. (Huizinga 1949: 32–3)

This connects to Polanyi's description of 'dwelling in and breaking out' as a means of working with intellectual passions (Polanyi 1958: 196) as well as the notion of play as a contest of representation. There are two aspects of this relationship which are significant: the cognitive processes that compel a designer to design and subsequently their approach to, and individual experience of, their design process.

It is established that there are three mental states: the cognitive, affective and conative (Huitt 1999; Gerdes and Stromwall 2008; Heylighen, Cavallin and Bianchin 2009). The conative can be described as volitional, the act of exercising will or desire. The etymology of conation is from the Latin *conari* (to try) (Gerdes and Stromwall 2008). In regard to the design process, this concept appears as a useful addition to our understanding of the goal of design, as the will or desire to try or attempt a transformation. Gerdes and Stromwall (2008) provide a history of the development of the conative, including the writings of William McDougall, who 'categorized the mind's components as cognition (a knowing, a thing), affective sensation (feeling something about that thing), and conation (a striving towards or away from the object)' (Gerdes and Stromwall 2008: 235). Lundholm (1934 cited in Gerdes and Stromwall 2008) pointed out that a conative process is best understood as one that impels action (drives it from within) while cognition and other outside forces compel action (drive it from external force or action).

Academic research into the conative tends to be discussed or applied in specific academic fields, such as child development and social work. Design is an activity that in varying degrees or phases requires all three mental states. Heylighen, Cavallin and Bianchin (2009) explain that the cognitive and conative can be seen as asymmetrical: the cognitive state aims at truth in order to fulfil beliefs, while the conative state aims to satisfy desire or will.

Heylighen, Cavallin and Bianchin (2009: 97) include a useful analogy that explains the phenomenon particularly well:

> If you believe that tomorrow will be a rainy day, you are ready to abandon the belief in case it turns out to be sunny. However, if you desire that tomorrow will be rainy, you are not necessarily ready to abandon the desire in case it turns out to be sunny: you might, but you are not irrational if you do not.

The conative is a search for a belief and the cognitive a search for truth. When considered in this way it would be easy to conclude that designing is heavily conative: as we survey and analyse existing objects, we imagine something new and set about making it, all the while involved in a chaotic and looping process of reflecting and perfecting. The designer believes (and capitalism encourages) that there is an alternative and strives to bring about that change. This helps to understand the imperative of designers as well as describing the nature or experience of the design process as desirous, not easily sated. Conative thought provides an explanation for the motivation, the attempt, but cognition and affect are applied throughout the design process and themselves give some context for rational and objective thinking (i.e. cost implications, choice of fabrication, suitability for customer or client) as well as those more connected to the subjective (i.e. haptic, aesthetic and intuitive choices) undertaken during the design process. At all times the three mental states are considered to be integrated and functioning. Thus, the notion of the tripartite brain provides us with some broader context for understanding how tacit knowledge and creativity engage during the design process towards the creation of designed objects.

One of the experiential elements of the design process that designers often relate to is the so-called creative leap. It is often compared to the 'eureka moment': an unexplained sensation bestowed as a reward for grappling with ideas. Dorst and Cross (2001) investigate creativity in the design process using quantitative research methods in the attempt to understand what is described as the 'creative leap'. They conclude by suggesting 'bridge building' as an alternative label for the leap. The analogy of 'bridge building' transforms the creative experience into an intentional and slower negotiated activity, perhaps involving a group of differently skilled people. However, in *Designerly Ways of Knowing* (2007), Cross describes it in a less structured way: 'throwing a bridge across the chasm between problem and solution' (Cross 2007: 78), an action more akin to building a rope bridge. This identifies the 'creative leap' as an opportunistic event that involves risk and complexity. Building a rope bridge requires tacit knowledge, embodied in intuition and a good aim so that the 'ropes' catch onto something on the other side. The initial 'throw' represents the conative aspects of the design process: once the first effort has been exerted it becomes an iterative process – the structure must be firmed up; the bridge-builder has to keep going over to each side to check strength. All the while a rope bridge remains a temporary structure, prone to instability that makes the act of traversing it, thrilling.

> I have crossed a gap, the heuristic gap which lies between problem and discovery .... We have to cross the logical gap between a problem and its solution by relying on the unspecifiable impulse of our heuristic passion, and must undergo as we do so a change of our intellectual personality. Like all ventures in which we comprehensively dispose of ourselves, such an intentional change of our personality requires a passionate motive to accomplish it. Originality must be passionate. (Polanyi 1958: 143)

The propulsion across a gap, as part of the bridge-building analogy for the creative leap, can be related to the concept of 'intellectual passion' as described by Polanyi. Intellectual passion provides an idea of the energy that propels designers across the heuristic gap described above. It is the personal passion to attain personal (tacit) knowledge towards intellectual beauty, while taking the risk that this passion may be misguided. Stefania Ruzsits Jha (2002: 130) clarifies Polanyi's intentions thus: 'Intellectual beauty is both that which is found by traversing the heuristic gap and the conative act.'

The creation of a more beautiful and enhanced representation of aspects of life and the world is the key aim of textile design. To create a visual and/or tactile representation of, say, a hyper-real floral display that rhythmically repeats unlimitedly, allowing the viewer and wearer to be consumed, is one of the pleasures of designing and wearing a printed fabric. The designer's tripartite cognitive function is exercised. The sense of enhancing an affect, experience or memory through cloth is often a key aim in textile design practice.

Poetic decorative

Textile designers see playfulness as a key characteristic of their design activity; Huizinga flatly refuted the notion of play in the context of the plastic arts, in contrast to music and poetry, which require performance. He grants that although the point of conceiving of a piece of art or design may feel free, the act of making it renders no scope for play.

> The man who is commissioned to make something is faced with a serious and responsible task: any idea of play is out of place . . . he has to make a vessel, a garment, an image, each of which may have to correspond to the idea it renders symbolically or in imitation. (Huizinga 1949: 191)

It appears that Huizinga here is referring only to the act of making to order, almost as manufacturing, and the activity of playful making within a subjective design process is not considered. He does later accept that designing or making art (specifically showpieces or masterpieces) does involve the element of contest, as discussed earlier. He does this by outlining a semantic link between ritual, art and play in the ancient Greek word *agalma*. Its primary meaning derives from the word *agallein*, 'to adorn' or 'to delight in', and refers to an ornament, showpiece, a precious object (Huizinga 1949: 192). He later says that a 'play sense' is involved in producing all forms of decoration – 'where the mind and hand move most freely' (Huizinga 1949: 227), referring to the innate urge to doodle and decorate a surface, but still minimizes the notion of play as a means to explain this activity.

However, by using the term '*agalma*' he puts emphasis on the use of decorative items for the purpose of play, even suggesting that these items are imbued with magical power and symbolic value. This returns me to Connor's explanation of paraphernalia as magical objects. The headscarves, the buttons, the old photographs, the examples of colour, the scraps of embroidery gathered by textile designers – these can be considered the *agalma*, the precious, magical objects, the paraphernalia of textile design as play.

The connection between poiesis as making and poetry is one that Huizinga clearly understands.

> In fact, the definition we have just given to play might serve as a definition of poetry. The rhythmical or symmetrical arrangement of language, the hitting of the mark by rhyme or assonance, the deliberate disguising of the sense, the artificial and artful construction of phrases – all might be so many utterances of the play spirit . . . . The affinity between poetry and play is not external only; it is also apparent in the structure of the creative imagination itself. In the turning of a poetic phrase, the development of a motif, the expression of a mood, there is always a play-element at work . . . the writer's aim, conscious or unconscious, is to create a tension that will 'enchant' the reader and hold him spellbound. (Huizinga 1949: 154–5)

Repetition, motif, expression of mood – all hallmarks of the visual language of textile design. The correlation between textiles, writing and making (Mitchell 1997) and the notion of textile design as a form of translating/transforming that I establish across the chapters of this book supports this understanding.

Playing and designing 'in real life'

Huizinga uses the term 'methectic' in contrast to the mimetic as he describes the sacred, ritualistic nature of playing (Huizinga 1949: 34). In considering methexis in play, those participating are a fundamental aspect of the playing, and the object of play is situated in a larger context or entity, which is collectively shared. The notion of methexis underlines play (and therefore designing) as inter- and trans-subjective, as described in matrixial, relational knowledge-making. Huizinga uses the metaphor of woven cloth to describe the interconnectedness of particular aspects of play:

> In nearly all the higher forms of play the elements of repetition and alternation (as in the refrain), are like the warp and woof of a fabric. (Huizinga 1949: 10)

Huizinga also suggests the social aspect of play, saying that it 'promotes the formation of social groupings which tend to surround themselves with secrecy and to stress their difference from the common world by disguise or other means'. 'This is for us, not for the "others". What the "others" do "outside" is no concern of ours at the moment . . . We are different and we do things differently' (Huizinga 1949: 12).

Playing as an enhanced, methectic representation of ordinary life, made up of elements of repetition and alternation, casts it, as Huizinga describes, as a form of poetics. He says that poiesis is a function of play which exists 'in the region of dream, enchantment, ecstasy, laughter' (Huizinga 1949: 141). This ancient Greek term, deriving from the verb 'to make'. Ettinger uses the term 'co-poiesis' to describe the trans-subjective matrixial encounter. By suggesting that textile design resembles a matrixial encounter, and therefore copoiesis – a 'making-in-partnership' (with the viewer or user) – in the secretive, poetic realm of pleasure that Huizinga describes both permits a recognition of the tacit relational knowledge and the subjective and often collective pleasure involved in the process of textile design. In my reading of *Homo Ludens*, the only aspect of textile design that disavows a definition of play is that it is functional, and the act of designing and making textiles exists in an industrial and/or commercial sphere, meaning that it does not operate in a truly free sphere of play. However, Huizinga himself says that play must always come to an end and becomes interrupted by ordinary life.

> The play-mood is labile in its very nature. At any moment 'ordinary life' may reassert its rights either by an impact from without, which interrupts the game, or by an offence against the rules, or else from within, by a collapse of the play spirit, a sobering, a disenchantment. (Huizinga 1949: 21)

These interruptions from ordinary life, in the context of play in design, take the form of a deadline, a technical issue, a bad decision or budgetary requirements. The purpose of the act of foraging/collecting paraphernalia for a textile designer is in preparation for play: to gather magical objects to nourish and be 'used up' in play as a methectic, representational contestable act that can be incited at any time by the designer themselves or a given brief or commission and stopped any time by external factors.

The ideas developed here through Baudrillard, Huizinga, Ettinger and Polanyi propose that textile design could be an activity in which the designer purposefully gathers and absorbedly plays with magical objects or paraphernalia. This is in the pursuit of affect – providing pleasure, expressing a mood, the representation of beauty or to end a tension, particularly when coupled with the notion of relationality and copoiesis. Simultaneously, the more common understanding and use of the concepts of 'paraphernalia' and 'playing' can immediately malign them through gendering and trivialization.

12

Patterns of objects

Tom Fisher

//In the attic:

A set of Lucite cutlery in their original purple card box, bought at a garage sale in rural Western Australia. The cutlery is of quite extravagant traditional shape; the box is slightly distorted with age.

A red vinyl 78 rpm record, in a leather-covered case of black shellac 78 records.

//in the kitchen:

A turned sycamore finial I made to go on the top of my wedding cake, briefly re-purposed as a toilet cistern pull. It worked well for both.

A turned sycamore finial from a bespoke cabinet.

Four turned sycamore feet from a bespoke cabinet.

//here and there, no fixed location:

an English hunting horn of indeterminate date, 200mm long. Much dented and repaired.

//in my university office:

a sycamore part-sphere made up of four segments; a sycamore miniature half-column, in two halves.

//buried:

A small ceramic bowl, containing a U shaped piece of brass tube stuffed with silver strands (15mm × 35mm × 13mm) and an old UK penny that is oval because it has been run over by a train.

This is a list of things that have persisted – they have stayed; been kept. I can relate them to different aspects of my life, as a child (the box of records I used to play in a damp house in northern Ireland, the hunting horn), as a furniture maker (the finials and feet), as a husband (the other cake finial), as an academic researching materials (the red 78; the Lucite cutlery), as a musician (the hunting horn), as an instrument maker (the buried spell). This chapter is about how I live with such objects, so it is about a self, myself. It responds to Chapter 11, *Paraphernalia and playing for design*, and I approach it both as an academic and as a maker, acknowledging that in respect of the themes I am responding to there may not be a useful distinction to be made between the two – many of the objects listed above belong in both 'worlds'. Just to hold this distinction in view for clarity though, the former attracts me to the abstract themes in the piece, ways of thinking about play and collecting, while the latter means I discuss some particular objects and personal experiences, relating the objects to those themes.

Many of the objects listed above originate in an earlier making career and are different in kind from the ones that Elaine talks about as part of 'paraphernalia'. Whereas those are objects found as stimuli, some of these are objects made as side effects from a materially engaged design and making practice. I am going to discuss two such objects in detail, the ones in my university office, that have been long-lived, accompanying me through several decades of academic life, tracking the arc of my making career. This is consequently a subjective piece, responding to Elaine's discussion of play and collecting, connecting particularly with the idea of 'paraphernalia' – those inalienable possessions that are simultaneously 'unnecessary and indispensable' that didn't have financial value, but existed to make a self. The objects I discuss are such things.

I am inspired by the writing of George Perec, among others. I cannot hope to match the wit and depth of his insights into our relationships with objects, their poetics, but I nonetheless hope that by approaching this writing as a maker with their work in mind I can engage with some of these things in a way that uses them to show how they work as part of my paraphernalia, and the subjective, reflective parts of my design process. In Perec's essay *Notes Concerning the Objects That are on My Work-Table* (1997) he uses the diverse ensemble of objects on his desk to let us understand something of the gentle connections that accrue between a person and particular things. He reflects on a process of sedimentation of relationships between a person and their material surroundings.

> A desk-lamp, a cigarette box, a bud-vase, a matchbox-holder, a cardboard box containing little multi-coloured index cards, a large carton bouilli inkwell incrusted with tortoiseshell, a glass pencil-box, several stones, three hand-turned wooden boxes, an alarm clock, a push-button calendar, a lump of lead, a large cigar box (with no cigars in, but full of small objects), a steel spiral into which you can slide letters that are pending, a dagger handle of polished stone, account books, exercise books, loose sheets, multiple writing instruments or accessories, a big hand-blotter, several books, a glass full of pencils, a small gilded wooden box. (Perec 1997: 146)

While I am motivated to understand such relationships with the objects I select here, these objects are different from those discussed by Perec in one crucial respect – I made them. I may have made them some time ago, but I have kept them close to the spaces I occupy day to day. This fact alone suggests that they play a role in my 'project of self', extended into objects (Belk 1990, 2001) and in some ways they illustrate that project but, up to now, I have not worried too much about what picture they form. Although they have been visible to others, in my office, around the house, displayed, usually quite casually, for others to see, the implications of their 'material community' has been implicit. In that sense they are private objects. Their 'community', to use Benjamin's word, includes objects of various materials. There are quite a lot of them, but for this essay I will focus only on two of them. Others are listed, in a nod to Perec, at the start of this piece.

Many, like the two I select, are wooden. Some are made of metal. Some are made of plastic. What are these two wooden objects? They are made of sycamore, made out of more than one component glued together. They are pale in colour, because sycamore is nearly white. The first is a wooden construction in the shape of the piece of skin left after the flesh is eaten from a segment of melon (Figure 9). It is made of four sycamore segments about 6 mm thick glued together along their long edges, each of which is a small version of the whole construction. The components differ from the whole in that they are of single curvature; in other words, they could be cut from the wall of a hollow cylinder. In combination they make an object of double curvature – like the segments of a globe or a hot air balloon. The whole is 150 mm long and 50 mm wide.

The second is a miniature half-column made of sycamore about 200 mm high and 40 mm wide, itself of two halves, each a quarter column (Figures 10 and 11).

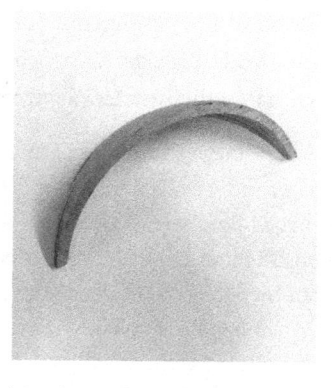

Figure 9 Image of melon-skin object. Source: Tom Fisher.

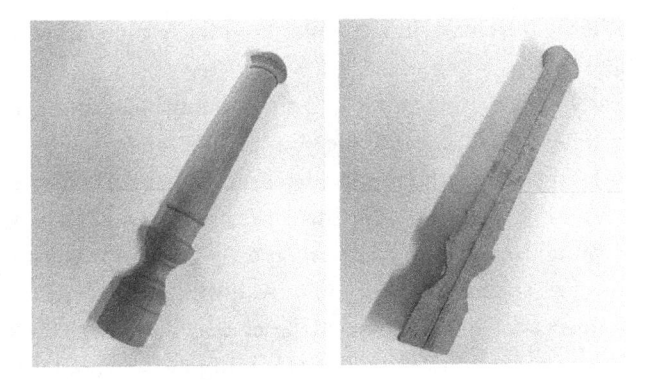

Figures 10 and 11 Images of half-column front and back. Source: Tom Fisher.

The glue joint between the two quarters includes a layer of newspaper. The 'missing' other half of the column was joined to its twin in the same way while the four pieces were turned to shape. The halves were separated along the plane of the glue/newspaper afterwards. The print on the newspaper is just legible, though reversed. On this flat paper surface there is written 'C3785Y' in faint pencil.

I made these objects between twenty-five and thirty years ago. Writing about them now means I have scrutinized them more closely and thought about them more deeply than at any time since I made them. Of course, doing this brings to mind memories of moments in my past, which may not be relevant to this piece, but it also presents some questions – about the objects themselves; about the consequences of focusing on them so closely; about the consequences of writing about them. It also brings up questions that relate to the themes that I pointed to above – are these objects the product of play? They have not served any instrumental purpose in thirty years. Are they part of a collection? I have kept them and displayed them. What do I achieve by writing about these things, as their maker? They have caused me to register their details and to recall the part they played in the work process that brought about.

To take the last question first, I hope that it is precisely because I made them that I can trace certain sorts of relationship with things in general, through these particular ones. It would be easy to suggest that the fact that I have brought these objects into physical being, and they have remained relatively private, give me rights over them in terms of the account I give of them. But this would be to overclaim. The copious literature generated by the 'material turn' in the humanities and social sciences, and its philosophical hinterland dubbed the 'new materialism', show that the being of objects is contested, it is common property

– we all have the right to make judgements about these 'material communities', and that makes sense.

Objects clearly have various aspects to their 'being'; Georges Perec, Walter Benjamin and Roland Barthes bring the objects they consider into a particular form of being by offering us their consideration of them. Thanks to Barthes's analysis of 1957, we can see the 1955 Citroen DS as the equivalent of a Gothic cathedral; we can appreciate a prayer written on a grain of rice for more than what it is thanks to Benjamin's account of it. And while what Perec and Barthes bring to their objects depends on their material actuality – Perec's small gilded wooden box has to be on his desk in order for him to write about it and the DS had to be visible to Barthes at the Paris motor show and on the streets – these are not arrangements of matter they have worked on directly. My objects are. I was in on the start of their biographies.

If I am to make sense of these objects as part of my paraphernalia I need to set out some of my biography. As a boy I was always keen to take things apart; I wanted to understand how things worked. But I wasn't great at science and maths, so my understanding was limited to what I could see and touch. I tried to understand a radio by removing its components one by one until it no longer worked, as if by this process I could find the one crucial, key, part that would explain the whole thing. I failed in that of course, though the radio . . . after a while it was no longer a radio.

I also took apart the musical instrument I was learning (a French horn) and successfully reassembled it. I studied art. I was better at drawing than at science and maths. I worked (untrained) as a joiner. I worked (trained) as a furniture designer and maker and it is from this period that the two objects I am discussing date. Then, after a period of combining it with an academic post, I gave up furniture design and making and researched materials (plastics) for a PhD while teaching product design. I have published several articles and books that draw on this research over the twenty years since. These relate to the emergence of interest in the human sciences in matter, objects. I started a Special Interest Group for the Design Research Society to help pursue that interest. I relearned the French horn. Again I took my instrument apart, this time modifying it and developing the skills of an instrument maker. I now make instruments for sale and collaborate on research about their performance and acoustics – the 'maker-self' represented by the two objects from my office has reasserted itself, in a particular articulation with both design as an abstract discipline and the study of 'matter' in the human sciences.

Attenuated though this description is, it indicates some of the points in time that are relevant to this story, some closer to and some more distant from the present. There are also spaces that fold into these objects' significance, some psychologically closer and some more distant from me – home, workplace, studio, workshop. The objects I am discussing belong in the past, really. In some ways they are what Elizabeth Shove calls 'fossils' (Shove and Pantzar 2005) – things that continue to exist, though the practice that gave them meaning has unravelled. Shove proposes that fossils are such in terms of social practice, whereas the practice that initially gave these objects meaning was an individual one – defined though it certainly was by shared expectations of utility, taste, economy and so forth. The practice that generated these objects certainly had the 'material/meaning/skill' components that make up a Shovian practice. These are once-meaningful components of a practice (of furniture design and making) that was my individual practice. Of course while such elements, such objects, must presumably exist for other people in their making practice, in Shove's terms they are 'situated' fossils, situated in my biography. They mark the lines I have taken through life, as Tim Ingold might put it (2007).

But they are strange. They remind me of the slightly spooky object that Kafka names 'Odradek' in his short story 'The Cares of a Family Man', from 1914 (1995). Odradek is a meaningless, subversive, but vital, object – always there, and tragically for the writer, likely to outlive him. Odradek is a bit of domestic material culture that gets in the way, threatens to destabilize the present – a fossil with agency. The two objects I'm discussing here are not meaningless (to me) but would certainly be so in my absence. The column is not a column. The text it carries is accidental and doesn't give it meaning other than by being indecipherable – faint and reversed. The writing on it is the code to a long-demolished workplace door. They have followed me about.

A collection or not?

Chapter 11 *Paraphernalia and playing for design* refers to the literature on collecting in discussing the material 'compost' of creative practice. I have kept these two objects some decades and keeping is necessary to collecting, whatever its purpose or meaning and they are two among a number of other objects I have also kept from that period. However, the terms that Baudrillard sets out for what items in a collection are, and their purpose as a collection, do not seem to fit these objects very well, perhaps because they are fossils. They are marooned, bereft of the practice that produced them. On the other hand, they are part of my paraphernalia, and have clear relationships to my identity as a maker – why else would I have kept them – and the key condition for them as being part of a collection, my existence, persists for now.

These objects are not part of a series, which according to Baudrillard's discussion of collecting as part of his 'System of Objects' (1968) means they cannot be a collection. Baudrillard's system is constrained by its attention to objects that are 'given', already part of the world of consumption, of goods. These are neither goods nor part of a series. Baudrillard also follows Freud by considering the fetish power that collections can have on their owner – these objects hold no particular power over me – there is no cathexis going on here – but I have kept them, so perhaps they are more significant than I realize.

Baudrillard assumes that objects are transformed by being collected, from being commodities to being 'possessed', and thereby possessing their owner as abstract elements in a series, defined only by their relationship to other objects in the series. He distinguishes such objects from those appreciated for themselves by connoisseurs. As he puts it 'in the passionate abstractness of possession, all objects are equivalent' (Baudrillard 1968: 88). The 'passionate play' he describes depends on the abstractness of the objects in play – this seems to lack the intense appreciation of and engagement with material qualities and potentials that characterizes creative material practice – a different sort of play.

He goes further, insisting the 'seriality' of objects as the defining feature of their objectness:

> [W]ithout seriality, no such play would be conceivable, hence no possession – and hence, too, properly speaking no object. A truly unique, absolute object, an object such that it has no antecedents and is in no way dispersed in some series or other – such an object is unthinkable. It has no more existence than a pure sound. Just as harmonic series, whatever their degree of complexity, brings objects up to their symbolic quality – carrying them, in the same movement, into the sphere of the human relationship of mastery and play. (Baudrillard 1968: 93)

This position is predicated on the absence of material engagement with the objects in question, their reduction to pure signs in a 'play of signification' as part of a series. This is play with objects as symbolic entities, not material entities, not the play of the maker. His reference to harmonic systems demonstrates his emphasis on pre-existing systems into which objects can be fit and misses the possibility that they may relate to emergent systems to which they might contribute.

He does identify a class of objects that are the obverse of those in a collectable series, which he calls things with 'practical specificity' (Baudrillard 1968: 93) – that is, particular things, for particular purposes. But it is characteristic of the objects I am concerned with here, and perhaps all elements in creative paraphernalia, that they don't (yet) have 'practical specificity' – they aren't for any particular purpose, though their origin may have been in purposeful actions or thoughts. And neither are they part of a series that can render them 'possessed objects' in his sense, with which I can play as a series, to show I am in charge. They are more mystifying, more Odradek-like, more material, more specific, more unsettling.

To say that they are playful does on the other hand ring true. They have been rendered the objects they are (partly) by accident, without intention; they aren't the answer to any question, rather the nearest they ever came to having a function was to help me in some sort of (long redundant) conversation with myself about formal, material, processual possibilities. They are reminders of those conversations, traces of them. But they are fossils in Shove and Pantzar's sense because the conversations that animated them are long silent.

Are they playful?

There does seem to be a relationship between the objects I am discussing here and the reference in Chapter 11 to play and playfulness. Alongside the copious academic literature on play, it is useful to think about everyday ideas about playing. Playing is not serious, so perhaps I made these objects while 'playing about', or more pejoratively 'messing about'. But I can't have been 'messing', since they came about in a craft process that includes using woodworking machines that can amputate digits in a blink and hand tools sharp enough to shave with. It is not sensible to mess with such things. You don't play with them.

So far, I have retained all my digits, so I clearly don't mess with the processes that produce these objects. But the actions that produced these objects did combine freedom from constraint in intrinsically motivated exploration with social rules that made the exploration meaningful, elements that are delineated in the academic study of play. As Brian Sutton-Smith puts it in a light-hearted 'quote': 'Play is intrinsically motivated, except if you don't do what the others tell you, they won't let you play' (1979: 173). Academic studies of play have tended to be sociological, to have related the actions and experiences of the playing self to the game they are participating in, for all that this participation is considered 'playful' by virtue of being intrinsically motivated. This sets communal play against individual play, though there are rich accounts of the individual subject's experience of playful states – Mihalyi Csikszentmihaly's encapsulation of this experience as a 'flow' state being the best known (1979).

Flow doesn't assume a distinction between work and play – work can include flow states, though this somewhat contradicts the idea of 'free' play of the 'creative' individual. Exploring the 'rhetorics' of play in our culture, Brian Sutton-Smith identifies this idea as an element in the Western, romantic, notion of the individual, from which are drawn many of our ideas about what creative people are like (Fisher 1995, 1997). To pursue these ideas in terms of these objects it may be helpful to think in detail about the processes that brought one of them about.

The part sphere is made of offcuts that I produced in the process of making a furniture component on a table saw. The component was geometrically a little complex – it was a semi-circular strip of sycamore about 6 mm thick tapered, so its depth at the tips was about 4 mm and in the centre of the curve about 15 mm. Before producing the offcut from the tapering process, I had produced the semi-circle. To produce the taper, the saw had to be set at an angle and the semi-circle passed over it. It was an inherently risky process because the shape was unstable and I can no longer remember how I minimized the risk, but I do remember the sense of triumph when I achieved a set-up that allowed me to make useable components.

The blade was rotating at 3,000 rpm or so. My fingers were within inches of it. I focused on self-preservation and used all my skill as a wood machinist, my intimate knowledge of my table saw, its blade and the set-up I had created to guide the work and avoid inadvertent amputation. So when I produced the offcuts, I was not playing. I was not 'messing about' – but my subjective state certainly had many of the elements present in play, according to the theory. I was intrinsically motivated; I was completely absorbed and in the deepest of flow states; I experienced a strong sense of joy when the rules that I had set up for these actions produced the result I wanted – when I 'won' the game that I had created, solitary though it was. There are other ways in which the actions I took that day to produce components for furniture that I would later be paid for were 'playful'.

In his discussion of the rhetorics of self that influence our ideas about play, Sutton-Smith refers to phenomenological perspectives on the subject, particularly Gadamer's. There is a strong affinity between that perspective and my experience as I set it out (as an example) above. I entered the game with the sycamore, the saw blade, the push stick . . . the motor, the dust extractor, the workshop – there was no obvious edge to the players who were active in the game, but it was a game, nonetheless. Having entered it, being in it, the game played me. Alongside the intense involvement it required, the rules that made it seem a closed and perhaps limiting game, but one that permitted and perhaps made possible the sort of speculation and delight that meant the offcuts became something else, a play object.

Gadamer refers to play as a 'to and fro' movement which is not tied to any goal which would bring it to an end' referring to the origin of the German 'spiel' in 'dance', and as Sutton-Smith puts it (2001: 183), the game 'frees you from yourself by binding you to another'. This paradox of limited freedom was certainly there in the making process that produced these two objects; it involved play, but not the apparently free play of leisure, rather the play of a certain type of work – work in particular (and exceptionally fortunate) conditions. I did not transition between a state of 'working' which produced the strange-shaped offcuts and 'playing' when I assembled them into the part sphere. All the actions in the game relied on all the others; they couldn't be separated, though they can clearly be distinguished.

So even the play of the creative maker follows its own rules. The playful edge of material practice involves 'stuff' that can hurt you if you don't keep focused and it also provides a more obviously playful excess, where wonderment and delight become prominent in this playful dance with materials. When I made the half-column I was perhaps more clearly playing, though perhaps experimenting would be more accurate. The experiment was to see if it was possible to make a half-column by gluing the wood together with a deliberately weak joint containing paper. It turned out that it was possible; the experiment was successful. I was also playing with shapes, with form, in the very direct way that is possible only in the process of shaping wood on a lathe. I was doing some design work through materials.

The material determined what was possible in a playful dance with my skill as a turner, my thoughts about the dining table I had in mind, the clients for it, the motifs that seemed appropriate. And I was clearly taken by the result of these more or less speculative actions – I held on to the result for thirty years. This seems the more obviously playful element in the trajectory of this object – the fact that I ended up with a curious shape, one surface covered with unreadable writing, perhaps a little reminiscent of a Dada object. This is not an unreasoned object – it resulted from a series of purposeful steps – but it is perhaps unreasonable, playful, to have kept it for so long, so close at hand, close enough to hand to have used it as a piece of note paper when I needed to remember the code to a door. This is an object that came from 'work' but exists in 'play'.

It is important to remember the conditions of work in which it came about. I may have been selling my labour to my clients, but this was not the alienated or estranged labour that Marx (2007) identified as characteristic of modern economies. As Marshall Berman (1982: 97) puts it, Marx 'proclaims, as the truly human alternative to estranged labour, work that will enable the individual to freely develop his physical and spiritual [or mental] energies'. My labour as a furniture maker was exceptional for our times in not being 'estranged'. Although I would have denied it at the time, the playful nature of these two objects demonstrates that I was not a worker in the sense of Marx's critique, but an artist in the modern sense, a member of a group that is allowed a greater degree of autonomy than is the norm and is defined by the Western tradition of a bounded self, responsible for its own playful states.

The objects show that the results of my work were not taken from me, but defined me, or as Marx put it:

> The object of labour is, therefore, the objectification of man's species-life: for he duplicates himself not only, as in consciousness, intellectually, but also actively, in reality, and therefore he sees himself in a world that he has created. (Marx 2007 [1844])

Through these objects, I have told myself who I am. My decision to keep them around me, as part of my paraphernalia, relates to my evolving sense of myself as a maker/designer as I have moved between the worlds of making practice and academia. On the face of it, these are quite different worlds, and certainly I found some strain in the adjustment from being a self-employed artist to an academic salaryman. The two objects I discuss above originated in the former life, but I chose to carry them into the latter, to tell others something about me. However, recently, I have come to realize that there is no clear distinction between the two 'worlds', and I have never believed there is a hierarchy. The qualities embodied in me that led me to make these objects, which meant I could make them and are therefore embedded in them (Fisher and Botticello 2018), do not divide into either cognitive or motor capacities. They do not map neatly on to a distinction between my work as a maker and as an academic; they are multiple and are enfolded with each other.

I can trace this enfolded complexity through the other objects in the longer list that starts this piece and realize that their relevance to me relates to an element of the ontology of any design or making practice – it's necessary connection to time – and that this infects the historical aspects of my academic interests. Our material focus gives us a distinctive relationship to the change we are involved in bringing about, albeit that this is most often small in scale. So, the red vinyl 78 record stands out from its shellac companions because of its colour, and also because it marks a moment in the history of plastics, as does the Lucite cutlery. These examples perhaps have an obvious connection with an academic interest in the history of design, whereas the tube stuffed with silver and then hidden is more abstract, and personal, in its relation to my biography.

Mesh four

I wanted to just use textiles to translate visual effects, not on paper or via paintings but in fabric. I never really went in the direction of trying to find solutions for anything or solving a problem. Textiles draw on questions rather than trying to answer problems. Following the gaps rather than a strategic line, I guess. But you are having to respond to a brief, as open as the brief may be. I wouldn't say that I solve problems, only my own problems. I wish in a way we did . . . . I wish problem-solving was more relevant in textile design. It's intriguing and I love the idea that we're capable of solving problems, even now, while technology is so advanced we're still finding problems to solve, but I don't think in textiles it's always the same kind of thing.

I suppose in, like, product design you're thinking about a need for something. I suppose right now we're thinking much more about kind of the future and things like sustainability obviously is, you know, huge, and . . . finding ways of . . . harnessing energy or solar energy through textiles . . . . I think potentially the kind of next five to ten years could be incredibly important for the textiles because of all those possibilities. Does that answer the question – no?

I guess in my situation the problem for me is that I like certain materials and they act in a certain way and everyone expects them to act in a certain way – how can I challenge that and make it act in a completely different way? I've got my own problem in my own mind with this material. I guess it's searching for a problem rather than encountering an actual problem. I guess a lot of the attraction to textiles, working in textiles, is that you're kind of making things for yourself. Sometimes when I'm weaving I do have a certain . . . . I do have an image of somebody that I could see wearing it. Somebody I might know, or somebody hypothetical . . . but I'm not doing it specifically for them.

My old tutor would always say 'everything is textiles'. The whole question of what is textiles – it is massive. Because I'm stitching on wood that's understood as a textiles process and therefore it doesn't matter that it's on wood, it's seen as textiles. But laser cutting into metal or experimenting with unconventional materials, that's not always seen as textiles because it's not a traditional textiles technique. I can see anything as textiles . . .

I think most textile designers in the industry and studios tend to see things much more from the aesthetic – what it looks like and maybe not beyond that. We think about colour and pattern from the beginning but everybody else doesn't. It's something they stick on afterwards and it shouldn't be that, it should be integrated . . . you know, if you go back to tribal ways of adorning ourselves they built their buildings in a pattern and it was all part of the same thing. When you think about, you know, the notion of pattern and of decoration, also surface texture if you're thinking about weave and knit, that's part of the pleasure, isn't it, the sensorial kind of concept . . . to build into a chair, to clothing or whatever. My understanding of textile design it's not just cloth, the surface, and it can be graphic, it can be textural, you can concentrate on the actual engineering behind it but to me it's always quite important that the outcome (I'm going to say beautiful and it might not be the right word) but the article has to be visually appealing, I just feel that within the process you're not thinking that much about beauty, necessarily. But if it doesn't emerge at the end, something has gone wrong. I mean, the thing is that in the end, the textile designer, designer being the operative word, brings, you know . . . the aesthetic that they're kind of developing is so, so important, you know. Even if it's all-singing, all-dancing and it does amazing, has amazing, kind of, properties and it forms in all sorts of extraordinary ways, if it doesn't look good, if it doesn't look like somebody wants to buy it or wear it or sit on it or surround themselves by it then what's the point?

I need to find it fulfilling, I'm not sure if I'm too worried about what other people think but I have to feel in tune with it. I want to focus on the actual technique and the piece and what that is, rather than, like, what's it going to go on to be used for. It does seem very self-indulgent that you do stuff and you don't really know what it's for. It's not necessarily a product or it's not functional in the sense that you can do things with it – you can put it on the wall but . . . . I don't know. It's slightly different in textiles, you see, we're not given a brief. It's the only industry, in design, where we're actually not given a brief by a customer and we interpret that brief. So yes, of course we're thinking differently. We must be approaching things differently because we're not coming at this from an angle of which new product do we need to develop, it's more about possibilities – it's more open-ended, isn't it, starting with textiles. Most industries, you know, if it's graphics you're told what they want you to design for, or an architect you want a building for, or a ceramicist, you want a set of china for. But as textile designers in the textile industry in the way it's working now is the most daft situation – you do the stuff in the way that a fine artist does stuff, and then you go out and you say: 'What do you think – do you want to buy it? Is it right for you or is it not?' If something's not right then it tends to be just discarded and we normally would design more than we need. I'd say probably almost at least double what we need.

So, it's a very bizarre situation . . . although I think I would probably never have pursued the notion of designing on paper very far had it not been for the extension of the idea into fabric and then the things that you could do having done that. It made you feel like you were a whole rather than just a part which then whatever you were producing went out into this industry and then you never saw it again, or maybe you did, but rarely. Although, I think I'd find it very, very difficult to just have a lovely, beautiful pile of fabrics – I would need to see what they looked like – resolved. It's a sad thing about textiles; the general public don't have the imagination to understand it without the product. If you just have flat fabrics people can so easily just walk past it or just ignore it just because people don't understand what it's for. By definition textiles needs something else. I think you just need to find a way to . . . find either the people or, yeah, I think you need to find the people who can look at your idea and find a use for it. I don't think that we need to necessarily know what to do. So, whether that means working with somebody else – either working with a, you know, someone in product design or in fashion, or just, you know, trying to sort of do that bit myself. It can be difficult though, often designers of clothing have their own ideas as to what fabrics they want to use and I very much had my own ideas as to what prints I wanted to put onto fabrics and the colours. Although, I'm not very good at applying my ideas to a useable thing.

I do think textiles is so fabulous. To be able to make things that are so beautiful. I mean art that you are wearing, or you are looking at as your curtains or whatever. So somebody can give me a kimono shape or an A-line dress or something really, really bog standard, normal pattern and your job is to make that into something that is fantastic and worth a fortune. Finding new ways of doing things. You have to keep giving yourself problems to find ways to move it on. And I think it's magic that you can sit there for a couple of hours and do something and it becomes worth something. The thing is changed totally.

It's funny, isn't it, because I think in the high-street scenario in a sense you're a problem solver in that you've got a kind of gap to fill. Okay we need a print for this story so you produce to order and I think that's wrong. That kind of goes against my grain in that sense, in that you're just filling in a box. Paint by numbers. Everything has to be fast but look expensive. At least, I suppose you're getting to see it develop from concept through to finished thing; you're getting the kind of feedback from the sales and you're kind of seeing the bigger picture. I think that's what textiles designers are able to . . . . I don't know, I think it's interesting because they're . . . they're very often creating their own brief aren't they and they're kind of setting out the series of question or problems for themselves, instead of that being imposed on them. I don't know, it's . . . it's a slightly different kind of way of approaching it. I think the other areas are more about problem-solving than we are. We just make things a bit more visual and you can kind of really make a statement with it or it can be hardly noticeable. I guess it's a slight challenge sometimes to kind of fit things together as a repeat and so I do quite enjoy that process. Definitely on some level it solves problems, even if the problem is just to make something superficially nicer that's solving it in itself. I think this engaging with the person that's seeing it is important. But I definitely think they can be kind of mood-enhancing as well, a beautiful print can kind of change the way you feel so I suppose that's why we have so much kind of print in our homes, yeah, it can give you almost a feel-good factor, I suppose.

But the whole making of beautiful fabrics isn't a fluffy thing. It's really not. I think we're are about discovery and innovation. And it's that that we've got to sell. Often my process, it's not structured or pretty-looking, it's not a pretty sketch book, it's very messy . . . you get a product at the end of it but the process is lost while doing it. It doesn't matter.

An engineer or a scientist will, kind of, reflect a lot on their work and spend a lot of time, kind of, looking and thinking about things before doing things. Because I'm very much a doer, very practical and hands-on, which comes from my creative side, I kind of, use design-speak and transfer the engineering knowledge, to maybe people who are more likely to use it, right down to people who are actually designing the products.

In a way, textiles don't need to be designed. Because textiles . . . it's a default. And organizing that default is something we are doing here, yes.

I think what's happening now is that in a way I think we are starting to . . . rather than just producing stuff, which I think, you know, can happen in textiles, has happened in textiles, I think there is much more reasoning and consideration in there and I think you know, if that's problem-solving then I think there is more of that now and it's important to have much more awareness of context and how the work is going to be used, how the textile is going to be used, what's it for. The danger is that if you don't think about the problem-solving bit, the ultimate kind of goal, then you know you just kind of produce things and it doesn't get pushed and pulled and challenged in ways that it is challenged if you're thinking about applying it to the side of the building or you know or applying it to soft furnishings or all those different kind of diverse possibilities, so . . . I suppose the textile designer is setting those problems for themselves, it's not like somebody's coming along and saying: okay design a new kettle that does these kind of . . . fits these functions. So yes, so it is still a very kind of broad thing but they are setting themselves some challenges I think, more than problems, maybe. Maybe it's not so much about kind of problem-solving but it's about you know challenging and by putting it in those different contexts it kind of challenges what the textile is and where it goes and how it lives on and doesn't kind of end up as a little swatch in a portfolio. Another bit of stuff.

13

Making, problems and pleasures

The notion of the 'design problem' is in some cases, and in particular fields of design, interchangeable with the 'design brief'. In equal measure, providing 'solutions' is often seen as the purpose, or goal, of design, which then becomes the tangible designed outcome of design thinking and process. One of the key principles of mainstream design research is that design thinking deals with, and in, ill-defined problems (Newell and Simon 1972).

Cross states that designing is not normal problem-solving but that it involves 'finding', 'structuring' and 'formulating' problems, as well as solving them. He identifies that designers deal with 'ill-defined' problems and, in reality, designers usually begin the design process without fully defining the problem. He cites Thomas and Carroll's 1979 study which concludes that even when well-defined design problems are delivered to them, designers would treat them as if they are ill-defined and take liberty in transforming those given problems (Cross 2007: 100), remarking that designers behave as designers, even when they could be problem solvers. If this is so, I question the persistence of these terms of 'problem' and 'solution' within design research.

Kauffman (1991: 45) distinguishes different qualities of ill-defined problems for design thinkers. He notes that there may be aspects of 'novelty, complexity and ambiguity' involved in the problem, and that problems can also be 'deceptive'. He states that 'the difficulties observed in these tasks may often be aptly described as related to a too narrow problem space, where the problem solver has to enlarge the space and see new possibilities in order to succeed in solving the problem'.

He goes on to explain that ambiguous ill-defined problems require the problem solver (designer) to choose between 'different kinds of problem spaces that are conflicting alternatives', and the 'deceptive problem' presents the problem solver with a wrong or false problem space, one that could not yield a solution.

Kauffman reiterates the notion that when dealing with ill-defined problems it is often necessary to rethink or reform the problem by 'adding, removing or rearranging stimuli' from the problem space.

In Chapter 4, *Design, Thinking and Textile Thinking*, I outline how Moxey (2000) and Studd (2002) discuss notions of problem spaces within textile design and propose conceptualizations of 'triggers' for textile design practice that seeks to solve design problems in a commercial context.

> [T]he designers got fidgeting after trivial novelties; change for the sake of change; they must needs strive to make their woven flowers look as if they were painted with a brush, or even sometimes as if they were drawn by the engravers burin. This gave them plenty of trouble and exercised their ingenuity in the tormenting of their web with spots and stripes and ribs and the rest of it. (Morris 1882)

As William Morris describes, technical restrictions certainly provide specific design problems, and often frame the scope of the outcomes of textile design, forcing compromises and innovation, but these are merely technological problems that are different from the design problems that are discussed at length in academic design research (Cross 2007: 99), and that I wish to pursue here.

The concepts of design problems and solutions have been well explored within design research, supporting the idea that designers operate in particularly uncertain situations, relying on their skills. of 'abductive' reasoning. Cross (2011: 27) cites C. S. Peirce when he describes abduction as hypothesizing what may be – an act of proposing and conjecture – and draws on work from Lionel March, developed from C. S. Peirce, which defines this as a 'particular logic of design that provides the means to shift and transfer thought between the required purpose or function of some activity and appropriate forms for an object to satisfy that purpose' (Cross 2011: 10).

Alternative ways of considering problem-solving in design have been put forward that attempt to better represent how the nexus of the ill-defined design problem, the subjectivity of designers and the uncertain context operate together within the design process. Clive Dilnot proposes 'positing' as an alternative description for the act of designing (Dilnot 1982). Kauffman argues that creative thinking is more closely related with constructing problems than problem-solving. Kauffman, writing on creativity, introduces the idea of the 'constructed problem' (Kauffman 1991: 59). Where there may be 'consistently reinforcing' conditions maintaining a status quo, constructed problems can form. In creative thinking, an individual compares the existing conditions with a hypothetical future scenario that offers improvements on a current situation.

Beginning to understand a designer's approach to dealing with design problems may also elucidate an understanding of the designer's relationship with the outcomes of their design thinking and process. If we believe that designing involves constructing problems and positing hypothetical solutions in the way outlined above then both the approach to the design problem and the designed outcome embody the designer's personal impetus for designing: their conation, with the emphasis constantly shifting in a dialectic, chicken-and-egg-type scenario.

When I first began to read into design research literature, I experienced real difficulty in relating to the idea of a design problem, to which, as a designer, I should develop a solution. These terms had never been used within my design education or in professional work contexts. I reflected that either the discourse was overlooking my experience as a textile designer or that textile design was rejecting or neglecting the invitation to take part in it. Design problems for textile designs are not just ill defined but unknown, at best entirely tacit. Concepts of human problem-solving were developed within psychology and the cognitive sciences and have historically varied between the principles of behaviourism (with a focus on changes in external behaviour to solve problems) and gestaltism (focusing on whole-form perception of problems). Newell and Simon (1972) famously classified well-defined and ill-defined problems differentiating between the types of cognitive processes required to deal with each category. Research into human problem-solving emphasizes the fact that it is an innate human cognitive activity, traceable to prehistoric people. My difficulty is not with the concept of problem-solving but with the mechanistic, transactional language that often surrounds it within the design research field. The persistence of this language, coupled with the various representations of the design process as an enclosed cycle (Dubberly 2004), means there is little space to explore alternatives languages and concepts of design.

Studd's use of the term 'trigger' (Studd 2002: 43), which in her terms stands in for the design problem for textiles, is interesting, but, I feel, flawed. Triggering could provide some coverage of both behaviourist conditioning and Gestaltist perceptual views of problem-solving. I envisage an athlete at the starting blocks. They have mentally and physically prepared for this moment. They are conditioned to physically react to the sound of the gun firing, but mentally they focus on holding a visualization of the race, rather than first getting off the blocks and then taking each stride. The idea of one kind of behaviour being transformed by a trigger connects to notions of collecting and foraging for paraphernalia, the designer preparing himself or herself for the inevitable moment when the trigger initiates. Triggers can initiate generic linear and automatic responses – a bullet emerging from a gun, or the start of a race – but triggers can be highly personalized, causing unexpected subjective results, like allergic or emotional reactions. However, the separation between the trigger and the reaction or behaviour it initiates is problematic. Triggers cannot be affected by what follows them. They do not provide the means to illustrate the notion of a problem space and how the designer or the context can affect the problem. Triggers stimulate a reaction rather than a response, which is the case in problem-solving. I have explored notions of 'responding' in regard to the comparison of textile design to feminist translation theory which arose from talking to textile designers. In this context, design problem-solving becomes a responsive dialogue, not a transactional activity (see Chapter 5).

Supporting this view, in both his 2007 and 2011 books Cross describes the complex co-evolution of problems and solutions in design (Cross 2007: 102; 2011: 123). Ettinger's concept of the matrixial provides a critical framework for this co-evolution. Griselda Pollock discusses Ettinger's theories in a way that could easily express the dialogic relationship of problem and solution within the process of designing:

> [T]he boundaries between subject/object (subjects and their objects), or presence/absence, are not absolute. They are borderlines that become borderspaces which we begin to sense when aesthetically confronted with their workings. (Pollock 2008: 486)

This statement can be used to propose some new terminology for design research that avoids positivism and recognizes the intuitive, subjective behaviour and cognition that designers use. If 'problems' and 'solutions' co-evolve their boundaries are unclear, which renders their existence shifting and indistinct – (border)lines which expand into (border)spaces, once processed (through design cognition). Considering the problem and solution not as a pairing but as a dynamic collaboration represented as lines expanding and evolving into space, exposing 'their workings', for me relates in some ways to the sequence of hand-spinning fibre into yarn which is then used for weaving. Fuzzy fibres are gradually pulled, twisted and spun into a line, which may or may not then be plied to create a yarn. The yarn (the line) is then woven or knitted (expanded into space). Tim Ingold's exploration of weaving as the foundation of making (and design) (Ingold 2000: 346–7) refers to the concept of 'world-weaving' from the Yekuana tribe of southern Venezuela. Through this Ingold sets up a relationship between weaving and making knowledge. Ingold's metaphorical 'weaving' weaves a world of experience that is 'continually and endlessly coming into being as we weave' (Ingold 2000: 348). In Ettinger's words, it is co-emergent. Viewing the co-evolving design problem and solution (and additionally, through Ingold's lens, making) as the process of spinning and weaving, lines expanding into space, represents design as a continuously divergent activity.

Metaphors of textile processes and objects, with their adaptive tendencies and abilities to systematically expand beyond previous framing and limits, are an excellent metaphor for this. Fibre becomes a thread or yarn through the orifice of the spinning wheel, a yarn is knitted or woven into cloth on the loom as 'portal' or 'aperture' (Pajaczkowska 2005), then pieces of cloth are sewn together with thread or yarn through the focus of a frame or hoop, offering unlimited potentiality. The concept of continuously and endlessly expanding lines, which I suggest here as a metaphor for designing, an activity which co-evolves design problems and solutions, renders any closed, looping or cyclical model of the design process inappropriate. This paradigmatic patchwork quilt-in-progress is like an interconnected Deleuzian plateau, 'a continuous self-vibrating region of intensities whose development avoids any orientation towards a culmination point or external end' (Deleuze and Guattari 1980: 24).

An infinite, soft, matrixial material represents the expansive, divergent nature of design thinking; but how does this relate to the process of designing? Ingold, by observing the development of natural forms, highlights three key insights into the activity of making, and weaving as the foundation for making. First, that making has a narrative quality, with each action, movement and line building on the previous. Second, that making does not only come about through the exertion of external force on a material but requires care, judgement and dexterity. And third, that making is predicated by the 'field of forces' set up by the relationship between the maker and his or her engagement with the material.

Applying Ingold's essay on making to design, in the first case, reiterates what has just been discussed here, the dialogical, narrative and expansive characteristics of designing. His second point recognizes the impact of the subjectivity of the designer, their expertise and specific, general and tacit knowledge they hold. His third point illustrates the complexity of the context of designing, with forces impacting on designing and making. The divergent nature of designing can be seen to operate within a field of forces. What I also enjoy about Ingold's three points is that they allow scope not only to understand how designers think and work with and through actual materials in the co-evolution of the problem and solution but also to see the problem/solution pairing as a meta-material that the designer must cognitively grapple with. They must carefully, judiciously and dexterously, yet subjectively and narratively, engage with it in the context of the field of forces. This scenario reminds me of Gaston Bachelard's concept of 'the ideal paste' – a putty, a dough, a clay, incidentally which Steven Connor references as an ultimate plaything. Connor describes how we play with an ideal paste to get a sense of its give, stretch and variability, 'to see how much play it possesses', potentially to the point of destruction (Connor 2011: 5).

> A multiplicity has neither subject nor object, only determinations, magnitudes and dimensions that cannot increase in number without the multiplicity changing in nature (the laws of combination therefore increase in number as the multiplicity grows) . . . It might be objected that its multiplicity resides in the person of the actor, who projects it into the text . . . . An assemblage is precisely this increase in the dimensions of a multiplicity that necessarily changes in nature as it expands its connections. (Deleuze and Guattari 1980: 9)

A paste is a multiplicity, its very materiality poses the 'problem' and yet also possesses immeasurable 'solutions', through its sticky malleability. Intangible pastes invite interaction and playing. So perhaps designers could be said to deal with intangible pastes that contain problems and solutions? What occurs within design is, then, a transformative playful encounter over time between problem and solution, involving the context, designer and any other external factors. Its imperceptible surface is delicately but irredeemably imprinted with the subjectivity of the designer. What is done with the intangible paste can improve on what already exists (like putty or adhesive) or create new things (like dough or clay). What is problematic in this scenario, for the purposes of design research, is that the cognitive processing associated with design becomes very hard to trace, because playing with the intangible paste is instinctual and tacit, involving poesis and praxis. Its conceptual form, as is the case for any thought, naturally shifts continuously and can never return exactly to its original state. They are 'soft logics'.

Pennina Barnett, in her paper *Textures of Memory: The Poetics of Cloth* (1999), relates, through the work of Michel Serres and others, the principles of 'soft logics' to Deleuze and Guattari's concepts of smooth (a felted surface) and striated (a woven surface) space, as well as pleating and folding. Barnett's essay has been fundamental in drawing these theories together to expand understandings of textile thinking, but in regard to textile designing it requires further evaluation. Serres's notion of box-thinking versus sack-thinking in his definition of soft logics immediately defines textiles, 'the soft', as an object, a product, a sack. A metaphorical textile has been woven, cut, then stitched together. Yes, it is still soft, foldable and recursive, but it has been processed or 'resolved'. In soft logics such as sack-thinking, what is woven suddenly becomes a series of manageable bags – not the infinite soft matrix previously discussed. It implicates Deleuzian theories of folding and unfolding as cognitive mechanisms but does not support the continuity of 'world-weaving', an infinite matrix or multiplicities of plateaus as a metaphor for design thinking. How to fold something that is continuously evolving?

> Folding-unfolding no longer means tension-release, contraction-dilation, but enveloping-developing, involution-evolution . . . . The simplest way of stating the point is by saying that to unfold is to increase, to grow; whereas to fold is to diminish, to reduce, 'to withdraw into the recesses of a world'. (Deleuze 1988: 8)

Deleuze states that folding and unfolding work not in opposition but in unity: his definition calls to mind the folding and unfolding of a narrative. With the comparison between narrative and textile weaving already set up by Mitchell and Ingold, we can see this as the expansion of a textile-in-the-making. Folding as thinking is a provoked, experimental and space-giving activity occurring within an encounter: new concepts unfold in the process (Barnett 1999). Barnett uses an example of a baker kneading dough, and I wish to continue it to explore the relationship between design cognition and the design process. Here, the dough is the intangible paste of the design problem/solution – the soft matrixial material. Through the activity of kneading, punctuated by stretching and proving (folding and unfolding), the dough processes and expands the matrix. Eventually this procedure is truncated by the 'field of forces', the requirement for this dough to become something else: either it dries out or it must be baked. The smooth gives rise to the striated (Deleuze and Guattari 1980: 546).

Folding and unfolding. Smooth and striated. I am suddenly reminded of my antenatal classes and descriptions of the uterine muscles in pregnancy and birth. I was encouraged to trust that my body knows what to do. The experts explained how the various layers of muscles worked in contrasting ways but ultimately in unison. I was warned that being fearful of birth (they did not call it 'labour') would prevent my biological system from working in its natural and innate way. They said I would experience 'surges', not contractions. With each surge, I was directed to breathe into my body, to expand it, to give my body more room and space. Pushing the baby out was not advised, and, in fact, deemed unnecessary. Uterine muscles exemplify smooth and striated space. The striated, skeletal muscles grow and contract rapidly to expel the baby – they become smooth. The smooth muscles, the bundles of criss-crossed, felt-like muscles, reorganize themselves, in a slower and more sustained manner, into a porous mesh – they become striated (Stables 1999).

Smoothing and striation facilitate folding and unfolding. The shape-shifting muscle movements are like kneading. Birthing is an experience of folding and unfolding. The existence of the baby and its developing subjectivity represent expansion. The uterine muscles pause while the baby, now existing externally, develops and grows. But there are more to be born and some to fail. Enveloping/developing Deleuzian folding and unfolding, as well as the shifting nature of smooth and striated space, correspond with notions of the matrixial when seen through the metaphor of birth.

Convergence as rhizomatic breakages

Stories of baking and birthing all require some state change, the unborn being born, the dough becoming bread. The folding and unfolding design process requires an outcome. This activity is rhizomatic (Deleuze and Guattari 1980: 10). This activity can be broken or shattered at any given point, yet is able to start up again in new or old ways. A rhizome is a multiplicity; it has no beginning or end and is always between rhizomes as multiplicities are innately interconnected forming 'plateaus'.

> The rhizome is the conjunction 'and . . . and . . . and' . . . Where are you going? Where are you coming from? What are you heading for? These are totally useless questions. (Deleuze and Guattari 1980: 27)

In baking, birthing and designing, something is required to momentarily break off the rhizomatic activity (so that it may continue on an old or new line). But when and how should this change occur? In a straightforward birth, the baby and the birthing body instigate this. Modern science still can only suggest a due date but, of course, many births are medically induced. In baking, there is general knowledge of how long to knead a dough. Internet searches uncover a great number of forum conversations trying to find the explicit answer of when enough is enough. (Incidentally, most say when the dough has become 'smooth' and elastic.) Eventually a baker develops a tacit understanding of when to stop kneading and start baking. In designing, either the designer reaches a point where they feel they may have a suitable solution or time, budget or technical restrictions call for a breakage in the rhizomatic activity. The sketches, samples, prototypes and the magical paraphernalia must be transformed, smooth becoming striated, a design decision must be made. It is this concept that allows expansive metaphors of designing to coexist with conventional ideas of divergence within the design process, except that it is a shattering or a breaking that occurs. To shatter or to break is simultaneously folding and unfolding, closing down and opening up: they are forms of creative destruction in the capitalocene (Moore 2017). In the narrative, linguistic sense, these moments are the punctuation. The story continues. Play is stopped by the imposition of context but can start again at any given moment. The knowledge gained both explicitly and tacitly from the process fuels connected and subsequent design processes and other cognitive activities.

> 'My ideas are never static. I don't just design a print or a dress, produce it, and then drop it. The theme keeps worrying me to be developed and the original idea becomes linked to something new and is regenerated.' Zandra Rhodes, textiles and fashion designer. (Rhodes 2012)

The 'auxetic' metaphors (derived from the Greek, meaning 'that which tends to increase') of the design problem/solution pairing as expansive lines, spun yarn, woven cloth, patchwork quilts, intangible pastes that I have discussed here provide a recursive idiom that contrasts with the transactional language of design as problem-solving. Dubberly Design Office (Dubberly 2004) has collated a compendium of design process models that track the developments in design research from linear flow diagrams to circles, loops, diamonds, cogs and spirals. What is common in all these models is that although initial divergent design thinking is represented as essential to the solving of design problems, it then is represented as converging, returning or focusing on the delivery of a solution. The 'designers' of these models are trying to capture the complex co-evolution of the design problem and solution. Interrogating Cross's use of the phrase 'co-evolution' in this context may shed some light when referenced to Ingold's work on the growth of artefacts. Ingold compares the making of artefacts (a coiled basket) with the growth of natural objects (a gastropod shell), calling both examples of autopoiesis, a self-transformational process. Ingold says, 'The artifact in short, is the crystallization of activity within a relational field, its regularities of form embodying the regularities of movement that gave rise to it' (Ingold 2000: 345). Autopoiesis is a term originally devised by biologists Humberto Maturana and Francisco Varela in 1972 to describe the self-maintaining qualities of biological cells. Varela, with Evan Thompson and Eleanor Rosch, took this idea further, transferring it into the realm of cognitive science and philosophy in their book *The Embodied Mind: Cognitive Science and Human Experience* (Varela, Thompson and Rosch 1991).

Evolution, after all, is defined in biological terms as the growth, development and expansion of species. And so if we accept that working with a design problem/solution pairing, through design thinking, as an activity of making and growing, the representation of convergence in design process models is giving too much emphasis on the mundane, external factors of design. Of course, budgets run dry and deadlines loom, so design decisions are made to provide a 'jumping off point' within this recursive activity, perhaps seen as a deposit, a birthing or a rhizomatic offshoot or dendrite. The activity continues transformed. Thinking in this way shifts the focus of the design process from the problem/solution, as is the case in most design process models, to the subjectivity and experience of the designer, each design experience building on the last and existing in our lived worlds. Ingold's depiction of making as 'crystallization' in 'relational' fields, material form representing material engagement, emphasizes the notion of a co-emergent, trans-subjective spatially expansive activity. As an ethical imperative, designers must understand their process as such.

The rhizomatic metaphors for designing are ultimately concepts of creation and making, emphasizing the varying influence of subjectivity and external forces. They align with theories of embodiment and autopoiesis developed in the field of enactive cognitive sciences (Varela, Thompson and Rosch 1991). In the same way that Ingold describes the connection between making, thinking and material in a field of forces based on biological evolution, enactive cognition is seen as an ongoing interaction with the medium, situated inseparably in the mind and world (Whitaker 2001). Varela, Thompson and Rosch say that cognition is functioning, or in this hypothesis the outcomes of design thinking are effective.

> [W]hen it becomes part of an on-going existing world (as the young of every species do) or shapes a new one (as happens in evolutionary history). (Varela, Thompson and Rosch 1991: 206)

In their terms, cognition is seen to bring forth the world (reflecting the productive metaphors of baking and birthing). Within this view, dealing with design problems/solutions is activating, relational and contextual. 'Bringing forth the world' through design is at once an enormous claim and responsibility.

These concepts reconcile the experience of the textile designers (communicated in Mesh Four) with the language of problem-solving in design research, but the question of the nature of design problems for textile designers still persists. Textile designers often state that the fundamental requirement of textile design (its problem) is to create beauty and elicit pleasure. They perceive a textile design's function as engaging and enhancing by definition, its purpose is to decorate.

Deep decoration

> I begin to see what decoration is for. It completes. It brings buildings, objects and artefacts to completion in and for perception, by making them easier to see, more finished, more easily focussed upon. It completes in and for social use by making them into signs and symbols for our endeavours and beliefs. It completes in and for pleasure by inviting the eye to dwell and the hand to caress. It completes in and for thought by making objects memorable. Decoration, by completing our world, completes those who live in it. (Brett 2005: 264)

> [I]n many or most cases we have got so used to this ornament that we look upon it as if had grown of itself, and note it of no more than mosses on the dry sticks with which we light our fires. (Morris 1877)

The quotations from David Brett and William Morris illustrate the importance and insignificance attributed to the decorative. Brett's explanation of decoration identifies and legitimizes it as transformative, alluding to its visual and tactile qualities and its role in sensory perception and social function. He continuously talks of the role of decoration for providing pleasure. Textiles are, of course, integral to Brett's remit of decoration; however, textiles can be the opposite of decorative – functional and earnest – and still fill us with pleasure. Textiles can be forgotten, unspoken and unseen. It is the omnipotence and ambience of textiles, as well as their shape-shifting qualities, that make them at once all-encompassing and yet often imperceptible.

Jane Graves extends Brett's and Morris's inclusion of textiles as a form/mode of decoration by aligning textiles with pattern. She gives a psychoanalytical account of pattern (Graves 2002: 45) in which she describes how decoration is converted through repetition into pattern and suggests that textile is pattern, whether or not pattern is woven in as a design, as the natural texture resulting from weaving or knitting, or is printed onto a textile surface. The significance of pattern in the growth and development of universal natural structures is widely recognized, largely due to the seminal work of D'Arcy Thompson's *On Growth and Form*, published in 1917. Similarly to Brett and Morris, Graves correlates textiles (pattern as textiles) with decoration. However, Graves focuses on the connection between textiles' innate patterns with the stimulation of pleasure, and uses Freudian concepts to describe how the unconscious is drawn to pattern for its addictive and disorientating qualities. As Graves states, pattern in textiles is either integral to the structure of the material or applied to its surface. By suggesting that textiles is pattern, a case is made that textiles are a material interpretation of natural laws such as fractals and algorithms. Indeed, in their repetition, they often mimic algorithmic and binary patterns in their production: knitting and weave patterns, for instance. Textiles are a visual and tactile connection to nature. To cover our chairs, floors, bodies and even phones with textile as pattern is to give these objects a surface which applies a visual and tactile translation of natural principles to enhance the way in which we interact with it. In this way, textile designs are conducive to a mind-body-world encounter.

Jane Graves discusses the development of meaning and symbolism involved in the development of motif in pattern within textile design:

> Imagine, however, that the motif is transformed in such a way that it conveys the experience of the place without actual representation. In other words, convert the motif into a symbol. Symbols convey meaning, not information. They are a valid mode of shared thinking, part conscious, part unconscious, which act like a stone thrown into a still pond. The ripples continue to reverberate long after the stone has disappeared. (Graves 2002: 49)

However these encounters play out initially, almost entirely within our senses, they are somatic. Being so heavily sensory, what is experienced within the encounter is difficult to describe and our perception of the experience is personal. It seems this is the crux of the difficulty in defining design problems for textiles design. The problem and solution are so very dialogically close. So close that their dialogue is but a whisper, almost silent, yet so densely layered.

This intimate proximity leaves a short path for abductive reasoning, so short it is difficult to trace and therefore to articulate. When discussing the pleasure of decoration and the experience and knowledge it offers, Brett aligns with Polanyi's notion of personal/tacit knowledge and finds contentment in knowing that we will always know more than we can tell. Brett advises against inquiring into the nature of pleasure for the fear of losing pleasure itself. It is easy to understand the trepidation of those who feel that beginning to expose and scrutinize design thinking (or behaviour) is akin to a magician revealing her methods; the worry that when you see the trick again, you'll always be looking for the sleight of hand. This analogy works both ways. A magician is capable of explaining her tricks – her intentions and the practical means by which she achieves those intentions. Once she does explain her methods, we become interested in the trick from a different perspective. We no longer just look at the trick but look at the magician. We can marvel at the skill and dexterity she displays. We might want to try the trick out for ourselves, but we are not so swift of hand for any magic to be conjured up, which at once serves to underline the extent of skill required to achieve such a spectacle. The magical quality returns, not in a supernatural form but in the recognition of the connection between thought, expertise and practice that the magician has developed. After revealing her trick, the knowledge she possesses allows her to continue to design many more wondrous tricks that will again give unfathomable pleasure and surprise. The magician can show and explain her tools; she can describe her intentions and how she uses the tools to perform and realize her intentions. The elements of magic laid bare: yet the magic only happens when one practises as a magician. Attempting to articulate textile design thinking need not remove the magic from the tacit but may provide some recognition for the possessors of that knowledge.

A sense of beauty

In textile design as decoration, the problem/solution 'dough' is substantially constituted from the combination of notions of beauty and pleasure, two concepts that are both indefinable and indivisible. In *The Sense of Beauty: Being the Outline of Aesthetic Theory* (1896) George Santayana uses Shakespeare's *54th Sonnet* to explain the connection between decoration, beauty and pleasure:

> O, how much more doth beauty beauteous seem
> By that sweet ornament which truth doth give.
> The rose looks fair, but fairer we it deem

> For that sweet odour which doth in it live.
> The canker-blooms have full as deep a dye
> As the perfumed tincture of the roses,
> Hang on such thorns and play as wantonly
> When summer's breath their masked buds discloses:
> But, for their virtue only is their show,
> They live unwoo'd and unrespected fade,
> Die to themselves. Sweet roses do not so;
> Of their sweet deaths are sweetest odours made.

Santayana uses the sonnet to explain how 'beauty is the co-operation of pleasures' and that sensorial pleasures require a visual, tangible objectification, an ornament, to create beauty.

> [B]eauty is constituted by the objectification of pleasure. It is pleasure objectified. (Santayana 1896:52)

Santayana's words manage to capture the activity of textile design as expressed by the textile designers I conversed with. To design textiles is to organize a cooperation of pleasures, both as sensation and perception, objectified through decoration, to constitute beauty or, more broadly, affect.

> The passage from sensation to perception is gradual, and the path may be sometimes retraced: so it is with beauty and the pleasures of sensation. There is no sharp line between them, but it depends upon the degree of objectivity my feeling has attained at the moment whether I say, 'It pleases me', or 'It is beautiful'. (Santayana 1896: 51)

This definition of textile design illustrates an activity operating as a complex translation, in a deeply subjective field with no clear criteria. Textile designers use beauty, sensation and perception as the raw materials for the objectification of pleasure, yet simultaneously rely on their own sensation, perception and pleasure to create something beautiful. It explains why textile designers talk of being drawn to things they liked, paraphernalia, as inspirational objects for their design process. They both feed and navigate from their own experience of pleasure and beauty to fuel and direct their design process. It supports an understanding of why textile designers must create double the number of designs needed, because they must allow for many designs not to be considered pleasing or beautiful by others. And textile designs must express all this within the boundaries of a single swatch of fabric, or at best a collection.

Textile designers talk about the importance of seeing their work 'resolved': that is to say, incorporated into the design of an object. Without wishing to return to the problem/solution terminology, this does bring to light the problematic of the object of textile design. Without being applied to or in another design, a garment, an upholstered chair or processes in some other way, textile design is merely an exercise in aesthetics. However, as Jane Graves highlights, the functional form of textiles is significant to its decorative qualities: its weave structure and yarn type are both the basis for its function and its decorative qualities. Santayana (1896: 164) describes this quality: 'ornament is distributed so as to emphasise the aesthetic essence of the form; to idealize it even more, by adding adventitious interests harmoniously to the intrinsic interest of the lines of the structure.' This statement applies to decoration added to a textile, as well as a textile applied to another designed object. Even within printed textiles the relationship between the structure and decoration is innate: for example, the fabric structure determines the dyes used, the thickness of the printed mark permissible for a good finish and the density of colour achievable. The finished textile design, embodying the unified qualities of function and decoration, is then applied within fashion, or perhaps interior design, to another object.

> Historically [ornament] is applied to a form as merely useful. But the very presence of ornament attracts contemplation; the attention lavished on the object helps to fix its form in the mind. (Santayana 1896: 164)

Santayana's words support David Brett's statement about the importance of decoration in completing the world: transforming, defining and fixing meanings of other objects. The textile designers I spoke with confirmed this for textiles, relishing in the task of transforming a simple kimono into something fabulous.

But we must remember that textiles' role within another designed object goes further than this. They provide more than a surface decorative effect: they are decoration and substance. Without the material substance and structure of cloth, there would be no dress to wear. This notion requires me to reflect on the differentiation between applied arts and design and where textiles is located: this is an enormous area of historical and theoretical debate which I shall not enter into, but it does seem important to highlight some pertinent aspects of the textile design process.

The purpose of textiles is implicated and unquestioned in the way they are made or manufactured. They are destined for application into another designed product: this is precisely why cloth is woven to specific widths, suitable for the layout plans of pattern cutting for garments or upholsterers. The direction, size and nature of the motif and pattern repeat is determined, again to suit various applications. As was mentioned within my conversations with textile designers, they often won't know how, where or why their textile designs are applied, and unless they do know in advance, do not give it conscious consideration. This is because the ultimate fate of textiles is the assimilation into something else. Textiles-as-entity engages with others, its purpose is to make itself available for use, offering the potential of pleasure, beauty through matter (whether material or immaterial), flagrantly yet silently.

Edmund de Waal's essay entitled *Sticky/Smooth* (De Waal 2007) provides an understanding of the differentiation between commodities (designed objects) and applied arts objects as gifts. He describes the smooth, liquid characteristics of the designed commodity, the ease with which they transfer between people and places, and contrasts it with the sticky qualities of the gift: the sense that the recipient is stuck to the gift-giver via the gift object. He also connects the metaphoric terms 'sticky' and 'smooth' with the materiality of the object, stating,

> These smooth objects are the objects in which the object contains enough – but not excessive materialization as objects to keep away the risk of their corruption by any hint of sensuous presence. Their smoothness keeps away metaphysical presence, the magic by which objects become values, fetishes, idols, and totems. (De Waal 2007: 48)

Typically, textile design is placed in a liminal position between design and applied art. Textiles are designed commodities that gain a metaphysical presence through application in another designed commodity. They are smooth things that stick. The notion of the application of textiles in a designed object once more begs a reflection on designing as folding and unfolding through kneading the 'intangible paste or dough'. What is the relationship here? A dress cannot exist without a textile. A textile has no animation without being folded, cut and sewn to make into a dress. What change occurs if the textile is different, or what if the shape of the dress is changed? What if a different fashion designer uses that textile? These qualities epitomize shifting Deleuzian smoothness and striation and are represented in Ettinger's theory of metramorphosis.

14

Design does/does not solve problems

Mark Roxburgh

The conception of design as a problem-solving activity, and the allied and now populist concept of design thinking, has a rich history as evidenced in the fairly extensive body of literature that deals with it. While I might in turn deal with some of that history and literature, if only to point towards it, my key objective in this chapter is to consider a different conception of design activity. Conceptions about what design is or does, needless to say, we call theory, a term that carries with it the often-pompous weight of earnest and rigorous intellectual endeavour over an extended period of time and conducted by many people. But let's be clear about the notion of theory, or theories, that attend to something like design for they are not the same as the kind of theories that attend to something like science.

Scientific theories belong to a class of theories known as descriptive theories and are concerned with observing, understanding and describing phenomena that occur in what we like to call the natural world. Such theories are descriptive of what has been repeatedly observed and confirmed through rigorous testing, using the scientific method. Notwithstanding that the instruments and protocols used to observe, measure and test natural phenomena are human constructs, and therefore framed by ideology (Latour and Woolgar 1979), it is generally agreed that scientific theories produce models of an empirical existing reality verifiable through repeated observation and testing. We can also say that because scientific theories are descriptive of what is observed and largely concerned with the nature of observed reality they are primarily ontological (Ladyman 2007). Describe comes from the Latin words *de*, which means down, and *scribere*, which means write, from which we can understand means to write down. From this we can infer that a descriptive theory is a theory based upon a written record of what has been seen (observed) – hence the importance of empirical observation and rigorous (written) documentation to the scientific method.

Theories about design generally belong to a class of theories known as prescriptive theories. Prescriptive theories are concerned with the realm of ideas, therefore theories about design are primarily concerned with ideas about what design is, what is does, and how it works. Because prescriptive theories are concerned with the nature of ideas they are primarily epistemological. As design is a human activity through which we speculate on what might be rather than describe what is, design theories are also speculative theories, as are all prescriptive theories. However, unlike many prescriptive speculative theories we actively transform our material reality from its current state to a future state through the act of designing. Because of this, design theories are the point where the epistemological (ideas about knowing) and ontological (ideas about reality) intersect.

Furthermore, prescriptive theories are closely related to normative theories which in philosophical terms are concerned with how things should or might be and in sociological terms are additionally concerned with the social norms that are held about ideas. Thus, prescriptive theories are long-held views (social norms) established over time and through experience and argumentation and are based upon evidence that itself is typically prescriptive. In this way prescriptive theories are anecdotal. While the instruments and protocols we use to speculate upon and transform the world are a human construct, and the resulting transformation is in turn literally and metaphorically also a human construct, design theories prescribe the imagining and production of the artificial (human-made) world, based upon philosophical and social norms (ideology) as well as empirical observations of the world as it is. This is distinct from describing the existence of observed phenomena in the natural world and is, in part, the rhetorical dimension of designed 'things', design practice and design theories that Buchanan (1985) wrote about. These understandings of the differences between theories related to the natural and artificial worlds are nothing new. For example, Herbert Simon's seminal publication the *Sciences of the Artificial* (1969) covered all of this as has Clive Dilnot's harder to find paper *Design and the Science of Uncertainty* (1998) to name but two among many authors.

The notion of design theories being prescriptive is of further interest given design as an activity is primarily concerned with transforming reality and, at least in its industrial setting, usually decoupled the idea of the 'thing' the designer wanted to get made from the actual making of the 'thing' they imagined. In this setting some form of direction was required to indicate to the people making these 'things' what was to be made and this historically took the form of visible images such as drawings or plans. Even in its post-industrial setting where the things that get designed have little to no material properties, such as the practice of service design, various forms of visible images and diagrams are typically used to direct the configuration of the service experience. As it is images (visible and mental) that are central to process of transforming the world through design, these too could be conceived as a kind of prescription. I will return to the prescriptive role of images in design practice a bit later, for they are key to the conception of design I will outline shortly, but for now I would like to focus on the broader notion of design theories as prescriptions. Prescribe comes from the Latin word *praescribere* which means to direct in writing and is a conjoint of the Latin words *prae*, meaning before, and again the word *scriber* which we know means write. From this we can infer that a prescriptive theory is a written direction of how we should or might see (imagine) things differently – hence the numerous theories that have abounded about design as a distinct activity from craft since its emergence in the proto-industrial revolution.

For example, from William Morris's theories about the relationship between craftmanship, truth to materials, form and social good and his repugnance with the industrial revolution to the Bauhaus's embrace of it with their theories of design efficiency, form and function contributing to human progress, to more recent theories of design problem-solving and design thinking being used to address the wicked problems facing society, theories of design are contested and change, yet their antecedent and antithetical theories are often enmeshed within them. In this regard design theory, as a prescriptive theory, is always ideological, anecdotal and tautological. On this basis it is worth questioning the current prevailing orthodoxy in design that it solves problems, wicked or otherwise, and how relevant it is to the diversity of practices that are captured by the term 'design'. The literature in the field of the sociology of technology, and in particular that which falls under the auspices of actor network theory, is instructive in this regard for it takes a systems approach to the historical and empirical analysis of how technologies come into to being (see e.g. Bijker et al. 1987; Latour 2005; Law and Hassard 1999). It is evident in this literature that the complex network of human and non-human actors that inform the emergence, distribution and uptake of technology is such that solving problems is a lower-order issue and, perhaps more importantly, that the problems identified to be solved are fundamentally socially constructed.

It would be fair to say that prescriptive theories are also often reliant on metaphors and as Cazeaux (2003: 8) has argued that

> the production of metaphor is a fundamentally ethical act since it involves the question of finding the right word: it is a creative use of language on the part of the individual which nevertheless, in order for it to work and be recognized as

a metaphor, has to be sensitive to the linguistic and cultural associations which the hearers or readers of the metaphor are likely to share.

In this regard we can consider the application of the prescriptive metaphor of design as a problem-solving activity to the practice of textile design as potentially unethical if the metaphor does not resonate with those that practice it. Or to put it in terms of the appropriateness of a theory to a specific practice we can turn to Ranulph Glanville who reflects that 'theory is frequently developed in one area and applied to another – i.e., theory derives from a field distinct from the field to which it is applied' (2005: 6). He also argues this 'may have advantages and disadvantages' but when these 'are not explored and tested we no longer have a proper use of theory: we have polemic' (Glanville 2005: 6), and I would add dogma. So, Elaine is right to question the efficacy of the problem-solving metaphor to textile design and explore alternative metaphors and develop alternative and more appropriate theories, for the field that the problem-solving metaphor of design emerged from is not necessarily the same as the field of textile design.

Without going into specifics, it is generally understood that design problem-solving and design thinking were key ideas developed during the 1960s by Herbert Simon in the United States and those aligned with the Design Methods Movement in Europe, although the intellectual antecedents of these concepts can be traced further back. For example, the Ulm School of Design, founded in 1953, was explicitly interested in the perspectives that sociology, economics, psychology, systems-thinking and so on could bring to design and it is no coincidence that the father of wicked problems, Horst Rittel, was a key member of staff there. Buchanan (1992: 6) traces the interest in the 'new disciplines of integrative thinking', as exemplified by Ulm, back to John Dewey's 1929 publication *The Quest for Certainty: A Study of the Relation of Knowledge and Action*. Regardless, the primary concern that emerged in the work of Rittel, Simon and Design Methods, more broadly, was with understanding the increasingly complex (wicked) design problems encountered at a systems level. Systems-level design addressed large-scale, technological challenges and emerged in the broad field of engineering (Rittel 1972: 5; Simon 1969: 118). It then morphed into management science in business schools (Simon 1969: 58) and found its way into urban planning in the form of human behaviour research (Rowe 1987: 158–62). As an intellectual endeavour and emerging form of theory it went from being focused on designing material objects and complex systems of technology (as configurations of diverse material objects and ensembles of technologies) to being focused on the management of decision-making systems (as immaterial networks of human relations) in which those material objects and ensembles of technologies were situated. It would be fair to say that the intellectual contexts and fields that contributed to the development of the concepts of design thinking and design problem-solving have largely been technocratic and managerialist and the adoption of these concepts into mainstream business thinking – as evidenced, for example, in the work of Roger Martin (2009) of the Rotman School of Management, Tim Brown (2009) of IDEO and Thomas Lockwood (2009) of Lockwood Resource – is indicative that design thinking and problem-solving have both jumped the shark and have been universally co-opted by neoliberal economics.

Susan Stewart argues that the history and trajectory of the design problem-solving metaphor is a far cry from the intellectual journey of disciplines such as visual communication design, interior design and fashion design in which 'issues of communication, embodied experience and sensation are to the fore' (2011: 516). Setting aside issues of communication, for that is partly related to semiotic theory and I don't have the space to write about what a waste of time that has been for much of design practice, embodied experience and sensation point to phenomenology and perception and this is the territory I have been exploring in formulating an alternative conception (theory) of design practice from my own practice as a photographer and visual communicator. Notwithstanding the fact that textile design is a radically different practice to photography and visual communication design, these conceptions might be of interest because of their phenomenological perspective, which when you strip down to its essence is the relationships that exist between designers (as subjects) and the world we inhabit and transform (as objects) through our experience of designing. It is also reasonable to assume, from my novice perspective concerning the history of textile design, that it has more in common with design practices such as visual communication, interior and fashion design than it does the worlds of engineering, systems and product design where design problem-solving emerged.

In the *Sciences of the Artificial* (1969), Herbert Simon argued for a rigorous programme of study of the human act of designing which he saw as being concerned with transforming the world we inhabit to one that better suits our perceived needs and desires. This transformation of the world, through the act of design, has meant that we have created and inhabit an increasingly human-made, or artificial, world. Simon's characterization of the human-made world as 'artificial' was not to pass judgement on it but to distinguish such a world from the 'natural' world which, he argued, was the object of study of science proper.

This binary distinction between the artificial and natural worlds, while somewhat simplistic, provides a useful and necessary analytical construct to highlight the shift that has occurred as a result of our constant intervention in the natural world through our propensity to design. Something that Villem Flusser addresses in perhaps a more provocative manner in arguing that the key function of design is 'to deceive nature by means of technology, to replace what is natural with what is artificial and build a machine out of which there comes a god who is ourselves' (1999 [1993]: 19). This points to the power of design as a vehicle for creating the world in our own image, which again points to the prescriptive nature of images in design. Additionally, this also implies human perception, which I will come to shortly, but if we needed any further evidence that our capacity to design has resulted in us transforming the world in our own image we have only to turn to the geological phenomena of the Anthropocene to find it. Although dealing with the consequences of the Anthropocene is pressing, the focus of my chapter is not concerned directly with that. Rather I seek to understand the basis of our urge to design, to illuminate a phenomenological perspective on it. I do this in contrast to the dominant discourse that sees design in largely instrumental terms as being concerned with solving problems, with doing design better to make it more efficient or effective.

Less we become seduced by the idea that by making design more efficient and effective and recasting it as more sustainable or eco-friendly – to solve problems in the natural world as it were – this does not get to the nub of why we design. While it is laudable, if predictable, that we turn to design to solve the ecological problems we have created through it such an approach is naïve at best and disingenuous at worst. To think that we can simply solve the problems we have designed into the natural world through design misunderstands the imperative to design, which is to transform the world in our image through acts of human imagination. Simply put it is through imagination that we perceive the world can be different from how we currently perceive and experience it. In this regard perhaps looking at the act of design as something that can be better managed, or made more efficient, might prove less fruitful in mitigating our impact upon the natural world than addressing the nature of these perceptions and the images that we have of the world we experience, on a day-to-day basis. I would now like to turn to articulating what I would loosely call a perceptual theory of design that explores the relationship between visible images (aka forms of pictorial 'representation'), human perception, human imagination and the transformation of the world.

Flusser argues that 'images signify – mainly – something "out there" in space and time that they have to make comprehensible to us as abstractions (as reductions of the four dimensions of space and time to the two surface dimensions)' and that 'this specific ability to abstract surfaces out of space and time and to project them back into space and time is what is known as "imagination"' (Flusser 2007 [1983]: 8). Merleau-Ponty argues, 'the word "image" is in bad repute because we have thoughtlessly believed that a design was a tracing, a copy, a second thing, and that the mental image was such a design, belonging among our private bric-a-brac' (1964: 164). Both Flusser and Merleau-Ponty are concerned with the relationship between visible images and human imagination and the role the non-visible, or mental image, plays in that. Flusser calls this relationship imaginary thought, whereas Merleau-Ponty calls it perceptual synthesis. Regardless of their differing terminologies and emphases (mind or body) both are interested in challenging positivist intellectual orthodoxy – in Flusser's case what he calls conceptual thought and in Merleau-Ponty's case classical thought – that they see as delineating the world in a series of binary constructs– subjects and objects, mind and body, image and reality, natural and artificial and so on.

Merleau-Ponty argues that mental images 'are the inside of the outside and the outside of the inside' and that they help us to 'understand the quasi presence and imminent visibility that make up the whole problem of the imaginary' (1964: 164). Likewise, he argues that the visible image is neither a copy nor representation of the world nor a thing separate to our perception of the world. Rather, as visible images exist in the world we perceive, they are a part of the world we experience and are not just a mechanism for showing us (representing) things absent from our immediate field of view. To illustrate the mutually constitutive relationship between these mental and visible images and our perception and experience of reality Merleau-Ponty explores artistic vision. The painter, he argues, 'sees the world and sees what inadequacies (manqué) keep the world from being a painting' and sets out to rectify these inadequacies through a painting (Merleau-Ponty 1964: 165). The painting then becomes a part of the world that we perceive and informs both our perceptual experience of that reality and our concept of what other realities could come into being. This resonates with David Brett's argument that decoration 'brings buildings, objects and artefacts to completion in and for perception' and that by 'completing our world, completes those who live in it' (2005: 264), although I would argue the world is never complete. This relationship, between the visible images of the world we see and the mental images we have of the world we'd like, Merleau-Ponty calls the image sensitizing itself and Rosalyn Diprose argues that it is how we transform 'the lived world' and 'is not an extraordinary event' (2010: 33). By arguing that what one sees (sight) and what one makes seen (visible images) the conventional view of the image as a regime of representation as articulated by critical theory is called into question.

In his critique of classical analysis, Merleau-Ponty argues that it regards the 'perceived world' as a 'sum of objects' and that consequentially 'our relation to the world' is 'that of a thinker to an object of thought' (1964: 12) which frames human perception as something that is independent of the things (objects) we (subjects) observe. Conversely, the things (objects) we (subjects) observe exist independent of our (subjective) observations of them. In contrast to that he argues, 'we cannot apply the classical distinction of form and matter to perception' (Merleau-Ponty 1964: 12), meaning that the nature of the form and matter of an object we perceive is entirely dependent on and not separate from human perception and experience. Conversely then we cannot 'conceive the perceiving subject as a consciousness which "interprets", "deciphers", or "orders" a sensible matter according to an ideal law which it possesses' (Merleau-Ponty 1964: 12). In other words, our perceptual experience of the form and matter of the objects we encounter is informed by our prior perceptual experience and, I would add, informed by what Charles Sanders Peirce (1998 [1893–1913]) would call collateral knowledge; that is our collective, and to some extent common-sense and everyday experience of them. It is through language, in its broadest possible conception (including visible images), that the apparent private world of the mind can surface in this collateral knowledge as Liddament (2000), in essence, argues.

As 'every perception takes place within a certain horizon and ultimately in the "world"' (Merleau-Ponty 1964: 12) and the things (objects) we perceive exist 'only in so far as someone can perceive it' (1964: 12) the existence of things (objects) for us (as subjects) is entirely dependent on our embodied, multisensory perception. This is I believe much like the mind-body-world 'encounter' Igoe has articulated in Chapter 13. Furthermore, the things (objects) we perceive are not stable entities in the way classical analysis would see them for they constantly change as the circumstances of our embodied perception change and it is for this reason that I think the world is never complete as Brett has claimed. As such perception does not reveal 'truths like geometry but presences' (Merleau-Ponty 1964: 14) and these presences 'constitutes the unity of perceived objects' (1964: 15), or what we might regard as the reality of the world we perceive. This does not occur as a form of intellectual synthesis but unfolds through 'perceptual synthesis' (Merleau-Ponty 1964: 15). In perceptual synthesis we first 'delimit certain perspectival aspects' of objects, that is, we see what is visible of them and then go beyond that to imagine what is not visible of them (Merleau-Ponty 1964, 16). Our facility to imagine what is not visible of the object that we perceive is based upon our multisensory, embodied, engagement and previous experiences of similar objects and indeed our multisensory, embodied, engagement and previous experiences of visible images of similar objects, given such images are as much a part of the landscape of the real as they are a representation of it. Because of the dynamic nature of perception and the horizons and contexts in which it unfolds, which I call the horizon of perception, the objects we perceive to be static unchanging things are actually ever-changing and not entirely fixed entities.

To highlight the role that imagination plays in perception, and its paradoxical nature, Merleau-Ponty further extends the idea of perceiving what is not visible by contending that even if we imagine a place we have never been to, the fact that we can imagine it makes us present at that place (1964: 16). For design, the place we imagine that we have never been to is the future and this too plays out within the horizon of our perception, even if we perceive an existing situation within that as problematic and wish to devise a course of action to change that into a preferred one. I contend then we do not design to solve problems, for problems are all a matter of perception, and that we design as a matter of perceptual course. We design simply because we have differing experiences and perceptions of the world, which are dynamic, and we can perceive the world being different and affording us different experiences. This is the point Merleau-Ponty made in relation to artistic vision and painting.

The human facility to 'abstract surfaces out of space and time' in the form of visible images and our capacity 'to project them back' into that, to return to Flusser, is both the foundation of imagination and a central aspect of our capacity to design, to transform the world in our image, both visible and imaginary. Images, and the manner in which they are bound up in the horizon of our perception, are therefore central to the human act of designing. They are manifest and operate on both a 'concrete' and 'abstract' level. They are simultaneously concrete and abstract when a designer observes an artefact or environment with a view to transforming it. Concrete in the sense that their experience of that object or environment is 'real' and abstract in the sense that the image they have of them, which is encountered through perception, is not physically manifest and is uniquely theirs and not transferable to anyone else.

Additionally, the images of design (for that is what I will call them) are abstract when they are the image a designer 'thinks' of (imagines) in relation to the changes they wish to make to that perceived artefact or environment. They then become concrete when that imagining becomes manifest in the plans, drawings, diagrams or photographs (all visible images) a designer produces to instruct others to manufacture the artefact or environment they have conceived. It is this specific relationship between the abstract images that designers perceive and imagine and the concrete images they encounter and produce that I have been exploring in my research for they are at the heart of how we design.

If we see design as a form of perceptual synthesis that results in the transformation of what we regard as the material world then it is reasonable to conclude that no designed 'thing' is a logical inevitability given that the horizon of our perception is uniquely ours. However, design is a transformative, creative and imaginative inevitability for it is bound up in our perceptual synthesis. This positions the image as key to both design and perceptual transformation. In particular it highlights the centrality of the non-visible image, the imaginary, to both. Additionally, however, if we regard both perceptual and design transformation as being an imaginative inevitability, as opposed to a logical one, then we cannot escape the question of morals or ethics. I say this because we absolve ourselves of a certain degree of ownership over the logically inevitable for it appears objective. Merleau-Ponty critiques this tendency, prevalent in the form of scientific thinking, to seeing the world as an object of study that leads to a view of the world in which we are determined by things other than ourselves and argues that such a science 'manipulates things and gives up living in them' (Merleau-Ponty 1964: 159). The imaginatively inevitable cannot be divorced so easily, on the other hand, from an experiencing human subject.

I will return to this ethical dimension shortly for I expect you are wondering what this has to do with how a perceptual theory of design might be more relevant to textile design than problem-solving. Thus far, I have explored perception primarily in relation to visible images and the images of our imagination and this is admittedly an ocular-centric view of perception. To be fair visual perception is one of our primary sensory mechanisms for, as neuroscientist V. S. Ramachandran (2011) has argued, there are approximately thirty areas of the brain that deal with visual perception and communication compared to two that deal with factual information and language. This suggests that we are more neurologically predisposed towards visual perception and communication than we are towards linguistic interpretation and communication. Furthermore, Ramachandran's research indicates that the line between 'visual perception and visual imagination' is blurred and that there is a clear link between perception and action (2011: 70), suggesting Merleau-Ponty's theories of perception are supported by the emerging neurological evidence. Setting this ocular-centricity aside, and returning to those theories, what I have been arguing is that the human subject is not simply a mind observing or constructing the world but is enmeshed in the world through embodied perception.

In keeping with his rejection of classical analysis Merleau-Ponty critiques the observational regime of modern (read positivist) scientific thought which 'looks on from above, and thinks of the object-in-general' (1964: 160) and argues that it needs to 'return to the "there is" that underlies it; to the site, the soil of the sensible and opened world such as it is in our life and for our body – not that possible body which we may legitimately think of as an information machine but that actual body I call mine' (1964: 160). This is in essence a call to reunite the observing subject with the observed object and conceive of reality as not based only upon a neutral observing mind (positivism) nor based only upon a consciously constructing mind (constructivism) but based upon our experience of being in the world as a perceiving thoughtful and embodied being. Again, this reinforces the idea that the world is not a fixed entity available to our perception, nor is our perception simply determined by the world, rather that they are mutually constituted. That is, the world changes its shape, and hence reality changes, as we orient ourselves through it via embodied perception and that as a consequence of this orientation our perception of the world also changes. In this regard, 'vision is not an operation of thought' for we are 'immersed in the visible' by our body and as such 'the see-er does not appropriate what he sees; he merely approaches it by looking, he opens himself to the world' (1964: 162). The boundary between the self and the world, the body and reality is permeable and ever-changing, for a 'body is a thing among things; it is caught in the fabric of the world' (Merleau-Ponty 1964: 163). In this way 'we experience a perception and its horizon "in action" [...] rather than by "posing" them or explicitly "knowing" them' (Merleau-Ponty 1964: 12).

It is the mutually transformative dimension of the relationship between the perceiving embodied self and a perceivable reality that is particularly relevant here for it again signals the perceptual foundations of design and expands the concept of perception to encompass senses other than sight. It points also to the sense of touch as part of our perceptual ability and the tacit dimension of knowing through touch and knowing through action, concepts generally referred to as aesthetic or kinaesthetic knowing. Setting aside the significance of the image in design as a perceptual activity, it is these aesthetic or kinaesthetic dimensions of perception that I think might be of particular interest in developing a phenomenological theory pertinent to the field of textile design. While I have previously argued, from a largely ocular-centric view, that the image is central to both perception and design this might be called into question when considering perception premised on non-ocular senses, such as touch, or where knowing through doing might be more valued, such as I would imagine might be the case in textile design despite the largely industrial framework it unfolds in. It may be questionable that visible images as a form of instruction to manufacture may be less common in textile design than they are in, for example, product design; nonetheless, the non-visible image, the imaginary, is arguably even more significant in design practices that privilege tactility and tacit knowledge.

Second-order cybernetics likewise challenges the binary constructs typical of positivism but specifically in relation to the observation of systems (social or otherwise) rather than perception in general, although an argument can be made there are analogous connections. Second-order cybernetics is interested in the desired goals of systems and the actions undertaken to achieve those goals, hence its relevance to design theory. Where positivism sees the observer being separate to that which is observed, second-order cybernetics understands the observer of a system to be a part of the system being observed not separate to it. Not unlike being caught up in the fabric of the world. Additionally, the act of observation causes the system to change (typically known as reactivity in research terms) and the systems observed condition the observer to observe in particular ways. Not dissimilar to Merleau-Ponty's view of the relationship between human perception and the world we perceive. Ranulph Glanville outlines the two key imperatives for second-order cybernetics, these being the ethical imperative which is 'to act so as to increase the number of choices' as opposed to limiting them and the aesthetical imperative which is that 'if you desire to see, learn how to act' (von Foerster qtd Glanville 2004: 12). The underlying inference here is that as observers within a system we need to take responsibility for our actions (or reactions) because they have consequences for all constituent parts of that system.

Observation, or indeed perception, and action are fundamental to design as they predicate desired change – imagining what-might-be. In his phenomenological interrogation of the relationship between imagination and design Mads Folkman argues that design 'investigates the latent opportunities of reality and employs its aesthetic means of sensual expression, creation of meaning, and contextual impact in order to integrate these aspects within the domain of reality' (2013: 221). A similar argument to that which I have made thus far. Folkman also argues that because design helps designate structures of experience it 'is essentially imbued with ethical concerns' (2013: 220). This relationship between aesthetics (conceived in terms of embodied perception and not just the 'look' of things) and ethics in design I have conceived in terms of what I call the design imperative. Building upon the two imperatives outlined above I have previously described the design imperative as 'if you desire to act (design) then learn how to see (aesthetically)' (Roxburgh 2010). In light of my broader interest in perception this could be reframed to be – if you design then learn how to perceive (aesthetically) because how we perceive, while conditioned by the horizon of our perception, in turn conditions how the world might be.

At the outset I wrote that theories of the design are prescriptive and in looking at the etymology of that term I noted that prescribe comes from the Latin word *praescribere* which means to direct in writing. I also noted that *praescribere* comes from *prae* which means before and *scriber* which means writing. I also noted that prescriptive theories are related to normative theories which are concerned with how things should or might be. It is not surprising then that many social theories are often written 'directions' about how society should or might be. However, it is interesting to note that before writing there were visible images, some of which we know became pictograms which became writing. As we had pictures before writing it is fitting that in a prescriptive phenomenological theory of design, which is concerned with perceptual synthesis and design as a consequence of perceptual transformation, that it is the image (visible or imaginary) that directs how the world should or might be. I also argued earlier that theories of design are ideological, anecdotal and tautological but so too are the images of design and it is for this reason that the world we inhabit and transform through design is increasingly artificial. Where theories of design might prescribe how design should be understood and practised, it is through our embodied perception of the world we encounter as it is, as it is depicted, and how we imagine it could be that prescribe what that world becomes. These various kinds of images (visible and mental) that we produce are always ideological for they are products of our perception of the world and how we imagine it could be; anecdotal because they are based upon human experience; and tautological because the traces of the world we encounter are enmeshed in the images we create to depict that world as it is and as it could or should be. As the visible images, as instructions to manufacture artefacts or configure experiences, are prescriptions of how the world has been imagined – and how it could or should be – the form and materiality of those images condition both the imaginary and soon to be perceived world created through design. As such the world we design is already and always an image, conditioned by human perception and the visible images we create, and is therefore always becoming, never being. Never complete.

Because we transform the world through design in our 'own image', or as the case may be in our own images (visible and mental), this presents us with two questions to consider. Not the predictable questions as to whether or not the creation of an artificial world is a good or bad thing for that is inevitable as long as humans exist. Rather the questions we might want to consider are, first, 'what image do we have or would we like to have of ourselves as a species?' or to paraphrase Flusser, 'what kind of god do we want to be in the world that we create in our own image?' Lest this sounds like hubris it is not for Flusser's characterization of us becoming gods through our capacity to design is cautionary and droll, but nonetheless accurate, and reminds us that pride goeth before a fall. Rather, it is a question of the extent to which we think we can, or attempt to, impose ourselves upon the world OR the extent to which we realize we are inextricably a part of it and that we experience and transform it through embodied (aesthetic) perception. Second, because we transform the world in our image, we might want to ask, 'what kind of artificial world do we want to create and inhabit?' for our image is within the gift of our imagination. This is the ethical dimension I alluded to earlier and is at the core of the design imperative. Not to ask these questions when we design is possibly the greatest failure of imagination we confront for I suspect our future might depend on it.

Elevated surfaces

Metaphors make meaning.
Textiles is a geisha
Textiles is a spinster.
Textiles is a mother.
Stories theorize experience.
Poetry is playing.
Playing represents.
Stories represent.
Design is representation.
Representation is one of two contests.
Playing ends tension.
Translation is transformation.

Translation is response.
Textile designers translate.
Textiles are pattern.
Pattern is universal.
Pattern is pleasure.
Beauty is the cooperation of pleasures.
Beauty is the representation of my pleasures.
Design is the representation of my pleasures.
Paraphernalia is important to design.

Creativity is the tension of mental dissatisfaction.
Playing is tense.
Playing is part of design.
Design problems and solutions are co-emergent.
Decoration perceptually fixes objects.
Decorative objects are magical.
Design is expansive.
Design is matrixial.

Above are some of the 'entailments' and 'reverberations' towards concepts (Lakoff and Johnson 1980/2003: 140) of the metaphors I have constructed and applied in this book. Some of these entailments and reverberations become metaphoric pronouncements in themselves; others are key notes from other authors. They overlap, criss-cross, conflict and interconnect, pointing to concepts developed as well as opportunities for further exploration.

Established textile metaphors used in everyday speech (Kapp 2013) referring to linguistic and cognitive mechanisms of storytelling and problem-solving, or physical actions or attributes, clearly themselves have entailments and reverberations, but it often feels as though the significance of these textile metaphors has become so tacit that the reverberations have lost their piquancy. Harper (2012: Vol 2, ix) compares Brett's opinion of the diminishing of the meaning and significance of the 'cosmic metaphor of weaving' (Brett 2005: 229) and f. marquespenteado's plea for theoreticians to develop alternative metaphors and examples of textile thinking: he suggests tooth floss might be suited to the task.

Brett develops a 'semantic chain' for the metaphor of weaving that covers three aspects: useful activity, a means for structuring private feelings and social relations and our cosmos (Brett 2005: 229). Indeed the metaphor of weaving textiles has found new meaning in new contexts, albeit as meshes and networks in the fields of communication technologies and the internet. What these mesh and net metaphors lack, though, is a visualization of their *making* and growth in relation to human emotion, relations and activity. What is required is Brett's evolutionary semantic chain for weaving, as well as f. marquespenteado's plea for alternative metaphors for textiles. After all, textile practice is, and increasingly so, far more than weaving, knotting and stitching. In order to do this a new paradigm of 'textile thinking' must establish, in tandem and in unison with the innovative and conceptual textile design practice that exists today, to assert new value for old textile metaphors and new significance for textiles in concepts developing today.

The metaphorical concept of textiles (thinking and making) as matrixial broadens the weaving imagery in response to Brett and f. marquespenteado's concerns. In reference to her textile art, Catherine Dormor (2012) refers to the 'material-conceptual matrix'. Dormor uses Ettinger's concept of 'borderswerving' to explain the negotiated boundaries between explicit and tacit knowledge, and explores this concept through folding, fraying and seaming (as textile making and thinking methods) as metaphors for the interrelationship of text, textile and *techne*. Dormor's interdependent activities of making and writing interrogate in an embodied way the scope and suitability of these established philosophical and psychoanalytical textile metaphors for thinking. I move the concept of the 'material-conceptual matrix' into an additional context. Dormor's handling of the folding, fraying and seaming metaphors is rich and clear, helping to visualize and articulate the interconnection of the tacit and explicit knowledge of textile making. Where this book has addressed ideas of folding and fraying, they are set within concepts of problem-solving and translation and transformation in design, contextualized in the field of cognitive science and other academic fields. This activity has been driven by theories of generative metaphors, frame analysis and restructuring in the development of new metaphors for textile cognition as well as from other domains.

> Metaphors external to a piece of research prefigure the analysis with a 'truth-value' code belonging to another domain. (Jameson 1981 cited in Richardson 2000: 927)

In this volume, the matrixial is divulged as trans-subjective relationality in design. A matrixial approach to design is presented as the prevailing epistemological position in textiles and therefore it has always existed as a paradigm of design research; but it has not been articulated in this way. The action of frame restructuring using metaphor and narrative inquiry methods within a feminist methodology corresponds with the declining post-postmodern condition. Scholars such as Vermeulen and van den Akker (2010) have contributed to the development of 'metamodernism' – a set of theories emerging from postmodernism. They define this era by an oscillation between modern enthusiasm and postmodern irony, emphasizing an alternative condition of tension. Vermeulen and van den Akker (quoting the eighteenth-century German Romantic philosopher Novalis) describe the metamodern:

> Metamodern neoromanticism should not merely be understood as re-appropriation; it should be interpreted as re-signification: it is the re-signification of 'the commonplace with significance, the ordinary with mystery, the familiar with the seemliness of the unfamiliar, and the finite with the semblance of the infinite'. Indeed, it should be interpreted as Novalis, as the opening up of new lands in situ of the old one. (Vermeulen and van den Akker 2010: 12)

The very idea of resignifying textile and feminine matrixial metaphors for thinking and making appears to be distinctly metamodern.

> For us, the prefix 'meta' indicates that a person can believe in one thing one day and believe in its opposite the next. Or maybe even at the same time. Indeed, if anything, 'meta' intimates a constant repositioning: not a compromise, not a balance, but an at times vehemently moving back and forth, left and right. . . . without ever seeming reducible to any one of them. (Vermeulen 2012: 215)

It is tempting here to point out the clear connections between this definition of metamodernity and the act and object of weaving, another link in Brett's semantic chain. Here Vermeulen also describes the oscillating nature of metamodern thought which supports Ettinger's statement that the matrixial denotes *besidedness* allowing alternate ways of knowing to coexist. As Thiele (2014: 211) points out, Ettinger's matrixiality is not served well by a standpoint of opposition or replacement but that a diffractive approach is required to signal complexity and open up realms of thinking and world-making.

The relevance of metamodernism to the ideas developed here extends to the conceptualizations of design as expansive and conative. Vermeulen and van den Akker, citing Kant, describe the nature of metamodernism as 'as-if' thinking (Vermeulen and van den Akker 2010: 5), which itself sounds metaphorical in action.

> Metamodernism displaces the parameters of the present with those of a future presence that is futureless; and it displaces the boundaries of our place with those of a surreal place that is placeless. For indeed, that is the 'destiny' of the metamodern wo/man: to pursue a horizon that is forever receding. (Vermeulen and van den Akker 2010: 12)

The metamodern discourse describes a condition that is highly conative, striving towards an impossible possibility, much like the way in which Polanyi describes intellectual passions as 'a heuristic vision which is accepted for the sake of its unresolvable tension' (Polanyi 1958: 212).

By its nature, metamodernist thought, being one thing one day, another the next or more than one thing at any one time, is clearly governed by principles of relationality and subjectivity, and Vermeulen and van den Akker talk continuously of the tension of this oscillating position. They talk about metamodernism as expressing an atopic metaxy and define this in relation to their proposal of metamodernism:

> We could say thus that atopos is, impossibly, at once a place and not a place, a territory without boundaries, a position without parameters. (Vermeulen and van den Akker 2010: 12)

The atopic condition could be seen as indicative of textile design's liminal position in so many contexts. It is design, art, craft and applied art. We respond to textiles, yet they are often ignored. They surround our bodies for almost every second of the day, and yet we rarely mention them. Can textile design act metaphorically for the metamodern? A dimensional, entangled, matrix-multiplicity, pursuing a 'horizon that is forever receding' (or expanding?)

What Vermeulen and van den Akker are describing is already recognized in the field of quantum physics and mechanics through theories of quantum nonlocality and entanglement. My attempts at trying to understand this theory has only allowed me to comprehend its most basic theories; principally that two particles interact and then are connected, despite any arbitrary distance between them. The connection is innate and not based on the sending or receiving of information. The tension between the modern naivety and postmodern scepticism in metamodernism is evident here in universal laws of the quantum. Werner Heisenberg, one of the founders of quantum mechanics, described the phenomenon (1974/1990: 227), capturing his own position as well as Wolfgang Pauli's:

> Pauli once spoke of two limiting conceptions, both of which have been extraordinarily fruitful in the history of human thought, although no genuine reality corresponds to them. At one extreme is the idea of an objective world, pursuing its regular course in space and time, independently of any kind of observing subject; this has been the guiding image of modern science. At the other extreme is the idea of a subject, mystically experiencing the unity of the world and no longer confronted by an object or by any objective world; this has been the guiding image of Asian mysticism. Our thinking moves somewhere in the middle, between these two limiting conceptions; we should maintain the tension resulting from these two opposites.

If we accept Vermeulen and van den Akker's proposal of metamodernism as the prevailing (Western) cultural logic (and the authors clearly state [2017] that it is as yet a proposal, not a theory), then the tension of both relationality and oscillation will predominate.

Design research is beginning to recognize the need to develop a position of oscillation, as evidenced in Lucy Kimbell's promotion of practice theories for design research that recognize its 'messy contingent combination of minds, things, bodies, structures, processes and agencies' (Kimbell 2012). Ken Friedman also cautions that design thinking is not a useful or precise term to describe phenomena that are genuine but that we have not yet described well enough. He says, 'I think the time may have arrived where we are indeed moving beyond the problematic conceptions of design thinking that she (Kimbell) critiques to a broader range of insights' (Friedman 2013).

Academic design research has proposed a multitude of diagrams in an attempt to model the design process and its associated thinking (Dubberly 2004). Circles, diamonds (Design Council 2005), loops and even 'squiggles' (Newman 2002) have all been used to symbolize this complex process. Modelling the design process and associated thinking in this way, despite the various geometries used to represent it, emphasizes a linearity of thought – a binary, transactional epistemology. It disregards the subjectivity of the designer(s) and the time, place and context of the design experience. Visual representations certainly help us to understand abstract ideas, but perhaps a better option is to utilize metaphors, allowing multiple ways of reading for different people and in different contexts, in the mode of the metamodern (and quantum), allowing design processes and thinking to be several things at any one time.

Kimbell (2012: 143) explains that 'design is understood as relational'. She expands on this, saying, 'Design thinking can thus be rethought as a set of contingent, embodied routines that reconfigure the socio-material world, which are institutionalized in different ways' (Kimbell 2012: 141).

The concepts explored in the meshes that punctuate this book, developed from 're-storying' my experience as a textile designer and that of other textile designers, provide a visualization and metaphor for Kimbell's definition. Kneading and folding the dough of the problem-solution (see Chapter 13), being a metaphor, offers a deeper, truer understanding of the phenomenon, inviting in notions of tension in the 'socio-material world'-dough that metamodernism alludes to. As Kimbell (2012) and Wang and Ilhan (2009) recognize, design and its disciplines are institutionalized and sociologically wrapped in different ways (see Chapter 8).

Drawing directly from the theoretical content of previous chapters I present design, as developed through an investigation of textile designing, as

Activating a tripartite but highly conative, expansive process, which, through playful folding and unfolding in the Deleuzian sense, develops a multidimensional conceptual matrix-multiplicity, evolving rhizomatically. Its rhizomatic expansion is set in a co-emergent encounter with more tangible aspects of the design nexus, the tension of which will at times force breakages, and at others, continuation.

This is a densely descriptive passage, so to simplify, here design is understood as a continuously generative activity which occurs in relation to and subsequently affected by external forces. These forces may be client needs, a budget or a deadline, for example. These externalities are similarly affected by the act of designing. The tension between the act of designing and these external forces results in truncation, diversion or simply change. But not end. The typologically metamodern cognitive mode of conation and its role in creativity maintains the act of designing as perpetually transforming activity. This connects the act of designing to the subjectivity of those engaged in it and with it. It recognizes and builds in actions of reflective practice.

Textasis, as a textile in tension, recognizes etymological and metaphorical connection between text and textile, thinking, speaking, writing and making. It represents the definition of textile design cognition that I proposed in earlier chapters in its interconnection of the material and immaterial in tasis, and as such addresses ideas being developed through metamodernism. Textasis suggests a movement between stasis/enstasis, that which is unmoving, immobilized, subordinated, standing firmly within oneself, to ex stasis/ekstasis, flow, excess, ecstasy, joy, insubordination, to be outside of oneself, the transgression of boundaries. A thinking, speaking, writing and making in tension, textasis represents both the conceptual ill-defined design problem and the cognitive and concrete actions required to deal with it. As Huizinga suggests, to end a tension you can play, and play is characterized by being outside of ordinary life yet limited and ordered by it (Huizinga 1949: 26–9).

Kavanagh (2008: 708; Kavanagh, Matthews and Tyrer 2004: 3) talks about how textile design education now better prepares new designers for the industrial context by emphasizing 'What one wants to say, and to whom, and by what means'. These tenets are of course important to any design discipline. Precisely what is lacking for textiles is developed theory to support these activities in ways specific to the discipline. In her 2010 paper 'Textile Theory: Do We Need It?' Jessica Hemmings reflects on the process of editing *The Textile Reader* and the impact of such a publication on the textile discipline:

> Perhaps the vitality of a discipline relies on the uncertainty of its values? A discipline without a canon may in fact be lucky rather than lacking. . . . For textiles to establish its critical footing, publications such as these may help. But the critical footing publishing projects such as these establish must remain negotiable if the discipline is to be protected from lapses in complacency. (Hemmings 2010)

This publication sits at the interstice of the texts included in Hemmings's anthology *The Textile Reader* (2012) and those of academic design research, combining and exploring one with the other and responding (and pledging back) to both (see Chapter 5). The metaphorical concept of the expansive rhizomatic matrix of design lends itself well to the critical literary, philosophical and cultural slant of the type of texts included in Hemmings's volume, which, as she notes, tend towards the Deleuzian (see Chapter 13). However, what I explore in this concept also proposes an alternative conception of what is considered as convergence in design, as depicted in the various models that have been drawn up (Dubberly 2004). Convergence is re-visioned as a notional whittling before breakages or diversion in the rhizome. I have deliberately avoided entering into the discussion about the position textiles occupies as applied art, design and craft, instead taking a clear stance that textile design as a design discipline encompasses all these at the same time. Doing this has meant that I have had to confront particular questions and assumptions about design and textiles head-on, rather than retreating to some of the established texts on craft such as those by Pye (1968), Dormer (1994, 1997), Adamson (2007, 2010) and Sennett (2008), which have a more, in some cases direct, application to textile practice.

Firmly situating textiles as a design discipline makes it accountable to the discussions within the design research community on the future of design education. Ken Friedman (2012: 148–50) and his co-editor Erik Stolterman (Rosner 2018: ix) outline ten challenges for design (see Figure 12):

Performance challenges	Act on the physical world
	Address human needs.
	Generate the built environment.
Substantive challenges	Increasingly ambiguous boundaries between artifacts, structures and processes.
	Increasingly large-scale social, economic and industrial frames.
	An increasingly complex environment of needs, requirements and constraints.
	Information content that often exceeds the value of physical substance.
Contextual challenges	A complex environment in which many projects or products cross the boundaries of several organizations, stakeholder, producer and user groups.
	Projects or products that must meet the expectations of many organizations, stakeholders, producers and users.
	Demands at every level of production, distribution, reception and control.

Figure 12 Ten challenges for design education. Adapted from Friedman (2012).

Friedman presents the challenges as a numbered list, but I prefer to avoid any connotation of hierarchy, and instead focus on the groupings proposed. Friedman states that the first three challenges require 'frameworks of theory and research to address contemporary professional problems and solve individual cases'. The grouping of substantive challenges focuses on these challenges. It appears that the textile design discipline (along with others) has routinely focused on the groupings of 'performance' and a rather limited scope of 'contextual challenges'. In bypassing the theoretical questions, the 'contextual' challenges remain somewhat fixed and limited. This is not to say that there are not examples where textile designers, educators and researchers are already tracing a line through aspects of all the three categories. However, it could be said that, even in the most forward-thinking and innovative textile practice, there is a tendency towards certain of these challenges. Textile design practice must begin to address the 'substantive' challenges listed above, specifically confronting the ambiguous boundaries between designed objects, structures and processes and by highlighting the significance and value of textilic design beyond the physical artefact and into cognition and to the design processes of other design disciplines.

My point is that by becoming an active participant in the discourse of design research, textile design must start to articulate and develop a position for itself in response to all these challenges. Particularly by confronting the substantive challenges, the types of organizations, stakeholders, producers and user groups that textile design is currently involved with could be massively altered and expanded. Effects would also be felt in the way that the textile design discipline relates to and interacts with these groups. Friedman's challenges for the design profession (including education) correlate with Kimbell's notion of the messy 'design thinking' nexus. Layered up, Friedman's challenges provide the striation, Kimbell's nexus the smooth: this combination would truly represent the challenges of future design. There is a tension in the oscillating relationship between the specificities of textile design as an entity (or discipline) outlined in this book and the mainstream oeuvre of design research. It is important that this is explored through the development of textile design theory.

Per Galle (2011: 94) mentions that there are good reasons to differentiate between design professions but also compelling reasons to conceptualize and address commonalities, citing Victor Margolin (1991, cited in Galle 2011)

> to define new points of contiguity and to facilitate greater collaboration between different types of designers while making it possible for individual designers to address a greater range of problems than most now do.

Victor Margolin's statement supports the requirement for textile design to participate more fully in the discourse of design research, for the benefit of both its own discipline and associated ones. It is prudent to note that Margolin remarked on this decades ago, and it is still an ongoing concern.

What textile designers have to say . . .

What textile designers have to say is an important part of our future. They have yet to explore further the use of pattern as a tool for thought in the context of pleasure and dreams – bad dreams as well as good.

(Graves 2002: 53)

Jane Graves points to just one aspect of future design on which many approaches to design can have a major impact, not just textiles. As I have explored, the overarching design problem for textiles can be seen as the cooperation of pleasures towards beauty and affect. Graves sees all textiles as pattern, whether pattern is present through the woven texture alone or as print on cloth: exploring and articulating textiles' action and agency in relation to human experience and emotion will of course be important in future design practice and theory across all disciplines.

In her distinctive style, Catherine Harper manages to give a poetic synopsis of some of the most innovatory practices and processes within textiles (Harper 2012: Vol 2, xiv–xv) and the impact of textiles on human experience. She follows it with a statement from textile innovator Carole Collet about how the future of textiles is not in responding to nature but with nature as its role model and mentor, working with biology and biomimicry to create sustainable future textiles. Although I also believe this to be true, it again exposes textile design's inefficacy in recognizing and articulating its significance to the history of design process, thinking and objects in general. The assumption that textile design has not so far been involved in mimicking nature overlooks the historical and archaic evolution of textiles and clothing (see Gilligan 2018) as well as the role that conscious variation has had in that. How was the idea of felt developed if not to mimic the matted fur and hair of humans and animals? How have the classic motifs of spots and stripes developed if not to imitate the natural markings of flora and fauna, for both aesthetic, spiritual, communicative and other functional purposes? Yet another long-established metaphor for cloth, textiles as a 'second skin', suggests that some form of biomimicry has implicitly and, in archaic terms, variously always been an aim of textile (design).

Innovation in textile design is strongly driven by developments in technology, fibre and materials, providing more explicit, defined design problems for textile designers. Many textile designers are indeed focusing on social issues than on aesthetic or technical concerns (e.g. Marr and Hoyes [2016], Goldsworthy and Earley [2018] and Sánchez-Aldana et al. [2019]) addressing some the 'substantive challenges' listed above, within higher education institutions and research and development projects for industry and policy. Growing awareness of the impact of textile consumption on the climate emergency as well as the connected issue of ethical design and production methods calls for urgent and impactful work in this area. Valentine et al. (2017) as well as long-standing projects such as *Girli Concrete* by Patricia Belford and Ruth Morrow have articulated the contribution textile designers make in collaborative inter-, trans- and multidisciplinary design projects that seek social or technical innovation. New researchers are developing works which explore the theories of textilic design practices; Lean (2020) traces textile thinking through her practice of facilitating workshops on materializing data; Miller (2019) practices textile thinking in collaborative projects in material science. The outcomes of these research projects are that the role of the (textile) designer, their collaborators and the design(s) is resolutely co-emergent. It is time for collaborators to recognize and value the impact of a textilic design approach to knowledge creation.

Imagine a hypothetical 'hospital gown' brief. The brief is to design a textile product that communicates the onset of increased body temperature. As long as the 'mechanism' for detecting and exhibiting heat sensitivity works, and there is appropriate consideration for the ethics of the scenario, the surface design could be anything at all: it could be text-based and graphical. Having a textile designer involved introduces affect – beauty and pleasure as a goal, functionality is in tasis with it (just as in the typical fashion and textile design context). Immediately, so many more aspects become important: the 'oscillating tension' between pragmatic technical and ethical considerations and the subjective and emotive are addressed through textile design. Simon J Williams (2001: 13) argues, 'Emotions . . . are embodied modes of being in the world, and the sine qua non of sociality and selfhood, conceived in intercorporeal, intersubjective, communicative terms.' He also sets up a social condition of eroticism as he explores the embodied gesture through the tension of the irrational and rational, focusing on the sociology of emotions of Marx, Simmel, Durkheim and Weber (Williams 2001: 6). Once again, we see scholars pointing to a social condition of oscillation; here its tension is eroticized by the context of emotion and sociality. To represent this, I wish to borrow (and corrupt!) Frayling's (1993: 5) adage for art and design research; I propose that design for affect, design into affect and design through affect will become key drivers for innovative textile practice and the development of textile design theory. This recognizes that affect or 'emotion' is not simply an outcome of the design process but part of it and aligns again with Kimbell's messy, contingent nexus. Williams (2001: 58) notes that Sartre (1962/1971) claims that 'Emotions . . . at one and the same time, involve both an imaginative mode of being-in-the-world and an imaginary "escape" from it. Confronted with a difficulty or impasse of some sort, for example, emotion "transform" the situation, making it somehow more "tolerable", "liveable" or "bearable."' This transformation of the situation seems to support Herbert Simon's 'science of design' where designers 'devise(s) courses of action aiming at changing existing situations into preferred ones' (Simon 1969: 111). However, this permeates the notion that design is an objective experience and disregards the subjectivity – and emotion – of the designers undertaking the process. Satre's statement notes that emotions help us to mediate situations; emotions are social, whereas affects are a 'pre-personal' state (Shouse 2005).

> The transmission of affect means that we are not self-contained in terms of our energies. There is no secure distinction between the 'individual' and the 'environment'. (Teresa Brennan 2004 in Shouse 2005)

More pluralist, feminist design research to represent multiple subjectivities in the field of design and emotion, pleasure, feeling and affect is urgently required. Transparency in and recognition of the creation of designed products and the ethics of design and manufacturing should have a bigger impact in this area.

In *On Understanding Emotion*, Denzin (1984/2007: 88) talks about 'emotional-interpretive practices' and goes on to offer several different kinds. Interpretive practices include those that are 'embodied', 'situated', 'personal', 'embedded' and 'accomplished', and he explains that these interpretive practices must be considered with regard to how the 'emotionality of the person attaches to these interpretive practices'. He then outlines 'emotional practices' as a complex coalition of these numerous interpretive practices and says, 'Any practice may become emotional, for all that is required is a transformation in the consciousness of the person out of the taken-for-granted into the world of emotional consciousness... To criticize and evaluate a practice is to criticize and evaluate the person who lies behind the practice' (1984/2007: 89).

This last statement resonates with me. First, as a lecturer of design I recall many years of the unenviable task of feeding back assessment and grades to students. The range in the emotional response is wild, sometimes instantaneous, sometimes brewing. We have judged their personal design work. They feel we have judged them. Feelings, affects and emotions are all at play. Second, it summarizes my own research experience, in particular my adoption of an autoethnographic approach which uses the personal, emotional, subjective experience to explore and critique the broader context of design research. It is my textilic design practice. It is an emotional and affective practice – a copoiesis.

> In the possibles of the practice, a world of doing that haunts and eludes the person is grasped and molded into concrete doing and accomplishments. The person claims ownership of these doings. The world becomes the person to the extent that practices produce actions that can be reflected on and claimed. The practices of the person produce things that are extensions of the person. In these practices the person is disclosed and revealed.... We give ourselves over to our practices, and in these practices we find ourselves. (Denzin 1984/2007: 89–90)

Denzin's 'practices' correspond with the notion of design as relational as well as other aspects developed across these chapters: the conative qualities of the 'possible', giving over oneself in the act of translation/transformation, designing as an ever-increasing, expansive matrix requiring physical and conceptual folding and playing, grasping and moulding emblematic of the rhizomatic breakage. Applying Denzin's idea of 'emotional practices' to design does seem to somewhat privilege the role of the lone designer, and this is a criticism of much established design research theory; however, when design is considered from a matrixial epistemology, design as a trans-subjective encounter is experienced by all those involved; it is at once personal and social.

What is textilic design?

Victoria Mitchell's defining work on textility (1997), further developed through the work of Tim Ingold (2010), is a key premise of this book. Textility is explained as a type of knowing through making which was debased in the era of the Enlightenment. Ingold describes how the textility of building gave way to architectonics – the relationality of making usurped by the cool rationality of technology. This ontological shift of course impacted in all areas of knowledge creation. Its effect in design was compounded in far more recent history by Simon's 'science of design' and perpetrated thereafter.

Textilic design is not about textile design. I suggest in this book that it is the most prevalent approach to designing textiles but it is not owned by it. If the field of textile design had been permitted to contribute to the development of design theory, that would be apparent. The closeness of the word 'textiles' and 'textilic' should not be an obstacle to understanding the nature of textilic design practice but an inbuilt metaphor to express its meaning fully and directly. A textilic approach is one that is entangled in relations with those agents we share our experiences of designing and our environments with; co-designers, makers or users, the materials and tools explored and selected for design and the context for designing. The process of designing with a textilic approach can be understood as moving from this metaphorical conceptual entanglement to one which is deftly woven – simultaneously smooth and striated. Textile design approaches rely on matrixial paradigms of being and knowing through trans-subjective encounters; that trans-subjectivity is not about connected yet individual bounded subjectivities; 'It is a weaving of affective and mental strings' (Ettinger 2006a: 219).

Textile design theory in the making

If this book represents an output of my textilic practice, what follows here is an act of frayage or facilitation (see Chapter 5) in the making of textile design theory. It is my translation-in-summary, a correlation and concentration of the main theoretical strands and themes explored across these pages. From a theoretical perspective, textile design can be captured as

Pleasure-giving aspects of natural and artificial decoration, ornament and texture (themselves recursively evolved from natural and archaic markings, colour, pattern and surfaces) are co-operated with and activated as transformations and expressions of phenomena, emotion and sensations in the trans-subjective design encounter, which uses repetition and composition in the creation of a visual and haptic multidimensional matrix to carry and communicate sensory and emotional information and messages of beauty in a multitude of commodified corporeal scenarios.

Summarized further:

Pleasurable aspects of nature and culture are processed through the act of textilic design by the subjective designer to express and activate affect. The experiential qualities of the resultant design, with particular emphasis on the haptic and visual repetition or composition of these qualities spatially, carry and communicate affect in socioeconomic contexts.

It is important to note that neither of these summaries mention textile design being distinctly about cloth or yarn or even surfaces. I am taking advantage of the etymology of the word 'textile' in addition to all the surreptitious occurrences of textile words with the English language (Kapp 2013). Textile designers are of course concerned with the materials of cloth making but, moreover, they can use any materials or media to design outcomes which translate, express, communicate and carry potential for affect, beauty, emotion and pleasure. As our lived worlds change, as our routes to pleasure expand into virtuality (Lee 2020b: 77) and therefore may be accessed and structured through artificial intelligence, it is important ethically to connect the materials and the immaterial and recognize that textilic practice and its associated 'textile thinking' transcend binarism and exist in human and non-human realms (Lee 2020a: 175). Understanding that textile design occurs largely through a textilic design epistemology supports this.

Ingold (2007: 14) in discussing matter and materials follows the path of William Gibson by focusing on substances and media and the surfaces between them which are the basic components of our environment. He distinguishes between the tangible existence of the physical world and the environment, which unfolds in relation to those having lived experiences within it. He goes on to say,

> And as the environment unfolds, so the materials of which it is comprised do not exist – like the objects of the material world – but occur.

Ingold describes how materials, and so, textiles, are set in a matrixial encounter with the environment in which they are created. They occur in relation to the space and time in which they are created. This is really a simple explanation for the history of materials and objects. Gold ore existed in our environment for millennia before humankind worked with it, exploring and multiplying its agency and properties. It existed then as it exists now but occurred – presented itself – in the prehistoric age differently to today.

> Thus the properties of materials, regarded as constituents of an environment, cannot be identified as fixed, essential attributes of things, but are rather processual and relational. They are neither objectively determined nor subjectively imagined but practically experienced. In that sense, every property is a condensed story. To describe the properties of materials is to tell the stories of what happens to them as they flow, mix and mutate. (Ingold 2007: 14)

And so what we understand textile design to be today must be expansive and set in relation to our lived worlds. Textile design as an entity encompassing textiles as objects (whether material or immaterial), textile designers and the textile design discipline, is always in tension between its 'occurrences'. Knowing that this situation provides an unresolvable complexity which is inclusive, expansive and adaptive allows us to recognize the privilege of working towards such ends. Through the development of new theories of textile design we can be at any one moment simultaneously exploring and developing new concepts of what we understand textiles and design to be. Buckley (2020: 29) reminds us that design (in relation to 'making') is an *ideologically loaded term* that needs to be questioned. Theories of textile design exist in an encounter. Theory occurs; it is in the making.

Epilogue

Toing and froing: On creating an oscillation-based practice

Marianne Fairbanks

In true rhizomatic form, Igoe's Chapter 15 *Elevated surfaces* offers myriad ideas as points of entry for my response, as evidenced by the false starts and abandoned drafts stored on my hard drive. In truth, my response to this chapter encompasses both text and textile, as my reflection on many of the ideas in this chapter reverberated and found expression in a body of work called *More Air-Like than Water*, more on which later.

As an artist and designer, I recognized myself and my practice in the preceding chapter. At each moment of recognition, I made a note in the margin: Metamodernism! Besidedness! Atopos! Rhizomatic! Textility! Before reading this chapter, I would not have applied any of these terms to my practice, not because they were not applicable but simply because I had not considered these concepts and terms in relation to my work. After reading Igoe, I have an essential new vocabulary with which to discuss my work, and so, perhaps the best response to this chapter will be to outline the ways in which my interdisciplinary practice as a maker engages many forms of knowledge that correspond to the interconnectedness and expansiveness of textiles. While a practice that encompasses multiple domains can at times feel scattered, my work always exists in the realm of innovation, wanting to create new ideas, solutions and processes. Though my practice has many threads, they all support one another, as with a braid, where each strand contributes to a stronger whole.

I have pursued this interdisciplinary, multipronged approach since I was an art student. As a maker with twenty years of experience, three threads of my practice have emerged – my solo work, my research into emerging textile technology and my social practice work. As I have worked to understand these systems in my practice over the years, I have often thought of them as polarities, or opposing forces. Though in light of Igoe's arguments, I'm persuaded that rhizomatic metamodernism might be an appropriate lens through which to see my practice, where the rhizome is the expansive, non-hierarchical piece, open to considering a wide breadth of influence and information, and the metamodern piece is active, constantly shifting, not a system of construction but rather a precarious movement, tilting, imbalance 'vehemently moving back and forth, left and right. . . . without ever seeming reducible to any one of them' (Vermeulen 2012: 215).

In reflecting on my practice, it is not about the oppositions but rather more about asking 'why' and hovering in the complicated interconnections between these ways of being and artist and designer. The relationship between these modes should not be measured on an old-fashioned weighing scale, one side having more value or stronger priority but set up on a seesaw motion, moving ideas back and forth, toing and froing.

While distinctly different in intentions and outcomes, each thread of my practice informs and supports the others. Whether engaging poetic and aesthetic pleasures, utilitarian applications or political and critical discourse, the unifying focus of my work is textiles and the role they will play in the future of our society.

My love for textiles began in 1994 in my sophomore year or college at the University of Michigan where the programme was titled 'Fibers'. In the United States, this terminology of Fibers versus Textiles is fraught with meaning and is indicative of the feminist history and a delineation between utility and art. I was largely unaware of these hierarchies and feminist histories being a nineteen-year-old student but was offered a glimpse into these pasts in the syllabus of my first Fibers course taught by Sherri Smith.

> All of these areas are to be approached as ways of making art forms. It is NOT a home economics course, and not a course for making useful little goodies. Garments and other useable objects are suitable only if they are original designs of very high quality. REMEMBER, THIS IS NEITHER THE TIME OR THE PLACE TO MAKE YOUR CHRISTMAS PRESENTS.

This inclusion in the syllabus didn't mean much to me at the time. I followed Smith's instructions and loved every aspect of Fibers process and theory. I went on to get my MFA at the School of the Art Institute of Chicago where I focused on developing conceptual art and collaborative practices.

Currently, I am an assistant professor of Design Studies in the School of Human Ecology at the University of Wisconsin–Madison. Students come to study textile design in the applied programme and receive a bachelor's of science. Having little clue about what Human Ecology meant when I first applied for the job, I was fascinated to learn that the original name of the school was Home Economics which had formed back in the early 1900s as a place to study domestic science and art. The transition from Home Economics to Human Ecology came in 1997 as a moniker that could better articulate the interdisciplinary nature of the programmes – the science of interrelationships. The School of Human Ecology now encompasses the departments of Civil Society and Community Studies, Consumer Science, Design Studies and Human Development and Family Studies.

I consider myself a conceptual artist using fiber media and focused on process and material meaning. I wasn't sure what to make of the idea of Human Ecology, though the idea of a 'science of interrelationships' was attractive and resonated with my own interdisciplinary and collaborative practice, and I was excited to move from an art school to a research university, and the possibilities that entailed. As a conceptual artist, teaching textile design was a bit of a departure for me, and entering this space of weaving, grounded in utility and, originally, in domesticity, I felt underqualified in many technical aspects of woven structures and finishing processes. I took this as an opportunity to pour over the information I found in the classroom, from journals to sample binders to books, which felt like a treasure trove of new practical knowledge about the subject of weaving I thought I knew. While I love conceptual work, I am not anti-utilitarian, and so what I encountered about structures, shrink rates, material estimates and other highly technical aspects of weaving impressed, inspired and intimidated me.

Simultaneously, I was engaging with old and new ideas and technologies in creating my new work. I learned about placemat, tablecloth and bedcover designs by reading journals like *Practical Weaving Suggestions*. I also learned the textile design software called Pointcarre so that I could create files to be woven on the Thread Controller 2 (TC2) loom. The entanglement of old and new, design and art, practical and impractical, low-tech and high-tech began swirling in my mind and became the seeds for my new work.

While my work had focused on the oppositional aspects of the form, practical versus impractical, masculine versus feminine and hard versus soft in a show titled *Impractical Weaving Suggestions* (Fairbanks 2016) after reflecting on the chapter by Igoe, I began to see my next body of work as rhizomatic rather than oppositional. The work in a show titled *More Air-Like than Water* investigates textile structures and systems and abstract vocabularies as they relate to image, architecture and graphic design. Using the processes of weaving, painting, photography and sculpture the work attempts to destabilize conventional value systems of hard and soft form-making while digging into more philosophical understandings of material versus immaterial.

Reading Michel Serres yielded for me new ideas about the relationship between hard and soft; ideas of 'hard' as physical and 'soft' as informational (as in hardware and software) entered my ways of understanding these dichotomies. Complicating the categories I had assigned to both was Serres's idea of 'hardness in softness and softness in hardness, [*de le dire dour*, Serres 1998, 165]' (Serres 2008: 129). Instead of a Boolean proposition, I saw nuance: if soft is a liquid and hard is solid that these things, like water, can change phase – they are dynamic and full of potential. Textility, as Igoe says, is knowing through making, and I came to better know the fluidity of soft/hard, information/object through the work I was making.

'The system's "matter" has changed "phase," at least since Bergson. It's more liquid than solid, more airlike than liquid, more informational than material. The global is fleeing towards the fragile, the weightless, the living, the breathing' (Serres and Latour 1995: 121).

I explore the change of states in the work *Gradient Slippage* (Figure 13). There are three layers of information, foreground, background, midground, but also

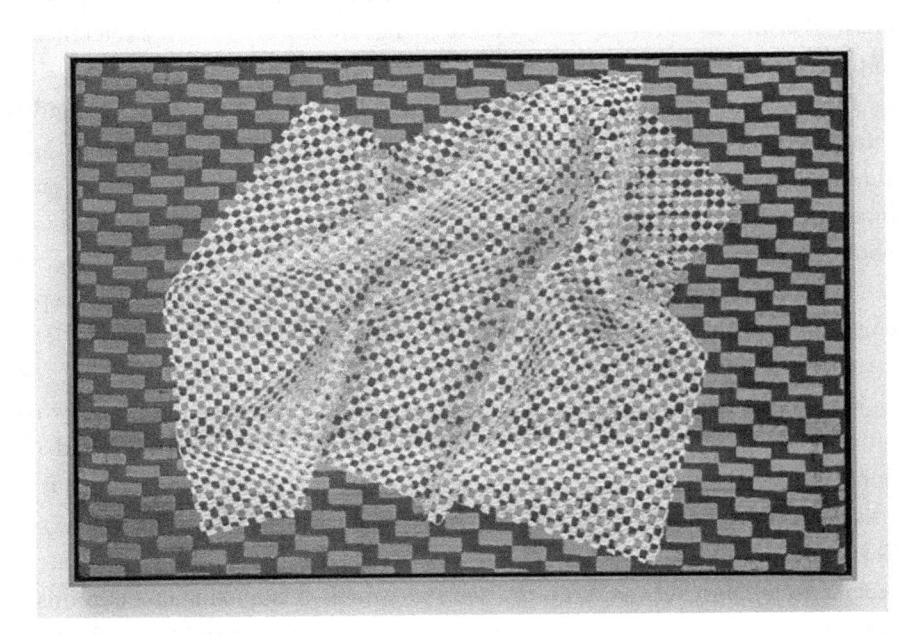

Figure 13 *Gradient Slippage* by Marianne Fairbanks (2018) 35.5 × 26 inches. Cotton, Tencel and polyester thread handwoven on TC-2 Loom (framed). Image by James Prinz. *Source*: Marianne Fairbanks.

structure, pattern and image. In the foreground, there is an image of a textile crumpled and full of form. The mesh is both beautiful and full of body, a nod to undulating and opulent textiles throughout art history, and pedestrian (in every sense of the word). It is a rug mat, a utilitarian piece of rubber with a grid-like system usually unseen beneath the rug itself. At once ordinary and domestic but also full of metaphors, simultaneously interconnected and open allowing for space and passage of information, a true mesh. While the work is serious and engages weighty concepts, it is not without humour as a point of entry.

The intersection of threads in the textile, a detail that often goes unnoticed because of the miniscule scale, has been enlarged to become the pattern filling the midground of the weaving. It looks a bit like bricks, but it is magnified glimpse at a satin structure. In the language of weave drafting a black square is used to indicate the warp is up and white for where the weft is up. This binary system of lowering or lifting of threads is the basis of all woven textiles. A satin structure is used to try to hide the tacking of the intersection of threads and requires both a repeat size and shift of the tacking threads. Beyond the integrity of the structure and the hand of the cloth, this structure can be used to create a gradient, where more warp threads up creates a darker value, or more weft threads up creates a lighter value. Using the gradient values is an attempt to illustrate the change in phase, the shift from image to object, the change from warp to weft a reference to the relationship of hard and soft, information and object.

The intersection of threads in the satin structure is both the background information and the building blocks that reveal how three-dimensional object is woven line by line, thread by thread. The jacquard loom enables me to weave an image or photo, the photo is still really a structure, structure is object, object is photo, photo is pixels, pixels are threads and on and on (Figure 14).

While the work fights for perceptual attention, it also encourages a deep engagement with our material world in the construction of philosophical belief systems and physical realities.

My interest in textile-based logic systems, philosophy and efficiency has drawn me to the work of Buckminster Fuller. I saw an image of his attempt to build a dome in a field at Black Mountain College where many students were holding up what looks to be limp flat lines – what look to be aluminium blinds (Díaz 2015). The angles were right but the material was wrong and the geometric structure seemed to fall into flatness, limp and soft (later dubbed 'Supine Dome'). In this early study of Fuller's signature domes, the aluminium was not rigid enough and folded under the weight. For me this image of structure and softness has always represented the closeness of these systems and logics, and also of failure and risk.

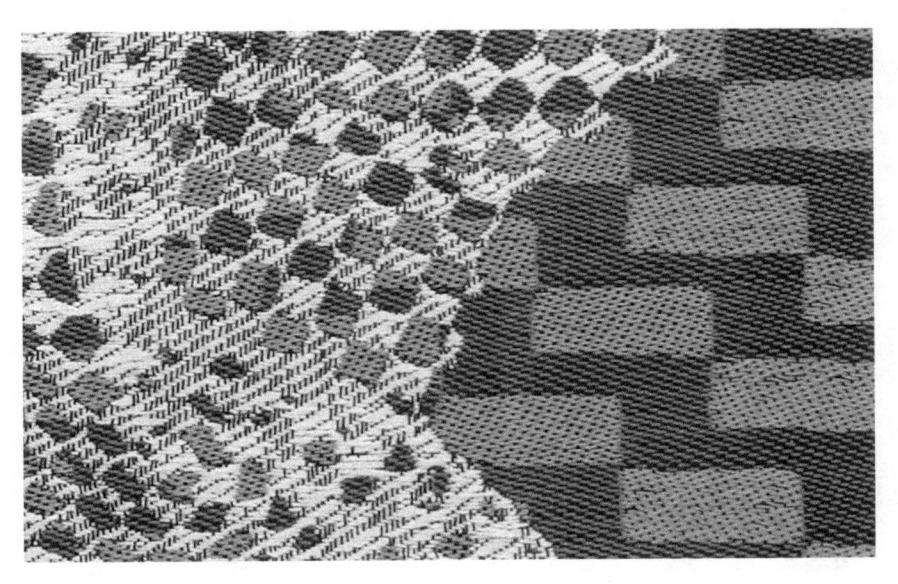

Figure 14 Detail of *Gradient Slippage* (2018) by Marianne Fairbanks (detail). 35.5 × 26 inches. Cotton, Tencel and polyester thread handwoven on TC-2 Loom (framed). Image by James Prinz. *Source*: Marianne Fairbanks.

Using the fold and flex of the aluminium blind material used in the dome experiments, I built new physical vocabulary of three-dimensional forms, or fonts, in a work called *Fuller Sampler*. Thinking through tension and compression and what is possible within one or two of these units. Restricting myself to a line or a string to hold the form, I worked to know the limits and structure through process. I use my hands as a way of knowing the materials but also as a way of experiencing structure and physics with my hands and body (Figure 15).

While inspired by Buckminster Fuller's hands-on approach to building a geodesic dome at Black Mountain College in the 1950s (Edmondson 1986), this work is also informed by the idea of samplers: a way of teaching young girls (who were not sent to school) their alphabet through the process of embroidered samplers – knowing through making. Fuller, also had a hands-on approach to thinking through math, geometry and architecture which is made evident through both his presence among artists but also in the trials and errors made visible in that image of students working together to build the dome.

My sculptural research is working to better understand math through making, but also, seen through the lens of Fuller's synergetics, it is inherently an attempt to 'comprehend feelingly the way nature works'. Therefore, the implications extend

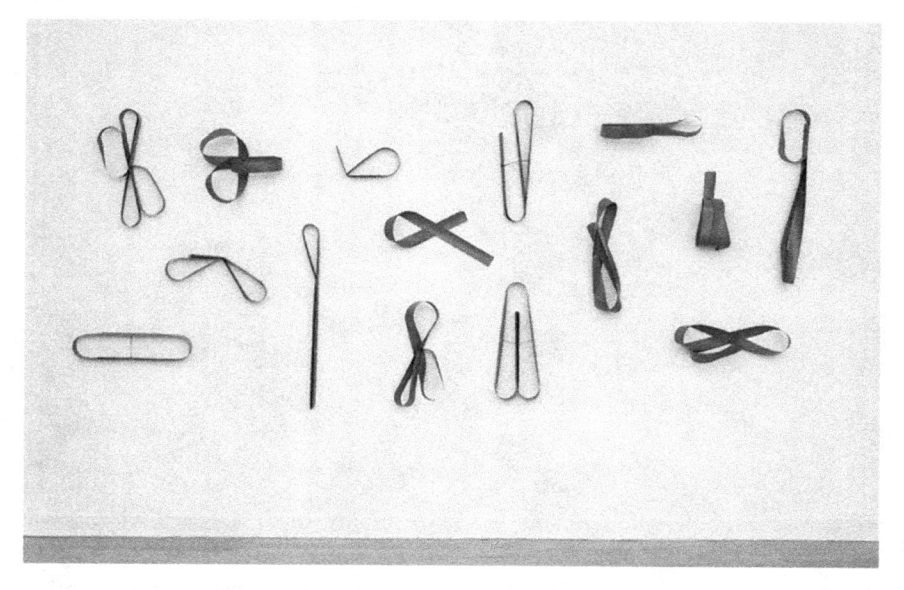

Figure 15 Fuller Sampler (2018) by Marianne Fairbanks. Size variable. Metal blinds, paint, waxed Kevlar. Installed at Living Room, Chicago, IL, United States. Image by James Prinz. *Source*: Marianne Fairbanks.

and connect the work of hands at a human scale to a greater understanding of the systems of nature and the cosmos.

Physicists speak of the fabric of the cosmos, and weaving metaphors abound in cosmology. My work embraces the idea that textiles, and their logic systems, comprise the micro and the macro, the utilitarian and the abstruse, the domestic and the cosmic. These are the spaces my work explores. My solo practice requires what Igoe calls the 'kneading and folding the dough' that I employ through process to find 'a deeper, truer understanding of the phenomenon, inviting in notions of tension in the "socio-material world"'.

Along with these material forms of making and knowing I have also developed a social practice called Weaving Lab, a project that marries theory, production and action in a method I call speculative weaving. Speculative weaving is the term I have used to encompass an approach that bridges the divide between craft-based traditions and conceptual work wherein weaving serves as the nucleus of community engagement and the catalyst for broad interdisciplinary explorations. Speculative design has emerged as a field that promotes the thinking openly about how things could be with an open-ended approach to solutions, formed actively as debate and discussion as in the book

Speculative Every: Design, Fiction, and Social Dreaming by Anthony Dunne and Fiona Raby (2013).

In many ways this approach resonates with the conceptual prompt of Weaving Lab but also veers away in the way that the social is promoted as an outcome, as is the process, not the product.

As a public site offering opportunities for hands-on experience and exploration, *Weaving Lab* recalls historical models of local production and asks whether access to looms as a social destination might create community. Participants are encouraged to approach and appreciate the process of weaving as an end in itself, while also considering the act in relation to conceptual domains of time, rhythm, meditation and materiality. As an artist, my practice has long included collaborative and community-based work. Weaving Lab takes lessons learned through those long-term practices and combines them with the disciplinary concerns of craft, design, art and social practice.

In researching weaving as a domestic and utilitarian design form, I began to question some stereotypes about the process and wondered if these could be explored, confirmed, debunked or demystified through a public inquiry.

One such stereotype, for example, is the assumption that weaving takes a lot of time. For the Hour Towel prompt, I set up a loom with a cotton warp and decorative twill pattern and asked each weaver to sit down for one hour to weave a towel. The resulting cloth acts as a physical representation of one hour of time, and shown together, the cloths become a timeline documenting process and labour invested into constructing a material for a period of time.

What is harder to reveal with this project is the social practice aspect. While the participants wove a lot of textiles collectively, how does that interaction get documented? A photo of a group of people in a room fails to get at the conversations and connections that were made in that space together. Perhaps the fabric we produced lives as a document of collected action or conversation. More intangible or ephemeral moments can be described as the spaces between the intersection of threads, just as important in the creation of cloth and yet immaterial. And to expand the weaving metaphor, Weaving Lab is about creating spaces for these intersections of people, processes and ideas.

In this case, the process is elevated over the product, and yet collectively there is a fabric being produced. The fabric gets processed, and sometimes sold as design objects to support the continuation of the project. One loom was set up to explore math through colour and pattern relationships. Participants were prompted to try different sequences of colours with different pattern variations.

The resulting cloth was a community endeavour and was cut into squares and made into pillows, each one is different, woven by many hands, anonymous in their exploration of pattern, colour and structure, but nonetheless individualistic in result.

This project has given me an opportunity to investigate weaving as an idea, an engineered system with a produced utilitarian artefact. I conduct this research collectively with community in the hopes that we can ask these questions together, not to get hard answers but to have conversations. Not to weave perfect cloth but to get our hands and minds involved in the process of making and knowing. This notion of textiles being a place where people come together socially is not new. 'The act of working together on textile-making has long been an important way of furthering a sense of group cohesion. This was true in traditional work "bees" for activities like processing fibre or making quilts and is equally evident in today's burgeoning craft groups.' Of these practices, I am most inspired by the textile practices that involve a collective making, not working on an individual item but a collective result. I am not interested in sitting down to weave myself towels or pillow covers but I am interested in skill-building, in the local production of cloth, in expansive thinking and in shared spaces where we can explore these potentials collaboratively and be together.

When I initially started working collaboratively as a young artist, it felt both risky and fresh to do so in an art world built on prizing individual genius. I also liked this form of making because of the ability for two people to build something bigger than one. I worked in a collaborative with Jane Palmer called JAM, and together we created projects that used technology, high and low, to create work that often asked for participation, involved some sort of alternative energy and strived to be poetic.

One of JAM's projects was *Personal Power*, a project that integrated flexible solar panels into garments, backpacks and handbags to create mobile power units for devices such as cell phones. Eventually we transformed this idea into a product and business call Noon Solar that marketed sustainably produced, high-fashion handbags with integrated flexible thin film solar panels. Where *Personal Power* was shown in galleries as a vision of possibility, one goal of Noon Solar was to realize the vision of a means to disconnect from conventional power sources while remaining connected to a larger network of information. We recognized the tremendous potential of this as a design solution and product, but it also was initially conceived as art, with poetic and aesthetic concerns. We had to be unafraid to explore terrains of technology and entrepreneurship, and we used our naivety and passion as strengths that allowed us to enter this new space.

As designers, inventors and business women, we had many successes with Noon Solar with international distribution and retail presence in over thirty stores, loads of press and eager customers who wanted more sustainable options. Nevertheless, in 2010 we closed shop, mostly due to burnout, but many of the lessons learned from that experience advanced forward.

Four years later, when I joined the faculty at the University of Wisconsin, Madison, I was still thinking about how solar technology could become more seamlessly integrated into portable goods. Being at a large research institution allows me to connect with engineers and scientists with whom I can collaborate to think about new multifunctional textile solutions. I reached out to a chemistry professor who had been working with developing an organic dye-based solar cell on paper and proposed we collaborate to conduct this research on a textile substrate. I have also started projects with an electrical engineering professor, an additive manufacturing and polymer engineering professor and a mathematics professor. While the collaboration to create the solar textile has progressed the farthest, with two published papers, conference presentations and test swatches, the pace of all of these collaborative efforts is slow. I have also worked with a mechanical engineer who specializes in additive manufacturing to develop a set of three-dimensional printed studies that test the pliability and rigidity of the print material and the textile structure. Unfortunately, both of the collaborations were cut short when my collaborators departed the university, one to work in the private sector and the other to a different research institution. I continue collaborative research with a colleague in electrical engineering to see if we can apply woven structures to motor construction (cannot disclose more until the research is published).

I have entered these research projects without much funding, and largely under the radar. This is partly due to focusing on solo primary research, institutional tenure pressures and time limitations. The informal (and unfunded) approach to collaboration lowers the stakes, to some degree, and it is delightful to enter the collaboration when the pressure of a determined result is not weighing heavily over the research. By the same token, such approach contributes to the slow advancement of the research.

In her discussion of textility, Igoe points to Tim Ingold's work, who wrote of textilic practitioners as 'wanderers, wayfarers, whose skill lies in their ability to find the grain of the world's becoming and to follow its course while bending it to their evolving purpose' (Ingold 2010). This, for me, is an apt description of my approach to collaboration. As I follow the grain of the world, and the grain of my work, I am often drawn to areas beyond my specific expertise. To continue to follow the grain where it leads, I must find collaborators whose own wandering had led them away from their own specialization. Together, enriched by each other's expertise and insights, we can continue to follow the grain.

With collaboration, however, comes challenges that must be an important part of the conversation about textilic design. When working collaboratively, each individual is challenged to invent collectively, to reach outside of comfort zones, and to rely on others. In my experience, the only way such partnerships can be fruitful is to have a shared investment in the process and outcomes, the time and space to think imaginatively and for each collaborator to be open and generous, all of which requires a relationship of trust. And yet, as important as collaboration is, there are many risks that make this kind of work difficult; in academic settings collaborators face additional challenges of funding, intellectual property, performance measures and a culture that often still prizes individual achievement over collaborative accomplishments.

Even with successes, each of these collaborations has been challenged by the cultural and institutional paradigms I have mentioned. I believe a textilic approach and interdisciplinary collaboration are essential to progress and innovation, though if textilic design is to be more widely accepted and practiced in the academy, we must also honestly and forcefully address the challenges I've described. Further, we must ward against the appropriation of textile thinking as a business strategy, as has been done with 'Design Thinking'.

All of these interactions with practitioners outside my field have inspired me to imagine new textile-based solutions to design problems, but also they inform my personal work, and how I might apply the lessons of my research in an artistic application as well. I relish the opportunity to use my technical expertise, and perhaps even more importantly, to apply my training as an artist in critical and conceptual thinking. My collaborations are possible in large part because of as a member of a large research institution, I am in contact with practitioners in many other fields. And yet, without the other strands of my practice, these collaborations would not be possible. My previous work and the success of Noon Solar and Weaving Lab has allowed me the credibility to approach researchers in other fields; these projects reflect my values, my way of thinking, inventiveness and ability to complete a project.

The potential of interdisciplinary collaboration is great and yet vastly underdeveloped. The value systems assigned to our areas of scholarship are intensely disparate; science research is well funded whereas art and design research is still the underdog. I am fully aware that when I enter these collaborations I am often at a financial disadvantage and it can be frustrating to see how much funding can become available in the arts when a STEM researcher joins the research, while there is rarely, if ever a grant funding advantage for STEM researcher who bring artists or designers into the team. The scientists and engineers might not think they need artists and designers, and yet there are solutions yet to be discovered that I believe can only come from collaborative effort.

I share all of this because it is my lived experience, as someone who is trying to embody a textile approach to my practice. There have been failures, starts and stops and abrupt ends, but the rewards have also been great. Beyond the success or failure of any end 'product', the process, the interactions and the communication involved in all of these forms of making yield their own invaluable dividends. Perhaps that is part of this equation that is also underappreciated: the value that comes from the effort. As Matsuo Basho said, 'the journey itself is home.'

As the threads of a braid intertwine, the resulting structure grows stronger. Each strand added to the braid is not straight, it must wend and bend around the others to become part of the whole, and strengthen the cord. Likewise, each of my ways of making – solo work, social practice and collaboration – reinforce and inform each other. Because there is no straight line to success, and because there remain undefined regions and relationships, encouraging the next generation to take it on as a course of study may be confusing. And yet, the slippery and oscillating relationship between creativity, utility, design and community holds a healthy tension that for the right practitioners can keep them engaged in innovative ideas and solutions for the future. Along with my call for taking more risks and thinking big will come failure but that is part of the oscillation, sometimes the seesaw is down, but sometimes it is up. I encourage going for the ride, toing and froing, following the grain of the world, knowing the buoyancy and beauty of the braid.

Glossary of terms

Please note, this glossary explains the key terms used by main author, Elaine Igoe.

Affect/affective A feeling or subjective experience in response to stimulus accompanied by thoughts or actions.
Atopos/atopic The ineffable, placeless state of experiencing rare phenomena and emotions.
Autoethnography An approach to research and writing that describes and analyses personal experience to understand cultural phenomena.
Autopoiesis Self-maintaining, productive organization and regulation. To develop a full understanding of this term, please read Maturana and Varela (1972/1980).
BAME A term used to group Black, Asian and Minority Ethnic people. The term is criticized for its homogeneity.
Borderspace/borderlinking For Ettinger, borderspaces indicate the spaces between conceptual and ideological borders, for example, binaries. Borderlinking is the linking together of borderspaces. To develop a full understanding of this term, please read Ettinger (2006a).
Conation/conative The volitional act of endeavour; expressing will or desire.
Copoiesis A joint process of creation used a key term in the definition of matrixial theory in Ettinger (2006a).
Diffraction/diffractive Here used in its post-humanist sense as a productive means or quality of gaining knowledge of the effects of difference through critical practices of material engagement from within.
Enact/enactive To actuate, represent or perform.
Entity Existing as a discrete unit. In this book textiles is seen as a complete entity encompassing its disciplinary behaviours, design process, designers as well as textiles as designed objects.
Epistemology/epistemological Theoretical discourse on knowledge and understanding.
Fabulation To fabulate is to fabricate a narrative. In this book, critical fabulations are referred to as semi-non-fictional narrative creative practices. To develop a full understanding of this term, please read Hartman (2008: 11) and Rosner (2018).
Feminine (noun) Pertaining to the female gender in social constructed gender distinctions.
Feminist (noun) An advocate of feminism to bring equality to all genders. (adjective) Advocating for equality to all genders.

Frayages An activity that invites an understanding of unravelling as a facilitative step in the creation of understanding or knowledge. To develop a full understanding of this term, please read Spivak (1993).

Gender A social and cultural construct that distinguishes differences in roles and responsibilities between women, men, girls and boys.

Gendering (verb) Recognizing or integrating perspectives of gender into the understanding and construction of phenomena.

Hermeneutics Relating to or concerning interpretation.

Intersectionality A feminist sociological theory that refers to overlapping social identities and related systems of oppression, domination and/or discrimination. To develop a full understanding of this term, please read Crenshaw (1989).

Ludic Pertaining to play and playfulness.

Matrixial In a basic sense, meaning 'of the womb/uterus'. Ettinger (2006a) uses this term metaphorically to explain her feminist theory of relationality, which avoids notions of discrete subjectivity.

Metamodernism Is a structure of feeling that emerges from, and reacts to, the postmodern and a cultural logic that corresponds to global capitalism today (van den Akker, Gibbons and Vermeulen 2017: 5).

Metaphor Something regarded as representative or suggestive of something else. A novel or poetic expression of a concept outside of its conventional meaning to express a similar concept.

Metaxy An oscillating state of 'in-betweenness' that delivers a 'both-neither' dynamic.

Methectic/methexis Describing collective participation, here used in the context of the rituals of playing.

Metramorphosis A weaving-like process of change resulting in/of matrixial ontology and epistemology. To develop a full understanding of this term, please read Ettinger (2006a).

Multiplicity The quality or condition of being manifold. In this book this term refers to the use by Deleuze and Guattari (1980) to describe the concept of a complex structure that disavows division.

Ontological Theoretical discourse on the nature of reality.

Pedagogy/pedagogical Pertaining to learning, instruction and training.

Phallogocentrism Structures of understanding, communication and action that express and reinforce male or patriarchal privilege and dominance.

Pluriverse/pluriversal A concept that recognizes multiple constructions of the universe(s).

Poiesis Creative production.

Polyphonic Producing or involving many voices (or sounds).

Relationality A theoretical concept that gives importance to the relational nature of reality or interprets reality in terms of relations.

Rhizome/rhizomatic In Deleuze and Guattari (1980), the metaphor of a rhizome – an underground growing system or root that sends out shoots and leaves at intervals – is used to describe a model of culture with no origin or end that resists chronological organization.

Semantics The study of meaning in linguistics.

Tacit/tacit knowledge Unspoken or unvoiced. Tacit knowledge describes intellect that is not accessible or communicable through language.

Textasis The tension of separation and binding within textility.

Textility/textilic Derived from the linguistic roots of weaving, it suggests an approach to making that separates and binds fibrous substances or materials. In this book, this term is used to collectively describe the particularities of making objects, language and texts. To be *textilic* is adopt the approach of textility. To develop a full understanding of this term, please read Mitchell (1997).

Trans-subjective/trans-subjectivity Transcending notions of singular or individual subjective experience.

Tripartite Composed of three parts.

Woman (noun) An adult female human.

Worldview A set of fundamental beliefs or values that denote a perspective on life or the world.

References

Adams, T., Ellis. E. and Holman Jones, S. (2008) 'Autoethnography Is Queer'. In *Handbook of Critical and Indigenous Methods*. Thousand Oaks: SAGE Publications Ltd, pp. 373–90.

Adams, T., Holman Jones, S. and Ellis, E. (2015) *Autoethnography*. Oxford University Press.

Adamson, G. (2007) *Thinking Through Craft*. Oxford: Berg.

Adamson, G., ed. (2010) *The Craft Reader*. Oxford: Berg.

Adorno, T. W. (1944) *Minima Moralia: Reflections on Damaged Life*. Trans. E. Jephcott. London: Verso (2005).

Albers, A. (1962) *Anni Albers: On Designing*. Middletown, CT: Wesleyan University Press.

Albers, A., Cirauqui, M., Smith, T. L. and Josef and Anni Albers Foundation (2017) *On Weaving* (New expanded edition). Pinceton, NJ: Pinceton University Press.

Andrew, S. (2008) 'Textile Semantics: Considering a Communication-Based Reading of Textiles'. *TEXTILE*, 6 (1): 32–65.

Anni Albers: A Life in Thread (2019). BBC Studios. 21 August.

Archer, B. (1979) 'Design as a Discipline'. *Design Studies*, 1 (1): 17.

Armstrong, L. (2012) 'Commentary, Portraits: Women Designers, Arts and Culture'. Available at http://arts.brighton.ac.uk/collections/design-archives/resources/women-designers/commentary. Accessed 25 August 2019.

Attfield, J. (1989) 'FORM/Female FOLLOWS FUNCTION/Male: Feminist Critiques of Design'. In J. A. Walker (ed.), *Design History and the History of Design*. London, Chicago: Pluto Press, pp. 199–225.

Attfield, J. (2000) *Wild Things: The Material Culture of Everyday Life*. Oxford: Berg.

Barnett, P. (1999) *Folds, Fragments, Surfaces: Towards a Poetics of Cloth*. (exh. cat.) Nottingham: Angel Row Gallery, pp. 125–34.

Bateson, M. C. (2000) *Full Circles, Overlapping Lives*. New York: Ballantine.

Baudrillard, J. (1968) 'Subjective Discourse of the Non-functional System of Objects'. In F. Candlin and R. Guins (eds), *The Object Reader*. Abingdon. Routledge (2009), pp. 41–63.

Baule, G. and Caratti, E. (2017) *Design Is Translation: The Translation Paradigm for Design Culture*. Milano: Angeli.

Benjamin, W. (1923) 'The Translator's Task'. Trans. S. Rendall. In L. Venuti, ed. *The Translation Studies Reader*. 3rd edition, Abingdon: Routledge (2012), pp. 75–83

Benjamin, W. (1936) 'The Storyteller: Reflections on the Work of Nikolai Leskov'. In H. Arendt (ed.) and H. Zorn (trans.), *Illuminations*. New York: Schocken Books (1968), pp. 83–109.

Boehnert, J. (2014) 'Design vs. The Design Industry'. *Design Philosophy Papers*, 12 (2): 119–36.

Booker, C. (2004) *The Seven Basic Plots*. London: Continuum.

Brett, D. (2005) *Rethinking Decoration*. Cambridge: Cambridge University Press.

Buckley, C. (1986) 'Made in Patriarchy: Towards a Feminist Analysis of Women and Design'. In C. Harper (ed.), *Textiles: Critical & Primary Sources: Vol 1, History and Curation*. Oxford, London, Berg: Bloomsbury (2012), pp. 236–51.

Buckley, C. (2020) 'Made in Patriarchy II: Researching (or Re-Searching) Women and Design'. *Design Issues*, 36 (1): 19–26.

Butler, J. (2006) 'Eurydice'. In B. Ettinger, *The Matrixial Borderspace*. Minneapolis, MN: University of Minnesota Press (2006), pp. vii–xii.

Bye, E. (2010) 'A Direction for Clothing and Textile Design Research'. *Clothing and Textiles Research Journal*, 28 (3): 205–17. https://doi.org/10.1177/0887302X10371505.

Chadwick, W. (1993) 'Living Simultaneously: Sonia and Robert Delaunay'. In W. Chadwick and I. Courtivron, *Significant Others: Creativity and Intimate Partnership*. London: Thames & Hudson, pp. 30–49.

Chamberlain, L. (1988) 'Gender and the Metaphorics of Translation'. *Signs: Journal of Women in Culture and Society*, 13 (3): 454–72.

Connor, S. (2011) *Paraphernalia: The Curious Lives of Magical Things*. London: Profile.

Cook, F. H. (1973) *Hua-Yen Buddhism: The Jewel Net of Indra*. University Park: Pennsylvania State University Press.

Craig, C. and Huber, J. (2007) 'Relational Reverberations: Shaping and Reshaping Narrative Inquiries in the Midst of Storied Lives and Contexts'. In J. Clandinin (ed.), *Handbook of Narrative Inquiry: Mapping a Methodology*. Thousand Oaks, London, New Delhi: SAGE, pp. 251–79.

Crenshaw, K. (1989) *Demarginalizing the Intersection of Race and Sex: A black Feminist Critique of Antidiscrimination Doctrine, Feminist Theory and Antiracist Politics*. University of Chicago Legal Forum, 1(8): 139–167. Available at: http://chicagounbound.uchicago.edu/uclf/vol1989/iss1/8

Cross, N. (2007) *Designerly Ways of Knowing*. Basel, Boston, Berlin: Birkhauser.

Cross, N. (2011) *Design Thinking: Understanding How Designers Think and Work*. Oxford and New York: Berg.

Csikszentmihalyi, M. (1990) *Flow and the Psychology of Discovery and Invention*. New York: Harper Collins.

Damon, M. (2009, December 2) *Text, Textile, Exile: Meditations on Poetics, Metaphor, Net-work* [online]. Available at https://electronicbookreview.com/essay/text-textile-exile-meditations-on-poetics-metaphor-net-work/. Accessed 31 July 2019.

Damon, M. (2011) *B, tiny arkhive: for Adeena Karasick* [blog]. 24 February. Available at http://www.hyperpoesia.net/2011/02/b-tiny-arkhive-for-adeena-karasick.html. Accessed 1 August 2013.

De Waal, E. (2007) 'Sticky/Smooth'. In T. Harrod and E. de Waal (eds), *Gift: Papers and Exhibition 2007*. Gmunden Think Tank e.V., pp. 46–9.

Deleuze, G. and Guattari, F. (1980) *A Thousand Plateaus; Capitalism and Schizophrenia*. Trans. B. Massumi. London: Continuum (1987/2008).

Deleuze, G. (1988) *The Fold: Leibniz and the Baroque*. Trans. T. Conley. Minneapolis, MN: University of Minnesota Press (1993).

Denzin, N. (1984/2007) *On Understanding Emotion*. New Brunswick, NJ: Transaction.

Denzin, N. and Lincoln, Y., eds (2011a) *The Sage Handbook of Qualitative Research*. 4th Edition. Los Angeles, London, New Delhi, Singapore, Washington, DC: SAGE.

Denzin, N. and Lincoln, Y. (2011b) 'Introduction: The Discipline and Practice of Qualitative Research'. In N. Denzin, and Y. Lincoln (eds), *The Sage Handbook of Qualitative Research*. 4th Edition. Los Angeles, London, New Delhi, Singapore, Washington, DC: SAGE, pp. 1–19.

Design Council (2019) 'The 'Double Diamond' Design Process Model'. [online] Available at https://www.designcouncil.org.uk/news-opinion/what-framework-innovation-design-councils-evolved-double-diamond.

Dilnot, C. (1982) 'Design as a Socially Significant Activity: An Introduction'. *Design Studies*, 3(3): 139–146.

Dilnot, C. (1995) 'The Gift'. In V. Margolin and R. Buchanan (eds), *The Idea of Design: A Design Issues Reader*. Cambridge, MA, London: MIT Press (1996), pp. 144–55.

Dormer, P. (1994) *The Art of the Maker*. London: Thames & Hudson.

Dormer, P., ed. (1997) *The Culture of Craft*. Manchester: Manchester University Press.

Dormor, C. (2012) *Material Matrices: Haptic, Scopic and Textile*. PhD thesis, Norwich University College of Arts and the University of the Arts, London.

Dorst, K. (2008) 'Design Research: A Revolution Waiting to Happen'. *Design Studies*, 29 (1): 4–11.

Dorst, K. and Cross, N. (2001) 'Creativity in the Design Process: Co-evolution of Problem–Solution'. *Design Studies*, 22 (5): 425–37.

Downer, L. (2006) 'The City Geisha and Their Role in Modern Japan: Anomaly or Artistes?' In B. Gordon and M. Feldman (eds), *The Courtesan's Arts: Cross-cultural Perspectives*. Oxford and New York: Oxford University Press, pp. 223–42.

Dryden, J. (1680) 'On Translation'. In R. Schulte and J. Biguenet (eds), *Theories of Translation: An Anthology of Essays from Dryden to Derrida*. Chicago, IL, London: University of Chicago Press (1992).

Dubberly, H. (2004) *How Do You Design? A Compendium of Models*. Available at https://issuu.com/ciphermak/docs/how:do_u_design_design_process. Accessed 29 August 2019.

Eames Gallery (n.d.). Available at http://eamesgallery.com/medium-house-of-cards-blue-cover/. Accessed 31 August 2013.

Earley, R. (2017) 'Circular Design Futures'. *The Design Journal*, 20 (4): 421–34. https://doi.org/10.1080/14606925.2017.1328164.

Earley, R., Vuletich, C., Hadridge, P. and Andersen, K. R. (2016) 'A New "T" for Textiles: Training Design Researchers to Inspire Buying Office Staff Towards Sustainability at

Hennes and Mauritz (H&M)'. *The Design Journal*, 19 (2): 301–21. https://doi.org/10.1080/14606925.2016.1130380.

Ellis, C. and Bochner, A. P. (2000) 'Autoethnography, Personal Narrative, Reflexivity; Researcher as Subject'. In N. Denzin and Y. Lincoln (eds), *Handbook of Qualitative Research*, 2nd Edition. Thousand Oaks, London, Delhi: Sage Publications, pp. 733–68.

Escobar, A. (2018) *Designs for the Pluriverse*. Durham, NC: Duke University Press.

Ettinger, B. (2004) 'Weaving a Woman Artist With-in the Matrixial Encounter Event'. *Theory, Culture & Society* 21: 69–94

Ettinger, B. (2005) 'Copoiesis'. [online] *Ephemera*, 5 (X): 703–13. Available at http://www.ephemerajournal.org/sites/default/files/5-Xettinger.pdf. Accessed 11 September 2012.

Ettinger, B. (2006a) *The Matrixial Borderspace*. Minneapolis, MN: University of Minnesota Press.

Ettinger, B. (2006b) 'Matrixial Trans-subjectivity'. *Theory, Culture & Society* 23 (2–3): 218–22.

Frayling, C. (1993) 'Research in Art and Design'. *Royal College of Art Research Papers*, 1 (1). London: Royal College of Art.

Friedman, K. (2003) 'Theory Construction in Design Research: Criteria: Approaches and Methods'. *Design Studies*, 24 (6): 507–22.

Friedman, K. (2007) 'Disciplines, Fuss etc…PhD Design Jiscmail Discussion List'. [online] 29 September 2007. Available at https://www.jiscmail.ac.uk/cgi-bin/webadmin?A0=phd-design. Accessed 27 December 2010.

Friedman, K. (2012) 'Models of Design: Envisioning a Future Design Education'. *Visible Language*, 46 (1–2): 132–53.

Friedman, K. (2013) 'More on Design Thinking'. PhD Design Jiscmail Discussion List [online] Available at https://www.jiscmail.ac.uk/cgi-bin/webadmin?A0=phd-design. Accessed 23 July 2013.

Friedrich, H. (1965) 'On the Art of Translation'. Trans. R. Schulte and J. Biguenet, *Theories of Translation: An Anthology of Essays from Dryden to Derrida*. Chicago, IL, London: University of Chicago Press (1992), pp. 11–16.

Gadamer, H.-G. (1960) *Truth and Method*. Trans. and ed. D. G. Marshall and J. Weinsheimer, 3rd Edition. New York: Continuum (1997).

Gale, C. and Kaur, J. (2002) *The Textile Book*. Oxford: Berg.

Galle, P. (2011) 'Foundational and Instrumental Design Theory'. *Design Issues*, 27 (4): 81–94.

Gardner Troy, V. (2006) *The Modernist Textile: Europe and America, 1890–1940*. London: Lund Humphries.

Gerdes, K. and Stromwall, L. (2008) 'Conation: The Missing Link in the Strengths Perspective'. *Social Work*, 53 (3) 233–242.

Gilligan, I. (2018) *Climate, Clothing, and Agriculture in Prehistory: Linking Evidence, Causes, and Effects*. Cambridge: Cambridge University Press.

Goldsworthy, K. and Earley, R. (2018) 'Circular Transitions: Textile Design and the Circular Economy'. *Journal of Textile Design Research and Practice*, 6 (1): 1–4. https://doi.org/10.1080/20511787.2018.1505362.

Gordon, B. (2013) *Textiles: The Whole Story: Uses, Meanings, Significance*. London: Thames & Hudson.

Graves, J. (2002) 'Symbol, Pattern and the Unconscious: The Search for Meaning'. In M. Schoeser and Boydell (eds), *Disentangling Textiles*. London: Middlesex University Press, pp. 45–55.

Haraway, D. (2006) 'A Cyborg Manifesto: Science, Technology, and Socialist-Feminism in the Late 20th Century'. In J. Weiss, J. Nolan, J. Hunsinger, P. Trifonas (eds), *The International Handbook of Virtual Learning Environments*. Dordrecht : Springer.

Harper, C. ed. (2012) *Textiles: Critical and Primary Sources*. London: Bloomsbury/Berg.

Hartman, S. (2008, 1 June) 'Venus in Two Acts'. *Small Axe*, 12 (2): 1–14.

Heisenberg, W. (1974/1990) *Across the Frontiers*. Trans. P. Heath. New York and London: Harper & Row.

Hemmings, J. (2010) *Textile Theory: Do We Need It?* [online]. Edinburgh College of Art. Available at http://www.academia.edu/1886887/Textile_Theory_do_we_need_it. Accessed 26 August 2012.

Hemmings, J., ed. (2012) *The Textile Reader*. London: Bloomsbury/Berg.

Heylighen, A., Cavallin, H. and Bianchin, M. (2009) 'Design in Mind'. *Design Issues* 25 (1): 94–105.

Houze, R. (2006) 'The Textile as Structural Framework: Gottfried Semper's Bekleidungsprinzip and the Case of Vienna 1900'. *Textile: Journal of Cloth and Culture*, 4 (3): 292–31.

Huitt, W. (1999) 'Conation as an Important Factor of Mind' [online] Educational Psychology Interactive, Valdosta, GA: Valdosta State University. Available at http://www.edpsycinteractive.org/topics/regsys/conation.html. Accessed 18 March 2010.

Huizinga, J. (1949) *Homo Ludens: A Study of the Play Element in Culture*. London: Temple Smith / Routledge & Kegan Paul (1980).

Huyssen, A. (1986) *Mass Culture as Woman: Modernism's Other*. Available at www.mariabuszek.com/kcai/PoMoSeminar/.../HuyssenMassCult.pdf. Accessed 12 February 2013. In A. Huyssen (1986) *After The Great Divide: Modernism, Mass Culture, Postmodernism*. Bloomington, IN: Indiana University Press, pp. 44–64.

Igoe, E. (2010) 'The Tacit-Turn'. *Duck: Journal for Research in Textiles and Textile Design*. [online] Available at https://www.lboro.ac.uk/microsites/sota/duck/volume1.htm. Accessed 26 September 2019.

Igoe, E. (2013) *In Textasis: Matrixial Narratives on Textile Design*. PhD thesis. Royal College of Art London.

Ingold, T. (2000) 'On Weaving a Basket'. In T. Ingold, *The Perception of the Environment: Essays in Livelihood, Dwelling and Skill*. Abingdon: Routledge, pp. 339–48.

Ingold, T. (2007) 'Materials Against Materiality'. *Archaeological Dialogues*, 14 (1): 1–16.

Ingold, T. (2010) 'The Textility of Making'. *Cambridge Journal of Economics*, 34: 91–102.

Ingold, T. (2017) 'Surface Visions'. *Theory, Culture & Society*, 34 (7–8): 99–108.

Kane, F. E. and Philpott, R. (2014) *Textile Thinking for Sustainable Materials*. Making Futures 2013, 26–27 September 2013, Plymouth.

Kapp, E. (2013) *Rigmaroles and Ragamuffins: Unpicking Words We Derive from Textiles*. 2nd Edition. Oxford: Elinor Kapp.

Kauffman, G. (1991) 'Creativity and Problem Solving'. In J. Henry (ed.), *Creative Management*, 2nd Edition. London: Sage (2001), pp. 44–63.

Kavanagh, T. (2004) 'Designers Managing Technology'. *Journal of Textile and Apparel, Technology and Management*, 4 (1): 1–7.

Kavanagh, T., Matthews, J. and Tyrer, J. (2008) 'An Inter-Disciplinary Search for Innovation In Textile Design'. *Proceedings of the 86th Textile Institute World Conference*, 18–21 November 2008, Hong Kong. pp. 409–22.

Kimbell, L. (2011) 'Rethinking Design Thinking: Part I'. *Design and Culture*, 3 (3): 285–306.

Kimbell, L. (2012) 'Rethinking Design Thinking: Part II' [online] *Design and Culture*, 4 (2): 129–48.

Lakoff, G. (1993) 'The Contemporary Theory of Metaphor'. In A. Ortony (ed.), *Metaphor and Thought*. 2nd Edition. Cambridge: Cambridge University Press, pp. 202–51.

Lakoff, G. and Johnson, M. (1980/2003) *Metaphors We Live By*. Chicago, IL: University of Chicago Press.

Lean, M. (2020) *Materialising Data Experience Through Textile Thinking*. PhD thesis, Royal College of Art, London.

Lee, Y., ed. (2020a) *Surface and Apparition: The Immateriality of Modern Surface*. London: Bloomsbury Academic.

Lee, Y. (2020b) 'The Textilesphere: The Threshold of Everyday Contacts'. *TEXTILE*, 18 (2): 160–79.

Lerpiniere, C. (2009) 'The Inspiration Board: Visually Evidencing the Hermeneutic Circle'. In S. Wade and Walton, K. (eds), *Futurescan: Mapping the Territory*, Proceedings of the 2009 Association of Fashion and Textiles Courses Conference, November 17–18, Liverpool, 24–9.

Lincoln, Y. S., Lynham, S. A. and Guba, E. G. (2011) 'Paradigmatic Controversies, Contradictions, and Emerging Confluences, Revisited'. In N. Denzin, and Y. Lincoln (eds), *The Sage Handbook of Qualitative Research*. 4th Edition. Los Angeles, London, New Delhi, Singapore, Washington DC: SAGE, pp. 97–128.

Lottersberger, A. (2012) *Design Innovation and Competitiveness in the Textile Industry*. PhD thesis, Politecnico di Milano, Milan.

Maharaj, S. (2000) 'Optical Voicing: Janis Jefferies' Text-Tale-Telling'. In V. Mitchell (ed.), *Selvedges: Janis Jefferies: Writing and Artworks Since 1980*. Norwich: Norwich Gallery and School of Art & Design (2000), pp. 7–9.

Margolin, V. (2003) 'Paul Scheerbart, The Gray Cloth'. *Journal of Design History*, 16 (1): 89–94.

Marr, A., and Hoyes, R. (2016) 'Making Material Knowledge: Process-led Textile Research as an Active Source for Design Innovation'. *Journal of Textile Design Research and Practice*, 4 (1): 5–32.

Maturana, H. and Varela, F. (1972/1980) *Autopoiesis and Cognition. The Realization of the Living*. Dordrecht, Holland. D. Reidel Publishing Company.

Mazé, R. (2018, 25 June) 'Bookmaking as Critical and Feminist Practice of Design'. In C. Storni, K Leahy, M McMahon, P. Lloyd and E. Bohemia (eds), *Proceedings of DRS2018: Catalyst. vol. 1*, Design Research Society. London, Limerick, Ireland, pp. 568–79. Design Research Society International Conference, pp. 568–79. DOI: 10.21606/dma.2018.469.

Miller, C. (2019) *Crafting Material Innovation and Knowledge Through Interdisciplinary Approaches*. Proceedings of the 4th Biennial Research Through Design Conference. Available at https://doi.org/10.6084/m9.figshare.7855916.v2. Accessed 7 March 2021.

Mitchell, V. (1997) 'Textiles, Text, Techne'. In J. Hemmings (ed.), *The Textile Reader*. Oxford: Berg (2012), pp. 5–13.

Moore, J. (2017) 'The Capitalocene, Part I: On the Nature and Origin of Our Ecological Crisis'. *Journal of Peasant Studies*, 44 (3): 594–630.

Morris, W. (1877) 'The Decorative Arts, Their Relation to Modern Life and Progress. An Address Delivered Before the Trades'. Guild of Learning, 4 December 1877. Available at http://www.burrows.com/dec.html. Accessed 26 September 2019.

Morris, W. (1882) 'The Lesser Arts of Life. An Address Delivered in Support of the Society for the
Protection of Ancient Buildings'. Available at http://www.burrows.com/morris/lesser.html. Accessed 26 September 2019.

Morse, E. (2011) 'Dream Works'. *frieze*, 138: 23–4.

Morse, E. (2013) 'Outsider Theorist Paul Scheerbart for Los Angeles Review of Books'. Available at https://lareviewofbooks.org/article/outsider-theorist-paul-scheerbart/. Accessed 26 September 2019.

Mott, C. and Cockayne, D. (2017) 'Citation Matters: Mobilizing the Politics of Citation Toward a Practice of "Conscientious Engagement"', *Gender, Place & Culture* 24(7): 954–73.

Moxey, J. (1999) 'Textile Design: A Holistic Perspective', *The Journal of The Textile Institute*, 90 (2): 176–81.

Moxey, J. (2000) 'The Representation of Concepts in Textile Design'. *Point: Art and Design Journal*, 9: 50–8.

Moxey, J. and Studd, R. (2000) 'Investigating Creativity in the Development of Fashion Textiles'. *The Journal of the Textile Institute*, 91 (2): 174–92. https://doi.org/10.1080/00405000008659537.

Neuhart, M. and Neuhart, J. (2010) *The Story of Eames Furniture. Book 1* [The early years]. Berlin: Die Gestalten Verlag.

Newell, A. and Simon, H. A. (1972) *Human Problem Solving*. Englewood Cliffs, NJ: Prentice-Hall.

Newman, D. (2002) *The Design Squiggle*. Available at https://thedesignsquiggle.com/. Accessed 26 September 2019.

Noel, L.-A. and Leitão, R. (2018) 'Not Just From The Centre'. Editorial at Design Research Society Conference 2018. Limerick, Ireland.

Ochs, E., and Capp, L. (2001) *Living Narrative: Creating Lives in Everyday Storytelling*. Cambridge, MA, London: Harvard University Press.

Ortega y Gasset, J (1937) 'The Misery and Splendour of Translation'. In R. Schulte, R. and J. Biguenet (eds) and E. Gamble Miller (trans.), *Theories of Translation: An Anthology of Essays from Dryden to Derrida*. Chicago and London: University of Chicago Press (1992), pp. 93–112.

Ortony, A., ed. (1993) *Metaphor and Thought*. 2nd Edition. Cambridge: Cambridge University Press.

Pajaczkowska, C. (2005) 'On Stuff and Nonsense: The Complexity of Cloth'. *Textile: The Journal of Cloth and Culture*, 3 (3): 220–49.

Pajaczkowska, C. (2016) 'Making Known: The Textiles Toolbox-Psychoanalysis of Nine Types of Textile Thinking'. In J. Jefferies, D. Wood Conroy and H. Clark (eds), *The Handbook of Textile Culture*. London: Bloomsbury, pp. 79–94.

Pastor, E. and Van Patter, G. K. (2011) 'NextDesign Geographies: Understanding Design Thinking 1,2,3,4'. [online] New York: Next Design Leadership Institute. Available at http://issuu.com/nextd/docs/nextdfutures2011_v02. Accessed 14 August 2013.

Pelias, R. J. (2011) 'Writing into Position: Strategies for Composition and Evaluation'. In N. Denzin, and Y. Lincoln (eds), *The Sage Handbook of Qualitative Research*. 4th Edition. Los Angeles, London, New Delhi, Singapore, Washington, DC: SAGE, pp. 659–68.

Polanyi, M. (1958) *Personal Knowledge*. London: Routledge & Kegan Paul.

Pollock, G. (2006) 'Introduction: Femininity: Aporia or Sexual Difference?' In B. Ettinger, *The Matrixial Borderspace*. Minneapolis, MN: University of Minnesota Press, pp. 1–37.

Pollock, G. (2008) 'Maternal Object: Matrixial Subject'. In F. Candlin, and R. Guins (eds), *The Object Reader*. Abingdon: Routledge (2009), pp. 483–7.

Pollock, G. (2009) 'Mother Trouble: The Maternal-Feminine in Phallic and Feminist Theory in Relation to Bracha Ettinger's Elaboration of Matrixial Ethics/Aesthetics'. *Studies in the Maternal*, 1 (1) [online]. London. Birkbeck College, University of London. Available at https://www.mamsie.bbk.ac.uk/articles/abstract/10.16995/sim.114/. Accessed 26 September 2019.

Prado de O. Martens, L. (2014) *Privilege and Oppression: Towards a Feminist Speculative Design*. Design Research Society Conference. Sweden, 2014.

Pye, D. (1968) *The Art and Nature of Workmanship*. Cambridge: Cambridge University Press.

Redström, J. (2017) *Making Design Theory*. Cambridge, MA: MIT Press.

Rendell, J. (2011) 'Critical Spatial Practices: Setting Out a Feminist Approach to some Modes and what Matters in Architecture'. In L. Brown (ed.), *Feminist Practices*. London: Ashgate.

Rhodes, Z. (2012) 'Using Previous Work to Inspire New Designs'. [online] http://www.zandrarhodes.ucreative.ac.uk/2013/02/using-previous-work-to-inspire-new.html. Accessed 14 April 2013.

Rich, A. (1972) 'Translations'. In Rich. A. *Diving Into the Wreck: Poems 1971–1972*. New York: W. W. Norton & Company, pp. 40–1.

Richardson, L. (2000) 'Writing: A Method of Inquiry'. In N. Denzin and Y. Lincoln (eds), *Handbook of Qualitative Research*, 2nd Edition. Thousand Oaks, London, Delhi: Sage Publications, pp. 923–46.

Rosner, D. (2018) *Critical Fabulations: Reworking the Methods and Margins of Design*. Cambridge, MA: MIT Press.

Ruzsits Jha, S. (2002) *Reconsidering Michael Polanyi's Philosophy*. Pittsburgh, PA: University of Pittsburgh Press.

Salustri, F. and Rogers, D. (2008) 'Some Thoughts on Terminology and Discipline in Design'. In *Undisciplined! Proceedings of the Design Research Society Conference 2008*. Sheffield, UK. July 2008, pp. 299/1–299/10.

Sánchez-Aldana, E., Cortes-Rico, L. J., Patarroyo, J., Pérez-Bustos, T. and Rincon, N. (2019) 'Testimonial Digital Textiles: Material Metaphors to Think with Care About Reconciliation with Four Memory Circles in Colombia'. Available at https://nordes2019.aalto.fi/wp-content/uploads/2019/05/NORDES2019_AbstractBook_PDFversion.pdf.

Sanders, E. and Stappers, P. (2008) 'Co-creation and the New Landscapes of Design'. *CoDesign: International Journal of CoCreation in Design and the Arts*, 4 (1): 5–18.

Santayana, G. (1896) *The Sense of Beauty; Being the Outline of Aesthetic Theory*. New York: Dover (1955).

Sartre, J.-P. (1962/1971) *Sketch for a Theory of the Emotions*. Trans. P. Mairet. London: Methuen.

Scheerbart, P. (1914) *The Gray Cloth*. Trans. and with drawings by J. A. Stuart. Cambridge, MA: MIT Press (2001).

Schön, D. (1978) 'Generative Metaphor: A Perspective on Problem-Setting in Social Policy'. In A. Ortony (ed.), *Metaphor and Thought*. 2nd Edition. Cambridge: Cambridge University Press (1993), pp. 137–63.

Schön, D. (1983/1999) *The Reflective Practitioner: How Professionals Think in Action*. Aldershot: Ashgate.

Schulte, R. and Biguenet, J. (1992) *Theories of Translation: An Anthology of Essays from Dryden to Derrida*. Chicago, IL, London: University of Chicago Press.

Schumpeter, J. (1942) *Capitalism, Socialism and Democracy*. London: Routledge.

Semper, G. (1851) *The Four Elements of Architecture: and Other Writings*. Trans. H. F. Mallgrave and W. Herrmann. Cambridge: Cambridge University Press (1989/2010).

Sennett, R. (2008) *The Craftsman*. London: Allen Lane/Penguin Press.

Serres, M. (1985) 'Boxes'. In M. Sankey, and P. Cowley (trans.), *Five Senses: A Philosophy of Mingled Bodies*. London: Continuum (2008), pp. 85–151.

Shouse, E. (2005) 'Feeling, Emotion, Affect'. *M/C Journal*, 8 (6). Available at http://journal.media-culture.org.au/0512/03-shouse.php. Accessed 9 March 2021.

Shreeve, A. (1997) 'Material Girls – Tacit Knowledge in Textile Crafts'. In P. Johnson (ed.), *Ideas in the Making: Practice in Theory*. London: Crafts Council (1998), pp. 103–14.

Simon, H. (1969) *The Sciences of the Artificial*. 3rd Edition. Cambridge, MA: MIT Press.

Simon, S. (1996) *Gender in Translation: Cultural Identity and the Politics of Transmission*. London: Routledge.

Sinclair, R. (2015, September) 'Dorcas Legacies, Dorcas Futures: Textile Legacies and the Formation of Identities in "Habitus" Spaces'. *Craft Research*, 6 (2): 209–22. Intellect.

Sparke, P. (1995) *As Long as Its Pink: The Sexual Politics of Taste*. London/San Francisco: Pandora/Harper Collins.

Spivak, G. C. (1993) 'The Politics of Translation'. In *Outside In The Teaching Machine*. London and New York: Routledge, pp. 179–200.

Stables, D. (1999) *Physiology in Childbearing: With Anatomy and Related Biosciences*. Oxford: Balliere Tindall/Elsevier.

Steadman, P. (1979/2008) 'The Evolution of Decoration'. In *The Evolution of Designs: Biological Analogy in Architecture and the Applied Arts*. Revised Edition. Abingdon, London, New York: Routledge, pp. 99–118.

Steiner, G. (1975) 'The Hermeneutic Motion'. In *After Babel: Aspects of Language and Translation*. 2nd Edition. Oxford, New York: Oxford University Press. (1992), pp. 312–435.

Stuart, J. (1999) 'Unweaving Narrative Fabric: Bruno Taut, Walter Benjamin, and Paul Scheerbart's The Gray Cloth'. *Journal of Architectural Education*, 53 (2): 61–73.

Studd, R. (2002) 'The Textile Design Process'. *The Design Journal*, 3 (2): 35–49.

Tedlock, B. (2011) 'Braiding Narrative Ethnography with Memoir and Creative Nonfiction'. In N. Denzin, and Y. Lincoln (eds), *The Sage Handbook of Qualitative Research*. 4th Edition. Los Angeles, London, New Delhi, Singapore, Washington, DC: SAGE, pp. 331–40.

Temple, B. (2005) 'Nice and Tidy: Translation and Representation' [Sociological Research Online, 10 (2).
Available at http://www.socresonline.org.uk/10/2/temple.html.

Thiele, K. (2014) 'Ethos of Diffraction: New Paradigms for a (Post)humanist Ethics'. *Parallax*, 20 (3): 202–16.

Tonkinwise, C. (2016) 'Committing to the Political Values of Post-Thing-Centered Designing (Teaching Designers How to Design How to Live Collaboratively)'. *Design and Culture*, 8 (1): 139–54.

Valentine, L., Ballie, J., Bletcher, J., Robertson, S. and Stevenson, F. (2017) 'Design Thinking for Textiles: Let's Make It Meaningful'. *The Design Journal*, 20 (Sup. 1): S964–S976.

van den Akker, R., Gibbons, A. and Vermeulen, T. (eds) (2017) *Metamodernism: Historicity, Affect and Depth after Postmodernism*. London and New York: Rowman & Littlefield.

Varela, F., Thompson, E. and Rosch, E. (1991) 'Enaction: Embodied Cognition'. In *The Embodied Mind: Cognitive Science and Human Experience*. Cambridge, MA: MIT Press, pp. 147–82.

Venuti, L. (1994) *The Translator's Invisibility: A History of Translation*. Abingdon: Routledge

Venuti, L., ed. (2012) *The Translation Studies Reader*. 3rd Edition. Abingdon: Routledge.

Vermeulen, T. (2012) 'Timotheus Vermeulen talks to Cher Potter'. *TANK*, 7 (4): 215.

Vermeulen, T. and van den Akker, R. (2010) 'Notes on Metamodernism'. *Journal of Aesthetics and Culture*, 2 (1). DOI: 10.3402/jac.v2i0.5677.

Veys, F. W. (2017) *Unwrapping Tongan Barkcloth*: Encounters, Creativity and Female Agency. London: Bloomsbury.

Vuletich, C. (2015) *Transitionary Textiles: A Craft-Based Journey of Textile Design Practice Towards New Values and Roles for a Sustainable Fashion Industry*. PhD thesis. University of the Arts London.

Wang, D. and A. Ilhan (2009) 'Holding Creativity Together: A Sociological Theory of the Design Professions'. *Design Issues*, 25 (1): 5–21.

Webster, R. (1996) *Studying Literary Theory; An Introduction*. 2nd Edition. London: Arnold.

Weston, R. (2005) 'Introduction'. In N. Pevsner (1936/2005), *Pioneers of Modern Design: From William Morris to Walter Gropius*. 4th Edition. New Haven, CT, London: Yale University Press.

Whitaker, R. (2001) 'Enactive Cognitive Science in Context: Comparisons with Earlier Traditions'. [online] Available at http://www.enolagaia.com/ECSTables.html. Accessed 22 July 2013.

White, D. (2019, 20 July) 'Design & Capital'. Available at https://medium.com/@DominicJWhite/design-capital-9eabcb596681. Accessed 21 July 2019.

Williams, S. J. (2001) *Emotional and Social Theory: Corporeal Reflections on the (Ir)Rational*. London, Thousand Oaks, New Delhi: SAGE.

Wolf, M. (1992) *A Thrice Told Tale: Feminism, Postmodernism and Ethnographic Responsibility*. Stanford, CA: Stanford University Press.

Young, I. M. (1990) 'House and Home: Feminist Variations on a Theme'. In *On Female Body Experience: Throwing Like a Girl and Other Essays*. Oxford: Oxford University Press (2005), pp. 123–54.

Contributors' references

Chapter 6: Caratti and Calabi

Barthes, R. (1991) *L'avventura semiologica*. Torino: Einaudi.

Barthes, R. (1999) *Variazioni sulla scrittura seguite da Il piacere del testo*. Torino: Einaudi.

Baule, G. (2017) 'The Translator Gaze. Design and Translation in the Editorial Field'. In G. Baule and E. Caratti (by), *Design Is Translation. The Translation Paradigma for Design Culture. "Design and Translation": A Manifesto*. Milano:Franco Angeli.

Baule, G. and Caratti, E., eds (2017) *Design Is Translation. The Translation Paradigma for Design Culture. "Design and Translation": A Manifesto*. Milano: Franco Angeli.

Bruno, G. (2014) *Surface. Matters of Aesthetics, Materiality and Media*. Chicago: University of Chicago Press.

Calabi, D. (2016) 'Texture and Text. A Translation Process'. In G. Baule and E. Caratti (eds), *Design Is Translation. The Translation Paradigma for Design Culture. "Design and Translation": A Manifesto*. Milano: Franco Angeli.

Chomsky, N. (1978) *Topic in the Theory of Generative Grammar*. Netherlands: M.I.T.; The Hague: Mouton & Co. N.V., 1966.

Ciarrocchi, M. and Calabi, D. (2017) 'Texture Design and Environment. Translation Tools for Places Identity'. InM. Bisson (a cura di), *Proceedings of the IInd International Conference on Environmental Design, 30-31 March 2017*, MDA, De Lettera Publisher.

Derrida, J. (1967) *Della grammatologia*. Milano: Jaca Book, 1998. (II ed. ita).

Gaur, A. (1984/1992) *A History of Writing*. Londra: The British Library, 1997.

Gombrich, E. H. (1979) *Il senso dell'ordine. Studio sulla psicologia dell'arte decorative*. Londra: Phaidon Press, 2000. (II ed. ita).

Huff, W. S. (1984) *Geometrizzare e Percettualizzare*, Rassegna19, Il contributo della scuola di Ulm, Anceschi G. (a cura di), Anno VI, September 19/3, pp. 36-9.

Jakobson, R. (1959) *On Linguistics Aspects of Translation*, in On Translation, edited by R. A. Brower, Cambridge: Harward University Press 1959, and in 1971, 260-6.

Jones, J. C. (1992, second edition) *Design Methods*. New York and Chichester: John Wiley & Sons, Inc.

Lotman, J. (1984) *O semiosfere, in Izbrannye stat'i v trëh tomah*, 1:11-24. Tallin, Aleksandra, 1992. Translation: *La semiosfera*. Edited by S. Salvestroni, Venezia: Marsilio, 1985.

Marcolli, A. (1971) *Teoria del campo. Corso di educazione alla vision*. Firenze: Sansoni.

Marcolli, A. (1975) 'Il laboratorio della visione'. *Ottagono*, 39 (10): 98-107.

Merleau-Ponty, M. (1945) *Fenomenologia della percezione*. Milano: Il Saggiatore, 1965.
Morin, E. (1977) *Il Metodo 1. La natura della natura*. Milano: Raffaello Cortina, 2001.
Neergard, S., ed. (2013) *Teorie contemporanee della traduzione*. Kindle Edition.
Osimo, B. (2014) *La traduzione totale. Spunti per lo sviluppo della scienza della traduzione*. Kindle Edition, 2014.
Osimo, B. (2015) *Manuale del traduttore. Guida pratica con glossario*. Milano: Hoepli, 2015.
Panofsky, E. (1915-1932) *La prospettiva come "forma simbolica" e altri scritti*. Milano: Feltrinelli, 1989.
Peirce, C. S. (1931-58) 'Semiotica: i fondamenti della semiotica cognitiva'. In M. A. Bonfantini, L. Grassi, R. Grazia (a cura di). Torino: Einaudi, 1989.
Penati, A., ed. (2013) *È il design una narrazione?* Milano: Mimesis.
Popovič, A. (1975) *La scienza della traduzione. Aspetti metodologici. La comunicazione traduttiva*. Milano: Hoepli, 2006.
Steiner, G. (1975), *After Babel. Aspects of Language and Translation*. New York and London: Oxford University Press.
Torop, P. (1995) *La traduzione totale. Tipi di processo traduttivo della cultura*. Milano: Hoepli, 2009.
Veca, A. (2007) 'Figure di argomentazione'. In V. Bucchetti (by), *Culture visive. Contributi per il design della comunicazione*. Milano: Polidesign.
Zingale, S. (2017) 'Like a Translation. Translation of the Meaning in Design'. In G. Baule e E. Caratti (ed.), *Design Is Translation. The Translation Paradigm for Design Culture. "Design and Translation": A Manifesto*. Milano: Franco Angeli.

Chapter 9: Lean

Ballie, J. (2014) *e-Co-Textile Design: How Can Textile Design and Making, Combined with Social Media Tools, Achieve a More Sustainable Fast Fashion Future?* PhD thesis. University of the Arts London.
Ballie, J. and Aspinall, M. (2020) 'Sewing Box for the Future at V&A, Dundee'. Available at https://www.vam.ac.uk/dundee/info/sewing-box-for-the-future-resources
Hall, C. and Earley, R. (2019). 'Divide, Switch, Blend. Exploring Two Hats for Industry Entrepreneurship and Academic Practice-Based Textile Design Research'. *The Design Journal*, 22(1): 19–35.
Igoe, E. (2010) 'The Tacit Turn; Textile Design in Design Research'. *Duck Journal for Research in Textiles and Textile Design*, 1: 1–11.
Igoe, E. (2013) *In Textasis: Matrixial Narratives of Textile Design*. PhD thesis, Royal College of Art, London.
Lean, M. (2017) 'Design Research Methods: Exhibition Data Collection'. Available at http://marionlean.co.uk/Design-Research-Methods-Exhibition-Data-Collection. Accessed 8 March 2021

Lean, M. (2020) *Materialising Data Experience through Textile Thinking*. PhD thesis, Royal College of Art, London.

Nevay, S. (2017) 'Social Connectedness: All Sewn Up?' *The Design Journal An International Journal for All Aspects of Design*, 20 (4): 511–19.

Philpott, R. and Kane, F. (2013) 'Textile Thinking for Sustainable Materials, Textile Thinking for Sustainable Materials'. *Presented at Making Futures 2013*, 26–27 September 2013, Plymouth.

Philpott, R., and Kane, F. (2016) '"Textile Thinking": A Flexible, Connective Strategy for Concept Generation and Problem Solving'. In T. Marchand, *Interdisciplinary Contexts in Craftwork as Problem Solving Ethnographic Studies of Design and Making*. London: Routledge, p. 237.

Robertson, L. (2019) 'Sonic Flock: Using Textile Birds to Start Conversations within a Dementia Friendly Community in the Outer Hebrides'. *The Design Journal*, 22 (Sup. 1): 2171–2.

Sanders, L. and Stappers, P. (2008) 'Co-creation and the New Landscapes of Design'. *CoDesign International Journal of CoCreation in Design and the Arts*, 4 (1): Design Participation(-s).

ten Böhmer, M. (2016) *Designing Embodied Smart Textile Services, The Role of Prototypes for Project, Community and Stakeholders*. PhD thesis, Eindhoven University of Technology.

Valentine, L., Ballie, J., Bletcher, J., Robertson, S. and Stevenson, F. (2017) 'Design Thinking for Textiles: Let's Make It Meaningful'. *Design Journal*, 20 (Sup. 1): S964–S976.

Chapter 10: Sinclair

Barnes, A. (2013) 'Geo/Graphic Design: The Liminal Space of the Page'. *Geographical Review*, 103 (2): 164–76.

Berger, J. (2013) *Understanding a Photograph*. Ed. Geoff Dyer. London: Penguin Books.

Buckley, C. (1986) 'Made in Patriarchy: Toward a Feminist Analysis of Women and Design'. *Design Issues*, 3 (2) (Autumn): 3–14. Published by: The MIT Press.

Buckley, C. (2007) *Designing Modern Britain*. London: Reaktion Books.

Buckley, C. (2009) 'Made in Patriarchy: Theories of Women and Design- A Reworking'. In D. Brody and H. Clark (eds), *Design Studies. A Reader*. Oxford: Berg.

Checinska, C. (2017a) 'Althea McNish and the British African Diaspora'. In A. Massey and A. Seago (eds), *Pop Art and Design*. London, UK: Bloomsbury Academic.

Checinska, C. (2017b) 'Re-fashioning African Diasporic Masculinities'. In E. Gaugele, and M. Titton (eds), *Fashion and Postcolonial Critique*. Vol. 22. Publication Series of the Academy of Fine Arts Vienna. Berlin: Sternberg Press, pp. 74–90.

Checinska, C. (2018) 'Christine Checinska in Conversation with Althea McNish and John Weiss'. *TEXTILE, Cloth and Culture*, 16 (2): 186–99, DOI: 10.1080/14759756.2018.1432183.

Elinor, G., Richardson, S., Scott, Thomas, A. and Walker, K. (eds) (1987) *Women and Craft*. London: Virago Press.

Gauntlett, D. (2011) *Making Is Connecting: The Social Meaning of Creativity, from DIY and Knitting to YouTube and Web 2.0*. Cambridge, Oxford, and Boston: Polity Press.

Hamilton-Brown, L. (2017) *Myth-Black People Don't Knit*. Master thesis. Royal College of Art, London, UK. Available at https://www.lornahamiltonbrown.com/about-me/. Accessed 29 September 2019.

Hand, C., Mhondoro, C. and Ove, Z. (2019) *Get Up Stand Up Now: Generations of Black Creative Pioneers* (exhibition) Somerset House Trust, UK.

Harris, R., White, S. and Beezmohun, S. (2009) *Building Britannia: Life Experience with Britain*. London, UK: George Padmore Institute Publications.

Hlaváčková, K. (2019) *Ascher: The Mad Silkman: Zika and Lida Ascher, Fashion and Textiles*. Prague: Slovart Publishing Ltd.

Hicks, K. E. (2003) *Black Threads: An African American Quilting Sourcebook*. Jefferson, NC: McFarland & Company Publishers.

Hislop, V. (1966) 'My Ideal Room by a Bachelor Girl. Daily Mail Ideal Home Exhibition'. *Daily Mail*, Tuesday March 1, p. 15.

hooks, b. (2007) 'An Aesthetic of Blackness: Strange and Oppositional'. In J. Livingstone, and J. Ploof (eds), *The Object of Labour: Art, Cloth, and Cultural Production*. Cambridge: MIT Press, pp. 315–32.

Igoe, E. (2013) In *Textasis: Matrixial Narratives of Textile Design*. PhD thesis, Royal College of Art, London.

Jackson, L. (2005) 'Caribbean Blaze'. *Crafts Magazine*, 194 (May–June): 32-7. UK.

Jackson, L. (2009) *Shirley Craven and Hull Traders: Revolutionary Fabrics and Furniture 1957–1980*. ACC Editions.

Johnson, P. (2018) 'New Caribbean Design: Revitalizing Placed-Based Products (2017)'. In S. Walker, W. Evans, *Design et al (2017) Roots, Culturally Significant Design, Products & Practices*. London: Bloomsbury.

Martin, K. and Mirraboopa, B. (2003) 'Ways of Knowing, Being and Doing: A Theoretical Framework and Methods for Indigenous and Indigenist Re-search'. *Journal of Australian Studies*, 27 (76): 203–14.

McMillan, M. (2008) 'The 'West Indian' Front Room: Reflections on a Diasporic Phenomenon'. *Kunapipi*, 30 (2). Available at http://ro.uow.edu.au/kunapipi/vol30/iss2/7.

Mendes, V. D. and Hinchliffe, F.M. (1983) *Ascher, Zika and Lida Ascher, Fabric, Art, Fashion*. Victoria and Albert Museum, UK.

Patel, K. (2019) 'Supporting Diversity in Craft Practice through Digital Technology Skills Development'. Crafts Council Report.

Patel, K. (2020) 'Diversity Initiatives and Addressing Inequalities in Craft'. In S. Luckman, and S. Taylor (eds), *Pathways to Creative Working Lives*. London: Palgrave Macmillan, pp. 173–95.

Richardson, L. (2000) 'Writing: A Method of Inquiry'. In N. Denzin and Y. Lincoln (eds), *Handbook of Qualitative Research* (2nd edn). Thousand Oaks, London, Delhi: Sage Publications, pp. 923–46.

Ringgold, F. and Obrist H. U. (2019) Faith Ringgold, Verlag der Buchhandlung Walther Konig.

Robinson, E. (2012) *Women and Needlework in Britain, 1920–1970*. PhD thesis, Royal Holloway, University of London.

Sellers, L. (2017) *Women Design: Pioneers in Architecture, Industrial, Graphic and Digital Design from the Twentieth Century to the Present Day*. London, UK: Quarto Publishing.

Sinclair, R. (2015) 'Dorcas Legacies, Dorcas Futures: Textile Legacies and the Formation of Identities in "Habitus' Spaces". *Craft Research*, 6 (2). Intellect Ltd Article.

Sinclair, R. (2019) Windrush: Arrival 1948 at the V&A Windrush by Rose Sinclair, John Price and Will Cenci. Available at https://www.gold.ac.uk/research/about/public-engagement/windrush

Sinclair, R. (2020) Caribbean Front Room (October 1–January 4). Available at HYPERLINK "https://sites.gold.ac.uk/windrush/caribbean-front-room/" https://sites.gold.ac.uk/windrush/caribbean-front-room/

Thomas, S. (2018) *Fashion Ethics*. Oxford: Routledge.

Tulloch, C. (1998) '"Out of Many, One People": The Relativity of Dress, Race and Ethnicity to Jamaica, 1880–1907'. *Fashion Theory*, 2 (4): 359–82.

Tulloch, C. (2016) *The Birth of Cool: Style Narratives of the African Diaspora - Materializing Culture*. London: Bloomsbury Publishers, UK.

Turney, J. (2009) *The Culture of Knitting*. London: Bloomsbury, UK.

Twigger-Holroyd, A. (2018) 'Forging New Futures: Cultural Significance, Revitalization and Authenticity'. In S. Walker, W. Evans, T. Cassidy, A. Twigger-Holroyd and J. Jung, *Roots, Culturally Significant Design, Products & Practices*. London: Bloomsbury.

Walmsley, A. (1992) *The Caribbean Artists Movement, 1966–1972*. A Literary and Cultural History. London: New Beacon Books.

Warren, E., ed. (2020) *Bisa Butler, Portraits*. The Art Institute of Chicago, New Haven: Yale University Press.

Webb, M. (1968) 'Design as an Invisible Export'. *Design Journal*, 214: 63–5.

Chapter 12: Fisher

Baudrillard, J. (1968) *The System of Objects*. London: Verso.

Belk, R. (1990) 'The Role of Possessions in Constructing and Maintaining a Sense of Past'. *Advances In Consumer Research*, 17: 669–76.

Belk, R. (2001) 'Possessions and the Extended Self'. In Daniel Miller (ed.), *Consumption: Critical Concepts in the Social Sciences*. London: Routledge, pp. 180–238.

Berman, M. (1982) *All That Is Solid Melts into Air*. New York: Simon and Schuster.

Csikszentmihaly, M. (1979) 'The Concept of Flow'. In B. Sutton-Smith (ed.), *Play and Learning*. New York: Gardner Press.

Fisher, T. (1995) 'From Mute Genius to Agile Manipulator'. *Point*, (1): 29–34.

Fisher, T. (1997) 'The Designer's Self Identity - Myths of Creativity and the Management of Teams'. *Creativity and Innovation Management*, (April): 10–18.

Fisher, T., and Botticello, J. (2018) 'Machine-Made Lace, the Co-production of Knowledge and the Spaces of Skilled Practice'. *Cultural Geographies*, 25 (1): 46–69. DOI: 10. 1177/1474474016680106

Ingold, T. (2007) *Lines: A Brief History*. London: Routledge.

Kafka, F. (1995) *The Complete Stories*. Trans. Willa and Edwin Muir. New York: Schocken Books, pp. 427–8.

Marx, K. (2007 (1844)) *Economic and Philosophical Manuscripts of 1844*. New York: Dover Publications.

Perec, G. (1997) 'Notes Concerning the Objects That Are on My Work-Table'. In George Perec, *Species of Spaces and Other Pieces*. London: Penguin, pp. 144–7.

Shove, E. and Pantzar, M. (2005) 'Fossilisation'. *Ethnologia Europaea*, pp. 59–62.

Sutton-Smith, B. (2001) *The Ambiguity of Play*. Cambridge, MA: Harvard University Press.

Chapter 14: Roxburgh

Bijker, W., Hughes, T., and Pinch, T., eds (1987) *The Social Construction of Technological Systems, New Directions in the Sociology and History of Technology*. Cambridge, MA: MIT Press.

Brett, D. (2005) *Rethinking Decoration: Pleasure and Ideology in the Visual Arts*. Cambridge: Cambridge University Press.

Brown, T. (2009) *Change by Design: How Design Thinking Transforms Organizations and Inspires Innovation*. New York: HarperBusiness.

Buchanan, R. (1985) 'Declaration by Design: Rhetoric, Argument, and Demonstration in Design Practice'. *Design Issues*, 2 (1): 4–22.

Buchanan, R. (1992) 'Wicked Problems in Design Thinking'. *Design Issues*, 8 (2): 5–21.

Cazeaux, C. (2003) 'The Ethical Dimension of Aesthetic Research'. *Research Issues in Art and Design Media*, (5). http://www.biad.uce.ac.uk/research/rti/riadm/,

Dilnot, C. (1998) 'The Science of Uncertainty: The Potential Contribution of Design to Knowledge'. In R. Buchanan, D. Doordan, L. Justice, and V. Margolin (eds), *Doctoral Education in Design Conference Proceedings*. Pittsburgh: Carnegie Mellon University.

Diprose, R. (2010) 'In Light Relief the Image Sensitises Itself: On the Ontology, Ethics and Politics of Photography in Design Researc'. In M. Roxburgh (ed.), *Light Relief* (Part II). Sydney: DABDOCS, pp. 33–47.

Flusser, V. (1999 [1993]) *The Shape of Things: A Philosophy of Design*. London: Reaktion Books,

Flusser, V. (2007 [1983]) *Towards a Philosophy of Photography*. London: Reaktion Books.
Folkmann, M. (2013) *The Aesthetics of Imagination in Design*. Cambridge, MA: MIT Press.
Glanville, R. (2004/Rev.2008) 'Second Order Cybernetics'. In Francisco Parra-Luna (ed.), *Systems Science and Cybernetics*; In *Encyclopedia of Life Support Systems (EOLSS)*, Developed under the Auspices of the UNESCO, Eolss Publishers, Oxford, UK, [http://www.eolss.net]. Retrieved August 24, 2010.
Glanville, R. (2005) 'Appropriate Theory'. In J. Redmond, D. Durling, and A. De Bono (eds), *Futureground Conference Proceedings*. Melbourne: Design Research Society.
Ladyman, J. (2007) 'Ontological, Epistemological, and Methodological Positions'. In T. Kuipers (ed.), *General Philosophy of Science: Focal Issues*. Amsterdam and Oxford: Elsevier, pp. 303–76.
Latour, B. (2005) *Reassembling the Social: An Introduction to Actor-Network-Theory*. Oxford: Oxford University Press.
Latour, B. and Woolgar, S. (1979) *Laboratory Life: The Social Construction of Scientific Facts*. Beverly Hills: Sage.
Law, J. and Hassard, J., eds (1999) *Actor Network Theory and After*. Oxford: Blackwell Publishers.
Liddament, T. (2000) 'The Myths of Imagery'. *Design Studies*, 21 (6): 589–606.
Lockwood, T. (2009) *Design Thinking: Integrating Innovation, Customer Experience, and Brand Value*. New York: Allworth Press.
Martin, R. (2009) *The Design of Business: Why Design Thinking Is the Next Competitive Advantage*. Boston: Harvard Business Press.
Merleau-Ponty, M. (1964) *The Primacy of Perception, and Other Essays on Phenomenological Psychology, the Philosophy of Art, History, and Politics*. Evanston: Northwestern University Press.
Peirce, C. S. (1998 [1893–1913]) 'Pragmatism'. In *The Essential Peirce: Selected Philosophical Writings, Volume 2*. Bloomington, IN: Indiana University Press.
Ramachandran, V. S. (2011) *The Tell-Tale Brain*. New York: W.W. Norton & Company.
Rittel, J. (1972) 'Son of Rittelthink'. In E. Dluhosch, H. Blasdel, J. Henry, E. Bexton, and H. Bexton (eds), *DMG 5th Anniversary Report*, CA: Design Methods Group, pp. 5–10.
Rowe, P. (1987) *Design Thinking*. Cambridge: MIT Press.
Simon, H. (1969) *The Sciences of the Artificial*. Cambridge, MA: MIT Press.
Stewart, S. (2011) 'Interpreting Design Thinking'. *Design Studies*, 32 (6): 515–20.

Epilogue: Fairbanks

Dunne, A. and Raby, F. (2013) *Speculative Everything: Design, Fiction, and Social Dreaming*. Cambridge: MIT Press.
Edmondson, A. (1986) *A Fuller Explanation: The Synergetic Geometry of R. Buckminster Fuller*. Boston, Basel, Stuttgart: Birkhäuser.

Fairbanks, M. (2016) *Exhibition: Impractical Weaving Suggestions*. Madison, WI: Ruth Davis Design Gallery.
Fairbanks, M. (2018) *Exhibition: More Air-like than Water*. Chicago IL: Living Room.
Fairbanks, M. (n.d.) 'Weaving Lab website. https://www.weavinglab.com/.
Ingold, T. (2010) 'The Textility of Making'. *Cambridge Journal of Economics*, 34: 91–102.
Latour, B. and Serres, M. (1995) *Conversations on Science, Culture, and Time*. Ann Arbor: University of Michigan Press.
Serres, M. (1998/2008) *The Five Senses: A Philosophy of Mingled Bodies (I)*. Trans. Margaret Sankey and Peter Cowley. London: Continuum.
Vermeulen, T. (2012) 'Timotheus Vermeulen Talks to Cher Potter'. *TANK*, 7 (4): 215.

Index

3D printing   32, 34
54th Sonnet (Shakespeare)   169–70

abductive reasoning   158, 169
abstractness   146
academic design research   25, 31, 158, 191, 193
actor network theory   175
Adams, Tony   4, 9, 30
Adorno, Theodor. W.   49
aesthetic/kinaesthetic dimensions   183–4
aesthetics   10, 23, 33, 41, 48, 66, 76, 91, 102, 105, 112, 113, 119, 127, 135, 154, 171, 184, 185, 186, 196, 203, 210
affect   134–9, 170, 195–198, 200, 215
agalma   136, 137
Albers, Anni   2, 40–2, 77, 81
Albers, Josef   81
Alter Mind, Trigger Behaviour (Lean)   99
Andersen, Kirsti. R.   38
Anthropocene   178
applied arts   5, 50, 87, 93, 171, 172, 190, 193
Arcades Project (1927–40)   74
Archer, Bruce   31
architectonic model   2
architectonic practice   85
architectural design   74, 84, 88
architectural theory   75, 76
Armstrong, Leah   82, 119
art forms   7, 48, 203
Ascher, Zika   119
atopos/atopic   190
Attfield, Judy   50
autoethnography   3, 4, 7, 9–10, 29, 30, 115, 198
Autoethnography, Personal Narrative, Reflexivity: Researcher as Subject (Ellis and Bochner)   10
autopoiesis   166
avant-garde art   74

Bachelard, Gaston   162

Balfour, Henry   54
Ballie, Jen   102
Banham, Reyner   74
Barad, Karen   97
barkcloth koloa   128
Barnett, Pennina   40, 73, 163
Barthes, Roland   1, 62, 144
Basho, Matsuo   213
Baudrillard, Jean.   127, 129–30, 133, 138, 145–7
Bauhaus   64, 76, 77, 175
Baule, Giovanni   52
beauty   41, 139, 154, 167, 169–72, 187, 195, 197, 200, 213
'Bekelidungsprinzip'   78
Belford, Patricia   196
Benjamin, Walter   13, 17, 53, 55, 74, 142, 144
Berger, John   120
Berman, Marshall   150
besidedness   189
Bianchin, Matteo   124
Biguenet, John   48
biomimicry   196
Black, Asian & Minority Ethnic (BAME) women   113, 114, 122, 122 nn.1, 2
Black Mountain College   206, 207
Black Threads: An African American Quilting Sourcebook (Hicks)   112
Black women textile practice   112–14
Bochner, Arthur. P.   10, 13
Body in Pain, The (Scarry)   50
Boehnert, Joanna   51
bookmaking   4, 8, 12
borderspace/borderlinking   23, 160
'borderswerving'   188
box-thinking *vs.* sack-thinking   163
Brett, David   49, 82, 167–9, 171, 179, 180, 188, 189
Broadway Theatre   122

Brown, Tim   177
'B: Tiny Arkhive' (Damon)   1
Buchanan, Richard   174, 176
Buckley, Cheryl   89, 113, 115, 121, 201
Building Digital UK (BDUK)   108, 109
Butler, Bisa   116
Butler, Judith   21, 24, 25
Bye, Elizabeth   37

Calabi, Daniela   5, 56
calligraphy   62, 63
capitalism   132–134
Capitalism, Socialism and Democracy (Schumpeter)   132
Capps, Lisa   12, 16
Caratti, Elena   5, 52, 56
'The Cares of a Family Man' (Kafka)   145
Caribbean Artists Movement (CAM)   119
'Caribbean Front Room'   122
Cavallin, Humberto   134
Cazeaux, Clive 175
Cendrars, Blaise   81
Chadwick, Whitney   81
citation politics   8
cognition   2, 18, 33, 35, 36, 38–40, 51, 101, 132–6, 150, 159, 160, 166–7, 187, 188, 192
collaboration   25, 41, 51, 71, 100, 102–4, 108, 196–7, 203, 211, 212
collecting, accumulating and foraging   123, 127, 129–30, 138, 145–7, 160
Collet, Carole   196
coloured glass   73, 74, 80
commercial textile designs/designers   11, 33, 94
complexity   2, 9, 17, 60, 61, 118, 135, 146, 150, 157, 162, 189, 201
compositional skills   64
conation   49, 50, 52, 132, 134–6, 159, 190, 192, 198
conceptual art/artist   203, 204
concrete and abstract level   181–2
condensation   40, 41
Connor, Steven   127, 129, 137, 162
conscious variation   54, 196
contemporary textile design researchers   109
conversation   1, 7, 11–13, 28–29, 52, 108

copoiesis   23, 128, 138, 139, 198
Council of Industrial Design   82
crafting practices   111–14, 116, 118
crafting spaces   112
Crafts Council   33
craft textiles   33
Craven, Shirley   83
creative destruction   132–3, 165
creative leap   52, 135
Creative Media Survey (Arts Council)   122 n.1
creative practice   100, 145, 146
creative space   112, 118
creativity   23, 31, 40, 70, 90, 112–13, 132, 135, 158, 192, 213
critical fabulation   7, 14, 97
Critical Fabulations: Reworking the Methods and Margins of Design (Rosner)   7, 14, 39
Cross, Nigel   47, 135, 157, 158, 160, 165
cross-stitched textile works   1
The Crystal Chain   74
Csíkszentmihályi, Mihalyi   53

Daily Mail   121
Damon, Maria   1
data collection   102, 108–9
Day, Lucienne   82
De Bastide, Jean-François   74
de Beauvoir, Simone   85
decoration   41, 54, 55, 76, 78, 83, 92, 95, 101, 128, 136, 154, 167–71, 179, 200
decorative objects   128
Delaunay, Robert   81, 84
Delaunay, Sonia   81, 84
Deleuze, Gilles   42, 163, 164, 172, 192
Denzin, Norman   25, 198, 199
descriptive theories   173
design academia   6, 8, 9, 37, 43, 150
Design and the Science of Uncertainty (Dilnot)   174
'Design as Discipline' (Archer)   31
design convergence   59, 164–72
design culture   56–67
Designerly Ways of Knowing (Cross)   135
Design Et Traduzione (DET)   52
design evaluation   59
design imperative   185, 186
Design Issues   37

Design Is Translation (Baule and Caratti) 58
Design Journal, The 37
Design Methods Movement 176
design problems 36–7, 157–63, 165–8, 171, 176, 195, 212
Design Research Society 37, 144
Design Studies 31
design thinking 38–43, 73, 88, 89, 131, 159, 161, 163, 165, 166, 169, 173, 175–7, 191–2, 195, 212
Design Thinking (Rowe) 38
'devoré' 99
de Waal, Edmund 172
Dewey, John 176
diffraction 97, 98, 189
digital fabric printing method 32
Dilnot, Clive 49–51, 158, 174
Diprose, Rosalyn 180
discourse 7, 35, 58, 88, 130, 159, 178, 203
    academic 37
    design 118, 31, 94, 194, 195
    feminist 52
    metamodern 190
    theoretical 21
Dorcas sewing clubs 39
Dormor, Catherine 42, 188
Dorst, Kees 35, 36, 135
dough 162–165, 169, 172, 192, 208
Downer, Lesley 91
Dryden, John 47, 48, 51
D-TEX 37
Dubberly Design Office 165
DUCK Journal for Research in Textiles and Textile Design 37
Dunne, Anthony 209
Duncan of Jordanstone College of Art 99
dyeing 32, 45
dyes 171, 211

Eames, Charles 81, 83
Eames, Ray 81, 83
Eames Studio 83
Earley, Rebecca 38, 39, 94, 101, 196
Eco, Umberto 74
ecological problems 178
education 22, 33, 35, 39, 62, 64, 77, 108, 159, 193, 195, 196

Ellis, Carolyn 9, 10, 13, 30
Embodied Mind: Cognitive Science and Human Experience, The (Varela, Thompson and Rosch) 166
'embodied sense making' 104
embroidery 32, 34, 71, 123, 137
'emerging' design disciplines 109
emotions 13, 51, 81, 103, 107, 133, 160, 188, 196–200
enactment 2, 52, 97
enactive cognition 166
enmeshes 10, 16–18, 42, 131, 175, 183, 185
epistemology 3, 7, 15, 18, 23, 36, 40, 42, 43, 52, 62, 101, 174, 189, 191, 199, 200
Escobar, Arturo 39
E-text and Textiles Project 1
ethnography 9, 17, 109
Ettinger, Bracha Lichtenberg 4, 11, 15, 20–4, 43, 73, 95, 97, 138, 160, 161, 172, 188, 189
Europe 40, 176
Eurydice (Ettinger) 24
Evolution of Decorative Arts, The (Balfour) 54
Experiential Knowledge Special Interest Group (EKSIG) 37
experimenting and experimental methods 10, 28, 77, 101, 108, 109, 124, 149, 153, 163

fabulations 12–16
Fairbanks, Marianne 6, 17
Fashion and Textiles Museum, London 82
fashion design 87, 171, 177
fashion designers 70, 71, 89, 92, 100, 165, 172
fashion industry 72, 115
'fashion space' 115
femininity 23, 81–3, 91, 95, 97, 120
feminism 14, 73, 76, 82
feminist critique 17, 19, 38, 85, 96
feminist design practice and research 6, 8, 198
feminist history 203
feminist methodology 189
feminist technoscience 14, 97

'Fibers'   203
fiction   5, 7, 17, 22, 75, 80, 84
fidelity   54, 55
'Field Theory' (Marcolli)   64
First World War   75
Fisher, Tom   17, 129
fluidity   2, 205
Flusser, Villem   6, 178, 179, 181, 186
folding and unfolding   163–5, 172, 188, 192, 199, 208
Folkman, Mads   184, 185
'fossils'   145–7
frame restructuring   18–19, 96, 189
frayages   53, 200
Friedman, Ken   88, 93, 191, 193–5
Friedrich, Hugo   48, 53
'full-bleed' method   8
Fuller, Buckminster   206, 207
Fuller Sampler (Fairbanks)   207
furniture design   6, 144, 145

Gadamer, Hans-Georg   148, 149
Gale, Colin   32
Galle, Per   195
Gardner Troy, Virginia   76, 77, 81
geisha (textiles as)   90–92, 97–98, 102, 105, 107, 187
gender
 issues   119, 120, 122
 role   76, 77, 82
gendered textile design
 disciplinarity   86–9
 textile entity   89–98
Gender in Translation (Simon)   52
genres   5
Gerdes, Karen   134
'Gesamtkunstwerk'   76–8, 82
Gestaltpsychologie   64
Gibson, William   200
Gift, The (Dilnot)   49
gift-giving   49–51
Girli Concrete (Belford)   196
Glanville, Ranulph   176, 184
glass architecture   75, 76, 80, 82
Golden Harvest (McNish)   120, 122 n.3
Goldsmiths, University of London   99
Goldsworthy, Kate   39, 196
Gordon, Beverly   3
Gradient Slippage (Fairbanks)   205

Graves, Jane   168, 171, 195
Gray Cloth, The (Scheerbart)   5, 73–86, 89
Groag, Jacqueline   81
Groag, Jacques   81, 83
Gropius, Walter   74
Guattari, Felix.   42, 163
Guba, Egon. G.   15

Hadridge, Phil   38
Haraway, Donna   97
Hara, Hiroshi   20
hard and soft   73–85, 205, 206
Harper, Catherine   188, 196
Hartman, Saidiya   7, 14
Heisenberg, Werner   190
Hemmings, Jessica   5, 193
hermeneutic approach   51–3
heuristic gap   136
Heylighen, Ann   124
Hicks, Kyra   112, 113
Hillier, Bill   47
Holman Jones, Stacy.   4, 9, 30
Homo Ludens (Huizinga)   130, 138
hooks, bell   112, 113, 116, 118
House of Cards (1952)   130–2
Houze, Rebecca   39, 42, 78
Huff, William   64
Huizinga, Johan   130, 132, 133, 136–8, 192
Hull Traders   119, 120
Huyssen, Andreas   79, 82
hylomorphic approaches   2, 41, 85

Ideal Home Exhibition (1966)   121
'ideal paste'   162
IDEO   38, 177
Igoe, Elaine   101–4, 115, 119, 141, 176, 180, 202, 204, 205, 208, 211
Ilhan, Ali   87–9, 192
ill-defined design problems   36–37, 157–59, 192
imagination   16, 27, 45, 49, 53, 54, 56, 104, 120, 133, 134, 137, 155, 178, 179, 168, 174, 181–6, 197, 201, 212
immaterial   100, 104, 108, 172, 177, 192, 200, 201, 205, 209
Impractical Weaving Suggestions (Fairbanks)   204

'Indigo' 89
Indra's net 3, 6
industrial design 31, 42, 82, 88
industrial structure 5
Ingold, Tim 2, 41, 42, 161-3, 166, 199, 200, 201, 211
intangible paste 162, 163, 172
intellectual passion 50, 86, 132, 133, 135-6, 190
interior design 83, 88, 171, 177
interiority 4, 63
interlinguistic transfer 59, 67
International Conference on Intelligent Textiles and Mass Customisation (ITMC) 102-3
Internet of Things (IOT) 100
intersectionality 115
intersemiotics 59, 66, 67
In Textasis: Matrixial Narratives of Textile Design (Igoe) 101
intralinguistic translation 59, 67
Irigaray, Luce 23, 85
Italian textile market 37

Jackobson, Roman 58, 59, 67
JAM 210
Jefferies, Janis 40
Johnson, Mark 18
Johnson, Patty. 113
Jongerius, Hella 87
Journal of Textile Design Research and Practice 37

Kafka, Franz. 145
Kane, Faith. E. 42
Karasick, Adeena 1-2
Kauffman, Geir. 157-9
Kaur, Jasbir 32
Kavanagh, Terence 35, 193
Kimbell, Lucy 36, 38, 39, 127, 191, 192, 195, 197
Kirby, Vicki 97
kneading 163-165, 172, 192, 208
knitting and weave patterns 3, 32, 72, 97, 111, 112, 114, 116, 154, 161, 168
knowledge making 2, 9, 40, 137
Kristeva, Julia 23
Kyoto, Japan 20-2
Kyoto Railway Station 20

Lakoff, George. 18, 96
language of textiles 48, 137
laser-cutting method 32, 34, 153
Leaman, Bill 47
Lean, Marion 5, 97, 196
Lee, Yeseung 42-3
Leitão, Renata. 39
Lerpiniere, Claire 52
Lesabéndio (Scheerbart) 74
'les belles infidèles' 54-55
Liberty's 119
Liddament, Terry. 180
liminality 53, 56, 73, 92, 112, 118
Lincoln, Yvonna. S. 15, 25
linear design process model 35
Living Narrative (Ochs and Capps) 12
Lockwood, Thomas 177
Lockwood Resource 177
London College of Fashion 33
looping 6, 134, 161
Loos, Adolf 78, 79
Lotman, Jurij 67
Lottersberger, Anna 37, 38
Loughborough University 37
'Love Letter' (Plath) 21
Lynham, Susan. A. 15

Made in Patriarchy (Buckley) 82
Maharaj, Sarat 40
Making Design Theory (Redström) 2
Mallgrave, Harry. F. 78
March, Lionel 158
Marcolli, Attilio 64
marginalization 2, 55, 73, 76, 82, 95, 113, 115
Margolin, Victor 73, 84, 195
Marr, Anne 39, 42
Martin, Karen 117
Martin, Roger 177
Marx, Karl 50, 150, 197
'Material Girls: Tacit Knowledge in Textile Crafts' (Shreeve) 33
material innovation 110
'Materialising Data Experience through Textile Thinking' (Lean) 107-8
materiality 3-5, 13, 47, 82, 108, 124, 162, 172, 185, 209
matriarchal culture 128

matrix   3, 20, 21, 163
matrixial approach/concept   2, 15, 20–4, 43, 82, 95, 97, 98, 131, 138, 160, 188, 189, 199
Maturana, Humberto   166
Mazé, Ramia   4, 8
McDougall, William   134
McNish, Althea   83, 118–21, 122 n.3
mending   6, 18, 24, 25
Merleau-Ponty, Maurice   6, 179–84
meshes   3, 5, 7, 16–18, 20, 78, 80, 164, 167, 188, 192, 206
metamodernism   7, 189–92, 202, 203
metaphoracity   97
Metaphor and Thought (Ortony)   18
metaphors   18–19, 23, 49, 53, 56, 73, 78, 95–7, 102, 161, 165, 175, 176, 187–9, 192, 193
  gendered   5
  interventionist   52
  textile   7, 23, 53, 75, 187–189
metaxy   190
methectic/methexis   137, 138
metramorphosis   23, 24, 73, 95, 172
micro-graphie   63
Miller, Mitch   108, 196
Mirraboopa, Booran   117
Misery and Splendour of Translation, The (Ortega y Gasset)   55
Mitchell, Victoria   1, 2, 40–42, 47, 163, 199
modern architecture   75, 78
modernism   5, 7, 73–85
modernist movement   76, 78, 82
More Air-Like than Water (Fairbanks)   202, 204
morphogenesis   63, 65
Morris, William   74, 95, 158, 167, 168, 175
Morrow, Ruth   196
mother (textiles as)   95, 97–98, 102, 105, 107, 187
'Mother Trouble: The Maternal-Feminine in Phallic and Feminist Theory in Relation to Bracha Ettinger's Elaboration of Matrixial Ethics' (Pollock)   21
Moxey, James   33, 35–7, 158
multiplicity   1, 8, 59, 162–4, 190, 192

narrative inquiry methods   6, 189
National Health Service (NHS)   116
neoliberal capitalism   51
nets   3, 6, 20, 188
Neuhart, John   83
Neuhart, Marilyn   83
Newell, Allen   159
New Materialism   143
Nimkulrat, Nithikul   37
Noel, Lesley-Ann   39
non-fiction   13–14
non-linear design methods   101
non-woven construction methods   32
Noon Solar   210–12
Notes Concerning the Objects That are on My Work-Table (Perec)   141

Ochs, Elinor   12, 16
ocular-centricity   182–4
Odradek   145
On Designing (Albers)   40
On Growth and Form (Thompson)   168
On the Art of Translation (Friedrich)   48
ontology   15, 40, 43, 85, 151, 173, 174, 199
On Understanding Emotion (Denzin)   198
On Weaving (Albers)   2, 41
Ortega y Gasset, José   55
Ortony, Andrew   18
Osimo, Bruno   57, 67
Otto, Frei   42

Pajaczkowska, Claire   40, 42
Palmer, Jane   210
Panofsky, Erwin   63
Pantzar, Mika   147
paraphernalia   27, 127–9, 141, 144, 150, 160, 170. *See also* patterns of objects
  playing and designing 'in real life'   137–9
  playing with   130–6
  poetic decorative   136–7
Patel, Karen   113
patriarchy   76, 79, 80, 83, 84, 97, 113
pattern   45, 55, 124, 154, 168, 187, 195
patterns of objects   140–51
  collection   145–7

playing 147–51
Pauli, Wolfgang 191
pedagogy 5, 33, 35, 52
Peirce, Charles Sanders 65, 158, 180
Pelias, Ronald 14
pentimento 25
perception 62–5, 95, 100, 120, 130, 159, 167, 168, 170, 177–86
Perec, Georges 141, 142, 144
Personal Knowledge (Polanyi) 132
Personal Power (JAM) 210
Pevsner, Niklaus 73
phallogocentrism 97
philosophy 3, 4, 42, 57, 127, 143, 166, 174, 188, 193, 205, 206
Philpott, Rachel 42
Pilke, Hilde. *See* Groag, Jacqueline
Pioneers of Modern Design (Pevsner) 73
Plath, Sylvia 21
pleasure 49, 50, 90, 91, 95, 105–106, 111, 123, 138, 169, 170, 197
pleasure-giving 50, 75, 200
poiesis 137, 138
Pointcarre 204
Polanyi, Michael 53, 86, 132, 133, 135, 136, 138, 169, 190
Politecnico de Milano 52
Pollock, Griselda 21–4, 160
polymath designers 87
polyphony 5, 8, 14, 16
populist concept 173
'Portraits: Women Designers' (2012) 82, 119
Portsmouth, UK 22–3
postcolonialism 113, 116
postmodernism 189
practical specificity 147
Practical Weaving Suggestions 204
'practice-centred' approach 36
Prado de O. Martens, Luiza 39
Première Vision (PV) trade fair (2001) 45, 89
prescriptive theories 174–6, 185
printed textiles 8, 27, 32, 136, 171, 211
problem-solving 153, 155–7, 158–63, 165–8, 171, 173, 175–8, 181, 182, 187, 188, 192
product design 69, 144, 153, 155, 177, 184
professional space 113, 118

psychoanalytical theory 20–1, 168, 188

qualitative method 7, 9
qualitative research 96
quantum 2, 49, 191
quantum physics 190

Quest for Certainty: A Study of the Relation of Knowledge and Action, The (Dewey) 176

Raby, Fiona 209
race 5, 114, 115, 118, 120, 122, 160
Ramachandran, Vilayanur. S. 182
Rand, Ayn 74
rapid prototyping 32
re-codification process 59
Redström, Johan 2
reflexivity 3, 13, 23
relationality 7, 10, 18, 23, 43, 73, 139, 189, 190, 191, 199
relational textiles 2, 80
Rendell, Jane 4
repair 6, 18, 93
Representation of Concepts in Textile Design, The (Moxey) 33
'representing concepts' 33
research methods 5, 7, 10, 42, 110, 135,
Rethinking Design Thinking: Part I (Kimbell) 38
Rethinking Design Thinking: Part II (Kimbell) 36
reweaving 6
rhizome 6, 24, 164, 193, 203
rhizomatic activity 164–72
Rich, Adrienne 96
Richardson, Laurel 8, 18, 111
Ringgold, Faith 112
Rittel, Horst 176
Robinson, Elizabeth 114
Rogers, Damian 86
Rosch, Eleanor 166
Rosenthal, Macha L. 14
Rosner, Daniela 7, 14–15, 18, 38, 97
Rotman School of Management 177
Rowe, Peter 38
Roxburgh, Mark 6
Royal College of Art (RCA) 100, 106, 119
Ruzsits Jha, Stefania 136

Salustri, Filippo 86
Sanders, Elizabeth. B-N 109
Santayana, George 169–71
Sartre, Jean-Paul 197
satin structure 206
Scarry, Elaine 50
'scentsory' design 39
Scheerbart, Paul 5, 73–5, 78, 79, 81, 83, 84, 89
Schön, Donald 18, 19, 52
School of Human Ecology, University of Wisconsin-Madison 203, 204
School of the Art Institute of Chicago 203
School of Ulm 64
Schulte, Rainer 48
Schumpeter, Joseph 132
'science of design' 41, 197, 199
Sciences of the Artificial (Simon) 174, 177
scientific theories 173
second-order cybernetics 184
'self-disposal' concept 53
semantics 5, 47, 51, 59, 60, 62, 65, 66, 136, 188, 189
semiosphere 67
Semper, Gottfried 75, 78, 80
Sense of Beauty: Being the Outline of Aesthetic Theory, The (Santayana) 169
Serres, Michel 73, 163, 205
Shaw, George Bernard 74
Shove, Elizabeth 145, 147
Shreeve, Alison 33, 35
signs 61–7, 146, 167
Simon, Herbert 159, 174, 176, 177, 197
Simon, Sherry 48, 52, 54, 55
Sinclair, Rose 5, 39
smart textiles 28, 33, 102–5
Smart Textiles Salon 102–3
Smith, Sherri 203
smoothing and striation 163–4, 172, 195
social reality 48
sociological wrapping 87–9, 192
soft logics 73, 163
solar technology 211
solar textile 211
Special Interest Group (Design Research Society) 37, 144

Speculative Every: Design, Fiction, and Social Dreaming (Dunne and Raby) 209
speculative weaving 208
spinster (textiles as) 94, 97–98, 102, 105, 107, 187,
Spivak, Gayatri 52–3, 216
Spuybroek, Lars 42
Stappers, Pieter 109
Steadman, Philip 54
Steiner, George 51–3, 57
Stewart, Susan 177
Sticky/Smooth (de Waal) 172
Stolterman, Erik 193
Storyteller, The (Benjamin) 17
storytelling 7, 10, 12, 13, 19, 23, 75, 121, 187
Straub, Marianne 83
Stromwall, Layne 134
Stuart, John 74–6, 78
Studd, Rachel 32, 33, 35–7, 158, 159
surface embellishment techniques 32
sustainability 34, 38, 42, 101, 153,
Sutton-Smith, Brian 147–9
symbols and symbolism 2, 27, 61, 62, 63, 64, 65, 80, 91, 146, 167, 168, 191
systematic design process 36
'System of Objects' (Baudrillard) 146
systems-level design 176
S/Z (Barthes) 1

tacit knowledge 47, 53, 101, 108, 109, 135, 138, 162, 169, 184, 188
Tacit- Turn: Textile Design in Design Research, The (Igoe) 101
taciturnity 6, 42, 94, 97
tactile/visual language 42, 51, 63, 136, 106, 167, 168
Taut, Bruno 73–5
technical and technological textiles 33
technoscience research approach 14
Tedlock, Barbara 13
Temple, Bogusia 55
ten Bhömer, Martijn 104
textasis 1, 2, 192
Textile as a Structural Framework, The (Houze) 78
Textile Book, The (Gale and Kaur) 32
Textile: Cloth and Culture 40

Index

textile design 11. *See also individual entries*
  definition 170
  industry 32, 33, 51, 89, 97, 154
  patterns in 168, 195
  practice 8, 39, 89, 93, 94, 102, 104–8, 110, 117, 122, 136, 174, 177, 188, 194, 196–8, 210
  process 23, 28, 31–3, 35, 39, 42, 48–50, 58–60, 87, 89, 97, 102, 118, 132, 134, 135, 159, 166, 170, 171, 191
  research 29–31, 36, 37, 39, 42, 43, 85, 98, 102, 107–10, 158–60, 189, 191, 195, 197–9, 213
textile designers 7, 10–14, 17, 18, 32, 33, 35–7, 39, 42, 46, 47, 50–2, 61, 70–2, 81, 82, 88, 89, 97, 101, 104–6, 109, 123, 124, 127–30, 136, 154, 155, 156, 159, 160, 167, 170, 192, 195–200. *See also individual entries*
  Black 111–22
  contemporary 116
  role of 90–4, 102, 103
  as translator 48, 49, 52–6
textile designing 7, 27, 28, 32–8, 43, 47, 49, 52, 70, 101, 132, 159, 163, 181, 192
'The Textile Design Process' (Studd) 32
textile innovation 11, 37, 196
textile practitioners 6, 37, 40, 88, 101, 108, 116, 211
Textile Reader, The (Hemmings) 193
Textiles, Text and Techne (Mitchell) 41
textiles as designed objects 49–51
Textiles Intersections 37
textiles space 113, 114, 116
Textiles: The Whole Story (Gordon) 3
textile structure 7, 78, 204, 211
'Textile Theory: Do We Need It?' (Hemmings) 193
textile thinking 5, 38–43, 99–110, 163, 188, 196
  applied 42, 107, 110
  in practice 107–10
  testing 102–7
textilic design/practice 2, 5, 6, 43, 85, 194, 196–200, 212
textility 1–3, 40–3, 199, 202, 205, 211

Textility of Making, The (Ingold) 2, 41
textuality 1, 2
texture design 5, 56, 61–7, 154, 200
Textures of Memory: The Poetics of Cloth (Barnett) 163
Thick/er Black Lines 118
Thiele, Kathrin 97, 98, 189
Thomas 157
Thompson, D'Arcy 168
Thompson, Evan 166
Thread Controller 2 (TC2) 204
Thrice Told Tale, A (Wolf) 17
Tillotson, Jenny 39
Timorous Beasties 99
Tongan culture 128
Tonkinwise, Cameron 39
Tootals 119
Torop, Peeter 58, 59
'traditional' design disciplines 109
transformation 23, 39, 47–56, 58, 59, 65, 92, 93, 132, 134, 135, 137, 146, 157, 160, 162, 165–8, 171, 174, 175, 177, 178, 180–3, 185–8, 192, 197–200
translation 5, 6, 47–67, 75, 54, 115, 160, 168, 170, 188, 199, 200
Translations (Rich) 96
'The Translator's Task' (Benjamin) 53
trans-subjectivity 2, 11, 13, 21, 22, 95, 137, 138, 166, 189, 199, 200
trigger 37, 86, 159, 160
Tulloch, Carol 115
Turney, Jo 114

UK Arts Council and Creative Skills 114
Ulm School of Design 176
universal truth 75
University of Michigan 203
University of Wisconsin, Madison 211
'unlimited semiosis' 65
utopian thinking 75

Valentine, Louise 42, 196
van den Akker, Robin 189–91
Varela, Francisco 166
Veil of Maya 3
Vermeulen, Timotheus 189–91
visibility and hyperinvisibility 112, 115–16

visual communication design   52, 56, 61, 64, 109
visual effects   153
visualization   3, 131, 160, 188, 192
visual research   45
Vuletich, Clara   38, 42

Wagner, Richard   76
Wallpaper Manufactures Limited   119
Wang, David   87–9, 192
warp design   62, 63, 112, 124, 137, 206, 209
Warren, Erica   116
Ways of Knowing, Being and Doing: A Theoretical Framework and Methods for Indigenous and Indigenist Research (Martin and Mirraboopa)   117
wearable technology   103, 104
We Are Sorry for the Delay to Your Journey (2017)   118
weaving   23, 32, 70, 77, 97, 98, 153, 161, 163, 168, 188, 189, 199, 204, 206, 208–10
Weaving Lab   208–10, 212
Webber, Michael   119
Webster, Roger   1
weft design   62, 63, 112, 124, 206
Western normativity   39
Weston, Richard   73, 74
White, Dominic   51
Windrush Generation   116
Wolf, Margery   17
women
    Black   112–14, 118, 120, 121
    clothing   76, 84
    workshop   77
Women and Craft (Elinor, Richardson, Scott, Thomas and Walker)   115
women of colour   5, 112, 114, 120
wooden objects   142–3
'Work in Progress'   106
world view   15, 19
woven textiles   17, 23, 90, 98, 112, 116, 128, 137, 161, 163, 165, 168, 171, 195, 199, 204, 206, 210, 211

Young, Iris Marion   85

Zingale, Salvatore   52

CPSIA information can be obtained
at www.ICGtesting.com
Printed in the USA
LVHW021803200423
744798LV00004B/174

9 781350 254107